INSIDE OUT
INDIA AND CHINA

For David —

With appreciation
for all that you are
doing for the country and
the world, and with
best regards.

Bill

BROOKINGS FOCUS BOOKS

Brookings Focus Books feature concise, accessible, and timely
assessment of pressing policy issues of interest to a broad audience.
Each book includes recommendations for action on the issue discussed.

Also in this series:

A BROOKINGS FOCUS BOOK

INSIDE OUT
INDIA AND CHINA
LOCAL POLITICS GO GLOBAL

William Antholis

BROOKINGS INSTITUTION PRESS
Washington, D.C.

Copyright © 2013
THE BROOKINGS INSTITUTION
1775 Massachusetts Avenue, N.W., Washington, D.C. 20036
www.brookings.edu

Library of Congress Cataloging-in-Publication data

Antholis, William.
    Inside out, India and China : local politics go global / William Antholis.
    pages cm. — (A Brookings focus book)
    Includes bibliographical references and index.
    ISBN 978-0-8157-2510-7 (hardcover : alk. paper)
    1. Regionalism—Politcal aspects—India. 2. Local government—India.
3. Private enterprise—India. 4. India—Economic conditions—Regional
disparities. 5. Regionalism—Political aspects—China. 6. Local government—
China. 7. Private enterprise—China. 8. China—Economic conditions—
Regional disparities. I. Title.
    JQ220.R43A67 2013
    320.80951—dc23   2013023178

9 8 7 6 5 4 3 2 1

Printed on acid-free paper

Typeset in Sabon

Composition by Cynthia Stock
Silver Spring, Maryland

Printed by R. R. Donnelley
Harrisonburg, Virginia

For Kristen

my muse and my metronome

CONTENTS

China: Provinces and Key Cities

Figure created by author using basemaps from Esri ArcGIS Online, www.esri.com. Cities are indicated in black, and provinces or regions indicated in grey.

India: States and Key Cities

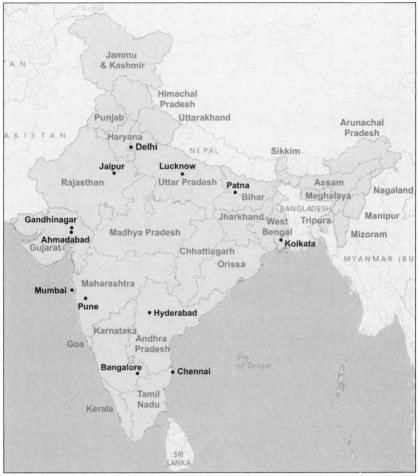

Figure created by author using basemaps from Esri ArcGIS Online, www.esri.com. Cities are indicated in black, and state names indicated in grey.

CHAPTER ONE

JIGSAW:
COUNTING TO 1.3 BILLION

ONE THIRD OF humanity is governed from two capitals, Beijing and New Delhi.

People who work in finance often speak of the magic of large numbers. The same applies to politics. To manage the biggest challenges facing the planet, China and India must be at the table. Steering the world economy, combating poverty, slowing global warming, preventing nuclear war—these are big and hard problems. You cannot get there from here without going through these two giants.

Yet few in Western foreign policy circles think about the dark magic of large numbers: what it takes to move two seemingly self-contained worlds. Connecting China's 1.3 and India's 1.2 billion people to the global economy—or protecting them from it—is no small task. And moving those billions to address common global challenges is even harder.

Imagine the challenge of solving a jigsaw puzzle made up of 1.3 billion unique pieces. Start with the population of the United States. Add Mexico, Brazil, and the rest of North and South America. Then add 500 million people living in the European Union. That is about 1.3 billion.[1]

India's seven biggest states have the combined population of about 740 million people. That is the same as the combined population of the seven largest industrial democracies: the United States, Japan, Germany, Great Britain, France, Italy, and Canada—also known as the G-7. China's seven biggest provinces are nearly as large. Few Americans can name the seven largest Chinese provinces or Indian states, let alone who governs them and what they care about. That includes many senior foreign policy professionals, political leaders, and business leaders.

By comparison, American and European diplomats, politicians, and business leaders intuitively understand federal politics and the big differences between American federalism and Europe's confederal union. They know how the Electoral College chooses the U.S. president—including the role of red states, blue states, and swing states. They know that while all states have Republicans and Democrats, each state has its own priorities and prejudices. They know that Senate voting blocs shape treaties and military spending, and that New York, Texas, California, and Illinois bring different strengths to our national economy.

Trade negotiators know the basics. Senators from Iowa care about corn subsidies. House members from northern California care about intellectual property. Governors and senators from West Virginia, Louisiana, and Texas will fight efforts to regulate greenhouse gases. All of these officials face crosscutting economic pressures and complex public attitudes within their states. Counterparts in Europe face similar puzzles but have an even more difficult challenge since the European Union's system is more decentralized and therefore more cumbersome.

This book is for people who wonder about the inside of China and India, and how different local perspectives inside those countries shape actions outside their borders. Though my family and I spent five months traveling in both countries to do research, this book is not a travelogue. Rather, it is an attempt to sketch how a few of China's and India's many component parts are being shaped by global forces—and in turn are shaping those forces—and what that means for Americans and Europeans conducting diplomacy and doing business there.

FIVE MONTHS, FOUR PEOPLE, THREE QUESTIONS

As my wife Kristen, my daughters Annika and Kyri, and I traveled across China and India in early 2012, we asked three simple questions: How do Chinese provinces and Indian states work? How do they blend local and national priorities and value systems? How do they view some major global issues? I addressed these questions to government officials, political leaders, business people, journalists, academics, and nongovernmental groups. But our whole family also asked the same questions of tour guides, taxi drivers, schoolteachers, and waiters.

Some locals seemed surprised by these questions. In Beijing and New Delhi, in Shanghai and Mumbai, in Chennai and Chengdu, in Ahmadabad and Hangzhou, I would get the same response: "Why do you care?"

I told them about my own small role, working in America's federal system. Over a decade ago, I served with the U.S. State Department's policy planning staff and then with the White House National Security staff. I helped prepare Secretary of State Warren Christopher and President Bill Clinton for dozens of meetings with foreign leaders. In addition, I worked on World Trade Organization trade talks, two G-7 summits, and climate change negotiations at Kyoto and Buenos Aires. The voices of senators or members of Congress from various states were a persistent reminder of the United States' federal politics. At the White House, in particular, we spent as much time negotiating domestically as we did internationally.

I also reminded my Chinese and Indian acquaintances about President Clinton and his own "provincial" past. Roughly twenty years ago, he moved into the White House having served as governor of a small, landlocked, largely agricultural state with high unemployment. As the first president inaugurated after the end of the cold war, he became the first American leader to speak of the promise and the challenges of globalization. His geographic

3

background was not his destiny, but his outlook was very much shaped by where he was from.

That president often successfully navigated America's federal system. As governor of Arkansas, he had led trade missions, including in support of Wal-Mart, a local Arkansas company that would become America's and the world's largest retailer. As president of the United States, Clinton assembled coalitions of senators to balance the national budget and to negotiate key trade pacts such as the North American Free Trade Agreement and the launch of the World Trade Organization. His bipartisan successes involved quilting together interests from a range of very different states.

At other times, he was unable to break domestic gridlock on nuclear weapons talks, trade deals, and a global climate change treaty. Regarding climate change, for instance, I witnessed Democratic senators from West Virginia, Louisiana, Nebraska, and Missouri join with Republicans to help kill a national approach to protect the climate. To this day, that stalemate still exists, and it still crosses party lines. That is federalism at work—or not.

Nonetheless, innovative state-level successes also have defied party lines. In the last decade, Republican governors named Schwarzenegger, Pataki, and Romney actually signed state-level climate change laws. Like President Clinton, these governors had priorities shaped by where they came from.

Europe's own confederal experiment in sharing sovereignty faces its own challenges—ones that are crucial to the health of the global economy. Europe continues to produce breakthrough industrial innovations in telecommunications, automobiles, high-speed rail, and renewable energy. Yet the European Union's finances are a wreck, and it is facing a major crisis about what richer, northern members such as Germany, the Netherlands, and Finland owe to Italy, Spain, and Greece—and vice versa.[2]

Establishing and maintaining unified political systems across a continent and across multiple and common belief systems is hard work. When the phrase *E Pluribus Unum*—"from many, one"—first appeared on the Great Seal of the United States in 1782, it was as much a hope as a statement of fact. Forging *unum* out of *pluribus* often requires crafting compromises or forcing odd coalitions. Our leaders often fail to put all the pieces together. Sometimes politics moves the process backward—the *unum* becomes *pluribus,* and the whole becomes less than the sum of its parts. But occasionally we do find a common good and reach a new consensus.

CHINA AND INDIA: FROM ONE, MANY

Americans and Europeans engaging with India and China cannot afford to treat these countries as monoliths. What happens outside Beijing and New Delhi is essential to those countries' economic and political futures, and also often directly critical to the West's future as well. So how do things work in each place? How does each country perform those acts of compromise or synthesis? When and how and why do they fail? And who are their internal regional leaders? Who might become the next Bill Clinton or George W. Bush—perhaps a former local leader who brings some of his or her region's views to the nation's capital? Again, geography is not destiny: Clinton and Bush were from neighboring states, yet each brought a very different philosophy to Washington. Still, their backgrounds did shape each of them in important ways.

To many professional diplomats and policymakers, China and India seem opaque internally. In political science jargon, both nation-states are often described as "unitary self-interested agents." Realist scholars of international affairs helped to shape this view by focusing on the core economic and strategic interests of nations. More recently, other students of world politics have interpreted national behavior using microeconomic theory and rational choice theory, assuming that states act the same way self-interested individuals would—as if nations had one mind and one interest.

There are good reasons for applying these assumptions to China and India. It is no accident that diplomats use "Beijing" for China or "New Delhi" for India. Both have streamlined foreign policy systems: in neither country does the parliament play a major role in foreign policy. Central governments are more powerful than in the United States or Europe. As a result, there is a tendency to think that if one could simply convince central leaders of their own nation's interest, a single centralized key will unlock their enormous systems.

Of course, the reality is far different. The politics between central and local forces in these places may differ from those of the West, but they are no less complicated. In neither country is the central government completely in charge. In both India's multiparty democracy and China's one-party "people's republic," a multicolored map exists that delineates not only territorial units but also multiple conceptions of the good life that need to be reconciled.

The power outside of their capitals has expanded dramatically in recent decades. Local governments have stepped forward, with global implications. Subnational leaders, in charge of country-sized jurisdictions, now drive economic development. They make critical decisions about energy and natural resources. Their jurisdictions are the proving ground for the rule of law—or lack of it. The most economically advanced and wealthy places have begun to emerge into the world's awareness. Real challenges exist in the poorer or emerging provinces, but even there, success stories exist.

It is not just that these places are diverse. Local leaders are truly starting to lead, moving these countries toward change from the inside out. And local leaders are becoming national leaders.

In coastal China's fast-growing Guangdong province, former party secretary Wang Yang just oversaw a decade of sizzling growth. He helped harness the global economy while also streamlining government, protecting intellectual property, and cutting greenhouse gases. He was just promoted to vice premier, and some hope he will head China someday. Still, his experiments in political and economic reform struck others in China as too much, too soon.

In India's state of Gujarat, Chief Minister Narendra Modi earned a reputation for bold leadership. He has overseen a decade of prosperity and has directed one of India's most effective bureaucracies.

Some Indians hope he might run the country someday. Yet his path to becoming prime minister is not assured. He is loathed by many who see him as, among other things, a Hindu communalist who steered murderous anti-Muslim riots and who might bring India to war with Pakistan.

In India's Bihar state and China's Chongqing province, local leaders became national celebrities by fighting corruption and tackling poverty. Bihar's chief minister Nitish Kumar and Chongqing's former party secretary Bo Xilai each aggressively prosecuted local hoodlums. Each used the very visible hand of state-led investment to bring dramatic economic growth. Yet they did so in very different ways. Nitish Kumar has few peers in India for being an upright administrator and has become a model for addressing India's endemic poverty. But his chances to someday run India are complicated by the narrow reach of his Janata Dal (United) political party, which is based largely in Bihar and is only India's fifth-largest party. Bo Xilai's career came to a crashing halt when Bo, his wife, and a top lieutenant were caught in a web of corruption and murder.

The impact of these leaders can be global. They can promote critical trade, investment, clean energy, and nuclear safety initiatives. Successful cooperation with foreign countries and companies is often anchored in a few select states or provinces. Yet states or provinces can also stall passage or fail to implement agreements. In both countries—in different ways—local strategies make it harder for Beijing and New Delhi to lead.

Given this context, American and European politicians, business leaders, media, and a range of civil society organizations must be more nimble and nuanced in dealing with emerging giants than traditional mental maps would suggest. Westerners must take local politics more seriously as a global matter and significantly revise how they organize and think about the conduct of global affairs.

The stakes are enormous. Taken together, India, China, the European Union, and the United States are home to half of the world's people, two-thirds of the world's economic activity, two-thirds of the world's greenhouse gases, and two-thirds of all nuclear power. Together the economic rise of China and India in the last twenty years has lifted at least half a billion people out of poverty.[3] In the next twenty years, those two nations are likely to become the largest and third-largest economies, respectively. Already, they are the largest and third-largest emitters of greenhouse gases on an annual basis. Furthermore, both countries have large stockpiles of nuclear weapons.

The rise of local leadership has led many to worry that a central leadership vacuum exists within the four great continent-wide unions. This may have led to greater economic dynamism locally, but it does pose huge barriers to cooperation on global challenges.[4]

This volume does not pretend to do the impossible by describing the full range of local experiences in either country. Instead, it focuses on a few critical places where innovation is happening. In addition to providing a mental map for China's provinces and India's states, this book also will try to give a glimpse into the promise and problems of local control. It describes what drives these places and their political leaders—either toward the global economy or away from it. After examining a few key locales, it then looks at energy politics and policy in both places, from the inside out.

China's provincial experimentation has transformed the world economy for the better. India's local leaders are making some of the world's most dramatic advances in human development. Yet India's paralyzed federal politics and China's authoritarian efforts to control its provinces also will be a central plot line as each nation evolves. These issues also will make it more difficult for them to lead on global challenges. Americans and Europeans need to start learning how to work with local leaders if they are going to address their own national priorities with these countries—not to mention global priorities.

CHAPTER TWO

LESS THAN PERFECT UNIONS

WHEN CHAIRMAN MAO ZEDONG and Prime Minister Jawaharlal Nehru established China's and India's modern systems in the late 1940s, both feared the power of provinces and states. Over six decades later, China's and India's most dynamic locales have pulled these two countries into leadership positions in the world economy. If China's five largest exporting provinces were independent nations, each would rank among the top forty trading nations. India sends as many highly skilled workers to the United States as the rest of the world combined—and half of those come from just four of India's thirty states. However, empowered local leaders are also making these countries harder to govern.

The promise and problems of local power should not be too hard for Americans and Europeans to grasp. The U.S. Constitution aims "to form a more perfect union," and Americans demonstrate near-religious reverence for that document. Despite this lofty aspiration, federal and state authorities often have had a less than perfect relationship. It took a civil war to forge the current union and strengthen central power.

Still, a century and a half later, Americans continue to recognize the need for states. They acknowledge a role for states to govern themselves and for states-as-states to tell the national government what to do. When U.S. negotiators engage in trade talks or investment agreements, they often are doing the bidding of senators from New York or California, Iowa or Michigan.

Europe's less than perfect union also has moved toward centralization, after an even bloodier past. After two major wars in a half century, Europe gave transnational central authorities greater power, designing a complex confederal system.[1] Most Europeans appear committed to the European Union (EU), even if they often remain befuddled and frustrated by it. Constituent states still remain "sovereign" over most internal matters. So when the EU's negotiators sit down to hammer out external agreements, they are often joined at the table by ministers from France, Germany, the United Kingdom, or others.

Both China and India have moved the other way. Each started with far more centralized systems, and only recently have they ceded power to local authorities. Both explicitly rejected sovereignty for their subnational units when creating their governments in the late 1940s. Only in the last thirty years have both governments granted greater local flexibility. When it comes to local control, perhaps the two most important markers are how local leaders are selected and how much freedom those leaders have in setting policy.

SELECTING LEADERS

"Sovereignty" suggests a "sovereign"—that is, a king, whose God-given right to rule is absolute, final, and perpetual. Modern parliamentary and constitutional democracies transferred authority from God and kings to people and their elected governors. "Popular sovereignty" has proven itself a sturdy foundation for modern industrial democracies. The body politic holds ultimate authority and uses it to ratify a constitution and select its leaders.[2]

In federal systems, however, popular sovereignty also can be a complex and unwieldy foundation. In the U.S. federal constitution of 1789, American states are considered "sovereign" over some matters. The people of those states are authorized to write their own state constitutions and choose their local leaders.[3] Of course, for nearly a century, the limits on that sovereignty were greatly and grievously debated. Many felt that state sovereignty allowed states to define rights and liberties, including the right to secede.[4] Union forces were required to settle what Americans now take for granted: that when the confederal states ratified the Constitution, they created a pact among all the people, not among separable states.

Europe's own confederal system is much more like the United States under the Articles of Confederation. Sovereignty remains the defining central feature of the members of the European Union—including the ability for each member state to design its own constitution and select its own governors. On the range of issues where Europe has established robust common institutions and rules—from trade to the environment—the legislative body that sets these rules and chooses administrators is composed of the sovereign states.

In neither China nor India are local jurisdictions close to being sovereign. Their ability to select leaders is thus more limited than in the United States or Europe. Both countries provide central oversight as a check against local abuses of power. In both countries, the central government has greater authority to remove local leaders on political grounds.

Of the two, India comes closest to being a federal system, since citizens in each state vote for representatives to the state legislative assembly, whose ruling party names a chief minister. But even there, India's central government holds the final authority to approve the chief minister and can invoke the "President's Rule" to unseat the incumbent at a moment's notice.[5] In China the top provincial officials are appointed by the national leadership in Beijing and usually do not come from the province in question. China has conducted direct elections at the most basic unit levels—villages and districts of cities—since the 1980s.[6] However, these elections are closely monitored, and candidates need approval to run from the Communist Party.[7]

But that does not mean that localities have no control. India is moving toward letting local authorities manage more of their own affairs. The rise of state leaders is one the most significant political developments in the six decades since India's independence. Moreover, much of the political energy in India is coming from these local authorities. That energy can be channeled because local leaders are presenting a new and appealing message to voters, challenging the once-dominant voice of the Congress Party. Local leaders are throwing their weight around on local issues and also shaping affairs in the national parliament.

In China top provincial officials are still chosen by Beijing, but the number of other local officials appointed by central authorities has declined. Provincial governments now have greater responsibility for appointing and promoting more of their own. Increasingly, the national government recruits the best and brightest from these localities. A rising leader's ability to govern—and *work with*—a locality is now a key test for higher office.

SETTING POLICY: TOP DOWN AND BOTTOM UP

Centralization remains a defining feature of both systems, particularly when it comes to national security. But on broader economic matters, the recent trend has been toward more and more local involvement and control in making and implementing policy.

In both countries, centralization remains strongest in national security and diplomatic policy. The Chinese and Indian national security establishments are bureaucratic forces without peer. Neither takes formal guidance from provincial or state governments or their representatives. Even in democratic India, when the foreign minister negotiates a treaty, the government is not required to seek parliamentary approval. In fact, in both countries, if central authorities feel that local governments pose a national security threat—particularly a threat of secession—they have the right and responsibility to act preemptively, including by deploying national security forces.

This is not that different from the U.S. national security system, where the design and conduct of foreign policy are centralized. But

America's sovereign states do have a voice, which echoes through the Senate's power to approve treaties by a two-thirds majority. The Senate also provides "advice and consent" to top national security officials. Still, even those powers are limited. And since the Civil War, the right of secession has been a nonissue in American politics, with central authority clearly established.

If states' voices echo when the United States articulates its national security interests, the EU's states bang like drums. Member states retain national armies, and each conducts its own diplomacy. The EU has tried to forge central institutions, creating a presidency and also a "foreign minister." Still, those officials take directives from the Council of Ministers—the heads of state from each member state, who form the equivalent of a single legislative body. That council does not advise and consent: it designs and decides. It does so by unanimous decisions only, creating a policy bottleneck that blocks the ability to forge common decisions. Diplomacy with Europe invariably means negotiating not just with Brussels but also with Berlin, Paris, London, and Rome, at the very least.[8] When designing their constitutions, both China and India feared any suggestion that their local units would have any such say in diplomacy.

When it comes to domestic economic matters, however, both China and India have moved toward decentralization, giving local authorities responsibility to manage their own affairs. In a global economy, decentralization gives these localities a role and stake in international affairs. China's provinces and India's states now have meaningful vested interests in industries and workers connected to global trade, investment, finance, and environmental affairs. So while localities are not formal negotiators for those matters, they do have interests to protect or advance.

Localities are increasingly racing one another to develop globally competitive industries, to market their region's goods to foreign customers, to build quality infrastructure, and to attract local and foreign investment. Local officials are at the leading edge of enforcing trade or investment agreements, cutting greenhouse gas emissions, or safely developing nuclear energy. Or, as is often the case, local authorities are *not* enforcing international agreements, protecting the environment, or stewarding resources.

To understand why they do or do not act on global matters, it is critical to understand at least four major domestic forces with which local leaders wrestle. Each has a global dimension.

Migration

In both China and India, a massive internal migration is taking place. Over the last three decades, hundreds of millions of rural poor in both countries have moved to towns and cities in search of jobs, and that trend is only expected to continue. Much of the global poverty reduction in the last thirty years has come from this enormous movement in China and India—in much the same way that the industrial revolution reshaped Europe, the United States, and Japan. This is happening both within and across provincial and state lines. These workers are fueling the global economy. They are also straining the capacities of local governments. Migrants seek not only jobs but also housing, health care, and education for their children, placing a huge social welfare burden on urban centers.

Land Acquisition

Local leaders struggle with a new land rush. Local and foreign companies are doing the rushing, trying to acquire land for factories, offices, and housing. It is a dangerous race, both for local politics and the global economy. The population density in China and India approaches that of the northeast U.S. outside New York or Boston—yet across much bigger territories, with many more people and with most living off the land. Many subsistence farmers near large and growing cities still live on ancestral lands and are reluctant to move, finding the trappings of urban life unappealing. Local governments in both countries often take matters into their own hands in unsettling ways. They often invoke eminent domain for private business projects, including high-profile sites for foreign investment. This has become a highly combustible formula, often leading to some of the most contentious political battles and violent protests in both countries. When that happens, private property and civil liberties often collide with investment capital and newer notions of economic progress.

Infrastructure and Fiscal Federalism

Global and local investors are desperate for quality airports, bridges, roads, water, and electricity. Local citizens themselves increasingly are demanding public transportation, hospitals, schools, and sewers. How local authorities pay for that infrastructure is a global concern. While localities get some support from central governments, they increasingly have to help foot the bill. Local authorities often become real estate developers of a sort. Many run fiscal deficits that the central government needs to cover, or they create elaborate credit systems to finance infrastructure or property development. In both cases, these can undermine more sustainable borrowing and lending, not to mention national finances.

Successfully balancing fiscal federalism is an issue in both developed and developing countries. How federal or other large political systems divide, assign, and monitor spending and taxing authority determines how successful they are in balancing their books, not unlike any large company or organization. The biggest risks occur when large subnational governments can borrow at will but have little autonomy to raise taxes. In these cases, local governments are not "sovereign" from the standpoint of international lenders. Instead, they are "wards of the center." This poses a liability for central governments, particularly if they find it hard to say no when subnational governments ask for bailouts.[9]

So as China and India have tried to liberalize their economies and seize global opportunities, both countries are experimenting with greater local political control and flexibility from central direction. They know that comes with advantages and disadvantages for

15

themselves, for other countries, and for foreign businesses. Both countries are trying to take advantage of their huge domestic markets while still delegating responsibility to the local level where entrepreneurialism can thrive. They are doing this while moving hundreds of millions from rural poverty to urban industrial life, and also while trying to have their local leaders not only be in charge but be responsible.

THE VIEW FROM BEIJING: UNTIL ALL ARE ONE

China is decidedly not a federal system. Above all, Chinese leaders care deeply—almost desperately—about the country's unity and territorial integrity. Yet local autonomy has been critical to China's economic boom. How the country's leaders balance their unity imperative with local innovation is key to understanding modern China and anticipating how it will continue to evolve.

China has been a united, continent-wide civilization under one government for over 2,000 years. Maintaining a single country is a core, dominant theme in both domestic and foreign policy. Still, the borders of what might be described as "the united provinces of China" have changed substantially over two millennia, with a number of minority ethnic populations resisting central Han Chinese control. The country's leaders—and many of its people—are particularly sensitive to a century of Western and Japanese attempts to carve regional spheres of influence. Those scars are still felt very deeply. They shape Chinese attitudes toward its various "autonomous regions" such as Tibet, Xinjiang, and Inner Mongolia, and former Western colonies of Hong Kong and Macau that are now "special administrative regions."

Chairman Mao stressed unity. He forged a centrally managed state that now has twenty-two provinces (plus, on paper, Taiwan), four provincial level municipalities, five autonomous regions, and two special administrative zones. Provinces have no formal independent authority. Beijing directly appoints province leaders (except in Hong Kong and Macao), much in the same way that the

Pentagon appoints base commanders. All provincial governments are local arms of the central government. The Central Politburo of the Communist Party and the National People's Congress can annul any local legislation that conflicts with national law. There is no "tenth amendment" that protects any sovereignty of constituent states. The federalist founders of the United States embraced states as laboratories of democracy. Modern China's revolutionaries feared "warlords' separatist regimes."[10]

The central government tightly holds onto the reins of power when it comes to national security and nearly all diplomatic relations. The People's Liberation Army does not even report to the top government officials but rather only to the top leaders of the Chinese Communist Party, especially the party secretary (who chairs the Central Military Commission) and the Standing Committee of the Politburo. Foreign diplomacy is also tightly controlled.

Still, local autonomy and experimentation have catalyzed China's rapid economic growth. Mao's centralism was a disaster: not only did China's economy shrink, but centralization directly led to a famine that killed at least 30 million people. So when Deng Xiaoping, Mao's successor, overhauled the system in the late 1970s, he allowed provincial and local economies to experiment. Local leaders were given two mandates: produce growth and maintain order. They were also given extraordinary control over collecting revenue and managing their own budgets—a degree of autonomy rivaling that of many federal systems.[11] Deng's experimentation extended to the phrase "one country, two systems" when negotiating reunification with Hong Kong and Macau—and prospectively to Taiwan.[12] Those special administrative regions were allowed the closest thing to some formal sovereignty, as they still choose their own leaders, write their own laws, and even negotiate international trade agreements.

On the mainland, Communist Party legitimacy came to rest on the mandate to create growth. In China economic growth was so central to three decades of politics that the approach might best be called "GDP monotheism"—a single-minded, near-religious devotion to increasing measurable GDP as the determinant of political success. Beijing provided local leaders with basic resources and guidelines. Local leaders determined how best to achieve growth. They were graded almost exclusively on their GDP performance and received points for growth beyond targets. In a country run by party member bureaucrats, the grading of local leaders was an essential national lubricant to economic growth. While other objectives were considered in assessing the performance of local leaders, measurable economic output was the overriding consideration.[13]

Decentralization in service of GDP monotheism helped to lift hundreds of millions out of poverty. Most of this happened on China's coast, home to two-thirds of the country's economy but less than half of its people. Deng Xiaoping supported the launch of the special economic zones in the 1980s, and his famous southern tour in 1992 largely spurred their rapid development and broader economic reforms. Deng knew that development in such a vast country would happen in stages: "The development of the coastal areas is of overriding importance, and the interior provinces should subordinate themselves to it."[14]

Export-oriented manufacturing first took off in Guangdong. It started in four special economic zones (three of which were in Guangdong), and then spread across the province and up the coastal provinces.[15] Tens of millions of inland migrants have poured into these provinces, working long hours under tough conditions and living in spare workers' barracks. Guangdong and the Pearl River Delta in the south have 110 million people jammed into a territory the size of Missouri. Shanghai and the Yangtze River Delta have 150 million people (think Japan squeezed into the New York Tristate Area). Beijing and nearby Tianjin have 35 million people (think California squeezed into the Washington-Baltimore metro area). In the far northeast, bordering North Korea, the aging heavy industry province of Liaoning is home to another 45 million. These coastal provinces have pursued greater market liberalization and shown the earliest elements of political pluralism.

In the last ten years, the central government has shifted focus inland, showering resources and attention on China's interior. Interior officials also have campaigned for foreign investment but in a way that protects their local power. That includes a robust role for state-owned enterprises, state-provided services such as health care and housing, and a much lower tolerance for political pluralism than found in the east. Figures 2-1 through 2-3 illustrate the shift of economic growth in China, from the coastal provinces to the interior, from 1990 to 2010.

Over three decades of liberalization, the center adjusted and fine tuned how much local control to allow. Some of China's most important recent political struggles have involved how much China should open up—both in its domestic politics and in its economic relations with the rest of the world. That has been particularly true since the 1989 Tiananmen Square crackdown and then the subsequent negotiation and implementation of new rules to join the World Trade Organization in 2000. Tiananmen was about the center maintaining domestic order; WTO accession was about the center imposing consistent rules to allow China to take advantage of global commerce. Central authorities also have had to control provincial and city leaders who had gone rogue. On the one hand, the central government has kept a more watchful eye on localities. Major corruption scandals in Beijing (1995), Shanghai (2006), and Chongqing (2012) saw the dismissal of party secretaries in the three most prominent municipalities. On the other hand, the center has come to see that national success depends on local economic success. The design and implementation of the 2009 stimulus were heavily influenced by inland local leaders.

The back and forth between center and localities is intentional. The central party manages a formal planning process that includes national and province-by-province five-year plans. Those plans are

FIGURE 2-1. China's Provincial GDP Per Capita in 1990
Dollars

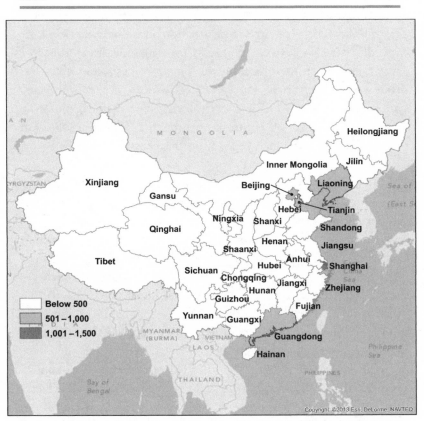

Source: Data from National Bureau of Statistics, *China Statistical Yearbook 1990* (Beijing: China Statistics Press, 1990).

ratified by the People's Congress. Actual implementation is another matter. "For China's local governments, laws, regulations, and contracts are often the beginning of business."[16] Bargaining between the center and the provinces, the provinces and localities, and the localities and businesses is the essence of governance. Some have called it "fragmented authoritarianism"; others, "consultative authoritarianism"; and more recently, "de facto federalism (or behavioral

FIGURE 2-2. China's Provincial GDP Per Capita in 2000
Dollars

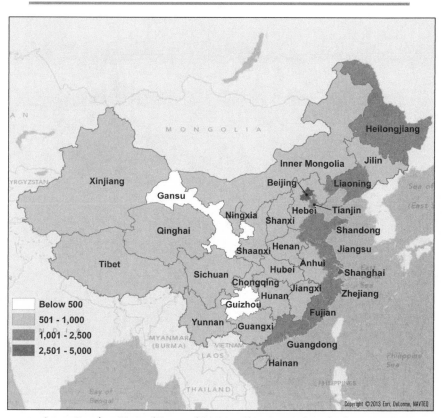

Source: Data from National Bureau of Statistics, *China Statistical Yearbook 2000* (Beijing: China Statistics Press, 2000).

federalism)."[17] In this way, power is spread across a number of authorities within the Communist Party and the various bodies of the Chinese state.

China's system of governance is not based on the rule of law. Instead, power is constantly being negotiated. Different authorities within the Communist Party and the government debate one another behind the scenes, and the final policy outcomes emerge from that

FIGURE 2-3. China's Provincial GDP Per Capita in 2010
Dollars

Source: Data from National Bureau of Statistics, *China Statistical Yearbook 2010* (Beijing: China Statistics Press, 2010).

back and forth. It is often difficult to determine who actually has made a decision or how long that decision stands in the public's mind. This system obviously has been successful in generating a surge of economic growth, but it also generates frustration for many citizens, private companies, and nongovernmental organizations, both foreign and domestic. Without the development of more transparent processes, it is unclear whether the economic miracle can continue.

Local governments are forces to be reckoned with. As a result, the central government works hard to keep officials loyal to Beijing and to prevent locals from having independent power bases. Central leaders use a "rule of avoidance": when appointing the seniormost positions—provincial party secretaries, secretaries of the discipline commissions, and policy chiefs—they make a point of avoiding candidates from home provinces.[18] Provincial leaders are regularly rotated—again, the same way the American military rotates base commanders. As a further incentive to keep local leaders loyal to Beijing, the most successful provincial leaders are promoted to national leadership. Three-quarters of the most recent Politburo membership served as provincial chiefs—a steady increase from the last two decades.

However, the center recognizes its limited capacity to manage all rungs of the party hierarchy. Other than a small handful of top officials, most local governments are staffed locally. Provincial party bosses appoint lower level officials and so on down to the local level.[19]

Regional interests actually are encouraged to shape the central government agenda. Competing local interests have emerged, based on networks and experience: "coast versus inland, north versus south, and metropolis versus small- and medium-sized cities."[20] Each provincial level unit of government has two full membership seats in the Communist Party's 350-member Central Committee. The four critical province-level "municipalities"—Beijing, Shanghai, Tianjin, and Chongqing—are regularly represented on the elite Politburo of twenty-five members.[21] Cities are often as important as the provinces to which they report: they are the main point of delivery for most social services, and more so than in the provinces, city leaders have the ability to raise revenues—particularly through complex real estate transactions. As a result, provinces often act simply as a "post office" between central government mandates and local government service delivery.[22]

So while GDP monotheism defined policy for thirty years, the devil of this religion lay in the local details. The central government

23

set broad directives and left the specific arrangements to each province and locality—whether it was the nature and extent of property rights, the ability to access foreign capital or goods, the development of infrastructure, tax authority, access to energy or mineral resources, the role of state-owned enterprises, or labor and environmental regulations.[23] However, the provinces and cities were not entirely free. Central ministries—each with its own priorities—jockeyed with provincial authorities for the best way to implement these broad directives.

In the most recent five-year plans, GDP monotheism has given way to goals such as environmental sustainability, harmonious development, and innovative growth. In the civics textbook version of Western democratic political systems, each of those goals would be a priority in various political parties, which would compete with one another by marketing those ideas to the public. The party that is elected, in theory, would have a mandate to advance that priority. In China, by contrast, all of those goals are adopted in principle by all units of government. In practice each goal then has a corresponding cluster of national ministries that are empowered to implement that goal. Ministry clusters compete with each other, and with provincial and local leaders, to control the national agenda.

National ministers (and even some state-owned enterprises) have the same rank as provincial party secretaries—perhaps the most important power balance in China, and what Brookings colleague Ken Lieberthal has aptly described as fragmented authoritarianism. The ministries' proximity to power in Beijing—and their formal inclusion in the State Council and Politburo—gives them leverage in formulating policy. Provinces are not powerless, however, since several of the largest provinces are also represented in the Politburo. That means that the provinces' and cities' ability to implement—or *not* implement—national policies "according to local conditions" gives them considerable leverage and has encouraged experimentation and entrepreneurialism.[24]

More broadly, Chinese society has become increasingly pluralistic. Debates among academics are widespread in universities across the country. The number of private businesses has grown exponentially in each decade. Civil society organizations are proliferating, particularly in providing services to citizens.

Still, while the country has formally adopted diverse goals and allowed a diversified economy and the proliferation of the Internet and social media, there is no official national recognition of *pluralism* as a value. The key official word is harmony: distinct pieces, working together and managed by a one-party state.[25] Provinces—let alone private individuals, associations, or corporations—do not have established rights to remain distinct entities. If there is a dark magic to managing China's very large population, it lies in the commitment to a single unified system and to burying disputes in an artificial language of harmony.

As the Chinese legal scholar He Weifang has argued, China's Communist Party still tilts far more in the direction of favoring "a competent leader" than it does "competent law." Despite a growing public demand for competent law, China's leaders still have not embraced an understanding of law that anticipates disharmony, varied values and rights, and the need for checks and balances. True rule of law will not be established in China until it is accepted that "lawyers inherently conflict with prosecutors, with judges, and even with public opinion. . . . Genuine harmony in a given society should be based on the respect for conflict through legal process."[26]

Across the country, the public has demanded the rule of law, particularly regarding land rights, social benefits, and the enforcement of labor and environmental laws. But this demand presents itself differently in different provinces. The uncertainty about the relative rights and power of the center and the provinces goes beyond institutions. It points to the back-room politics of modern China. Bargaining and reciprocity are the name of the game between officials with different priorities, beliefs, or interests—and often between them and business and private sector leaders. In the case of reciprocity, a policy is passed or implemented in exchange for a set of promotions or a decision to direct central resources. The center of gravity between Beijing and the localities has oscillated over the last thirty years, depending on which policies were being promoted, who was promoting them, and who was in place at the local level. In a few exceptional instances, the central power of the state is used to force change—such as the crackdown against local protests.[27] But even the central government has acknowledged that it has "implementation incapacity." One mainland publication plainly acknowledged China's internal reality: "While, to outsiders, China's effective single-party state speaks with a unitary voice, on the ground the reality is much more complex. At a news conference in 2012, prior to his retirement as premier, Wen [Jiabao] admitted his 'sadness' at failing to bridge the growing gulf between centralized policymaking and local implementation."[28]

Until recently China's fitful decentralization was largely considered a domestic matter. But local politics now are becoming central to how China engages with the world. In trade policy, coastal provinces have increasingly benefited from World Trade Organization accession and global finance. Many now support internationally accepted standards on a range of issues, from protecting the environment to intellectual property. Similarly, coastal cities like Shanghai and Tianjin want to become global financial centers, which means they must implement more transparent business practices. Still, a number of these provinces also promote "indigenous innovation" policies that seem designed to stall foreign competition—or even discourage the sale of goods produced in other Chinese provinces.

Inland provinces climbing up the economic ladder are even more likely to shun foreign scrutiny. Many low-cost industries have moved inland, where labor or environmental or intellectual property regulations are less actively enforced. Inland cities also have benefited from more opaque lending standards in their recent construction boom. And when coastal populations push for higher environmental standards, mineral-rich provinces in the west are either resistant or apathetic in enforcing them. Moreover, the economic development of western provinces is itself a national foreign policy priority that often gives those provincial leaders an upper hand in a wide range of national debates.

Beijing, in particular, prospers financially and politically by placing itself in the middle of this debate. Despite the commercial renown of Shanghai and Guangdong, Beijing is still a major force in Chinese business, particularly state-owned enterprises. It is still home to 100 of China's top 500 companies. Its GDP is the equivalent of Singapore's, and income per person is nearly that of Saudi Arabia. Only Shanghai has higher average income—just barely. Beijing has the best universities, museums, art galleries, and restaurants. And it is the epicenter of bargaining, where major decisions are still made and where inland China goes to seek help in catching up. But in many instances, the decisions made in Beijing are just the starting point for China's booming economy as it is really the implementation according to "local characteristics" that determines which regions prosper and lead the pack.

THE VIEW FROM NEW DELHI: FEDERALISM REDISCOVERED

India's challenge over the last two decades has been the same in practice as China's, even if it has been different in principle. In principle, India's national government has always embraced the goal of federalist local self-government, nominally carrying forward the spirit of Mahatma Gandhi, who led a nonviolent revolution against a colonial empire and who urged radical decentralization. Yet in practice, India has favored centralism. Only in the last two decades has it begun to give local leaders greater leeway to experiment with economic liberalization.

In principle, India's constitution promotes local control. The document binds thirty-five states and territories in a unitary government with federal features. It allows local autonomy in key arenas, with "schedules," or lists, of authorities for the central government, for the states, and for the center and states to share. More elephant than elegant, it is the lengthiest constitution in the world, at over 117,000 words—almost three times longer than this book. The U.S. Constitution with amendments is only 7,000 words—about the same length as this chapter.

The center was given prominence in national security and defense matters. To this day, regional and local leaders pay lip service to the center's primacy in representing India. Even the most nationalist of regional leaders or those who pursue a parochial foreign policy claim that they respect New Delhi's prerogatives to protect the country. In practice, the central government also has used its national security power to intervene to address a host of local ills.

At the top of the list are secession, repression, communalism, corruption, and incompetence. At first, secession was the greatest fear. In 1947 Pakistan had been carved out as a separate nation—which almost a decade and half later would experience the secession of Bangladesh. Control over Kashmir has remained in dispute, Hyderabad resented being subsumed, and Tamil Nadu would later contemplate secession.

In addition to secession, India's first prime minister, Nehru, feared communal violence. The magic of India is its diversity—its dozens of minority languages and religions, its multiplicity of castes and subcastes, all dispersed throughout hundreds of distinct regions. But since India's birth as an independent nation, its diversity has also exposed a birth defect—the local persecution of minorities. That persecution started with Hindu-Muslim-Sikh riots that scarred the infant nation, and such communal violence has recurred nearly every decade since independence.[29] So while local control was important in principle, in practice Nehru sought to promote and protect diverse populations and plural value systems across the states as a way of unifying the country.

Nehru was not content with being a benevolent traffic cop among states and various minority communities. To prevent secession and communalism, he used the massive national bureaucracy that India had inherited from the British to forge a common Indian identity. To this day, the national Indian Administrative Service (IAS) appoints elite bureaucrats in all of the states. State chief ministers and local mayors need IAS support to carry out local policies.[30] While local elected officials formally represent the grass roots of the world's largest democracy, they often are constrained from experimenting or being entrepreneurial by nationally appointed bureaucrats.[31]

As in China, a dark side of centralization emerged in India: an elaborate system of license requirements and regulations, as well as carefully crafted spoils and quotas to placate different communities. The "License Raj" has helped to stifle the economy and led to massive local mismanagement and corruption at all levels. And despite centralized control, communal animosities persisted. Communalist assassins have killed some of India's most revered figures. A Hindu nationalist shot Mahatma Gandhi. Nehru's daughter, Indira Gandhi, was gunned down by her own Sikh bodyguards, and her son Rajiv was blown up by Tamil extremists.[32]

India was slower than China to embrace decentralization. But finally in the early 1990s, with its economy about to collapse, the Congress Party slashed regulations. Among other things, it allowed state governments to further manage their own internal politics and to attract domestic and foreign investment. As in China, those policies produced growth, though—not surprisingly—in some states more than others.[33]

In some key states, prosperity and economic liberalization coincided. Some state governments were more successful in attracting investment, improving infrastructure, and educating their masses. But several states also had these advantages to begin with—particularly in the south and west. (See figures 2-4 and 2-5.) Wealthier states began to exert even more control over local matters.

Just as important, new regional parties began to influence policy at the national level, challenging the hegemony of the two national parties. The Congress Party had commanded a simple majority in

FIGURE 2-4. GDP Per Capita of Indian States, Fiscal Year 2000
Dollars

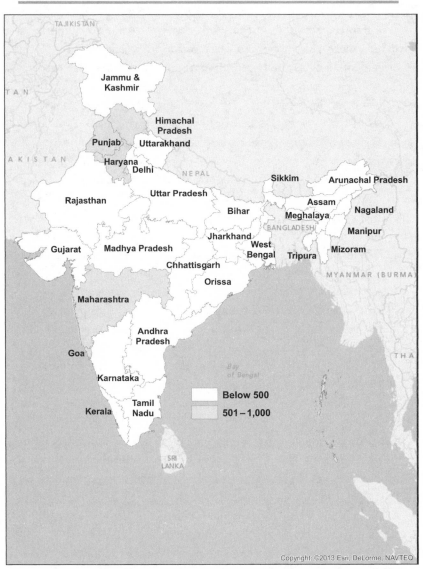

Source: Directorate of Economics Statistics of respective state governments, compiled by the Planning Commission, Government of India, "Per Capita Net State Domestic Product at Current Prices (as on 15-03-2012)" (http://planningcommission.nic.in/data/datatable/0512/databook_122.pdf).

FIGURE 2-5. GDP Per Capita of Indian States, Fiscal Year 2010
Dollars

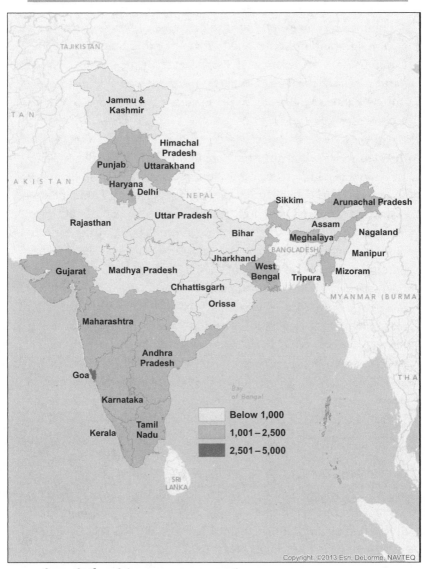

Source: See figure 2-4.

India's parliament for thirty-seven of India's first forty years. That dominance began to break down in the early 1990s. The other all-India party—the Hindu nationalist Bharatiya Janata Party (BJP)—could not get a majority, but it did succeed in welding together a governing coalition in the mid-1990s. Since that time, the BJP and Congress have traded power. But because of the rise of regional parties, neither the Congress Party nor the BJP is able to secure a full governing mandate by itself. Each has had to craft coalitions with regional parties.

Chief ministers who control regional parties now routinely threaten to leave the governing coalition to get what they want.[34] They now regularly block central efforts to make big public policy changes such as deregulating key industries or reregulating them in response to environmental challenges. That may be a good thing in those places where states are more effective laboratories for promoting economic growth or law and order. But it is significantly limiting the central government's ability to rule.

Ambitious states have stepped forward. The rise of India's more productive states—what we might call "forward states"—is reshaping India's view of the world as well as the world's views of India. A few key coastal states, in particular, have seized the initiative. The two great western coastal powerhouses—Maharashtra and Gujarat, with a combined population of nearly 200 million people—look to the energy resources and work opportunities in the Persian Gulf and the broader Middle East, as well as to the global diaspora of nonresident Indian financiers and traders, especially in the United States and United Kingdom. On the southeastern tip of the subcontinent, businesses in Chennai, the capital of Tamil Nadu, are forging closer trade relations with Southeast Asian nations. Moreover, a few cities dotting the spine of the subcontinent went global in the world of high tech. Starting in the south in Bangalore and moving north through Hyderabad and New Delhi (especially its suburb of Gurgaon), these newly emerging metropolises joined Chennai in taking advantage of a high-tech diaspora.

From a foreign policy standpoint, this outward orientation has, in its own way, undermined Nehru's centralized framework. It has begun to lessen the natural tendency to fixate on Pakistan and China as India's great national security threats. Central government officials in New Delhi had shaped this near obsession with India's northern neighbors, even if nearby poorer states with high Muslim populations, such as Uttar Pradesh and Bihar, had been less concerned. Coastal and southern states, such as Maharashtra, Tamil Nadu, and Karnataka, have a different perspective and want India to become a global economic player or at least to focus on other neighboring regions, such as the Arabian Sea, Southeast Asia, and Sri Lanka. Gujarat is pulled in both directions—on the one hand, enjoying the fruits of globalization; on the other hand, sharing a border with Pakistan and being a hub of Hindu nationalism.

Forward states also have tempered India's inclination to fight old third world battles in international organizations. India now is starting to seek high-end agreements on services, intellectual property rights, and investment. This shift has been gradual. It also has been a source of visible tension—especially with poorer states that cling to a preliberalization model of a closed economy.

A plurality of Indians still live in these so-called backward states—large, mostly landlocked, poorer, less literate, and less likely to be governed by globally focused leaders. "Backward states" is a technical term increasingly applied by the government to India's poorer locales—derived from the phrase "backward castes" that is used to describe lower social orders. The phrase even comes with its own formula, used to help determine which states qualify for additional assistance.[35] Local and regional parties are beginning to dominate here as well, representing unique ethnic and caste-based communities. That is, local leaders were elected not because they promised more effective, locally responsive governance but rather because they spoke the same language, came from the same caste, or held the same religious views as large "vote banks." As in the United States, when groups started to carve up electoral offices by ethnicity, it was often initially accompanied by cronyism. When favoritism is based on religion, it is pejoratively known as "communalism." Still, in the last few years, a second generation of regional parties in the backward states has now started to focus on the "politics of development." These new leaders carefully play the politics of caste, language, and religious identification when running for office, but they have tried to focus more directly on economic growth to lifts all boats, in both rural and urban areas.

New Delhi, as a province-level megacity of nearly 20 million people, is very much like Beijing in trying to balance local innovation, economic success, and economic failure. As a city, it has benefited considerably from the rush of business that has come to India. Most global companies now have New Delhi addresses, and real estate prices rival the most exclusive neighborhoods of Mumbai—not to mention Singapore or Beijing. It has an upper-middle-income standard of living, with modern subways and airports. But New Delhi also still bears the traditional central concern about standing up for lower castes, religious minorities, and the rural poor. And it still has its own challenges of local grinding poverty and lawlessness that are a reminder for India and the world that even India's centerpiece city still leaves much to be desired.

BE CAREFUL WHAT YOU WATCH, AND WHERE YOU WATCH

The Chinese saying "Be careful what you wish" was repeated to me countless times before taking this trip. As I traveled, what often was more apparent was my own inability to fully grasp what I was seeing. So before diving into China's and India's local politics, it is worth sharing a few cautions about what counts as an observable fact in each country.

First, there is the quality of the data. In both countries, good data are hard to find. The rapidly changing nature of the economy can make it difficult for officials to accurately measure industrial production, employment, and other key indicators.

In China local officials may intentionally raise or lower GDP figures to meet their desired targets. Data—from economic output to measures of air quality—are critical to evaluating officials for promotion. To address this, Beijing has encouraged more direct reporting by businesses to the National Bureau of Statistics. Still, these surveys are incomplete, and private and state-owned companies also misreport in order to avoid taxes and regulation.[36] As a result, national statistics and the aggregate of provincial statistics often do not add up to the same total.[37] For instance, the GDP calculated by the central government is often lower than the sum of figures reported by the provinces.[38] The tendency toward unreliable data is exacerbated by the lack of reportage from a fully free and investigative press.

In India the government recognizes this challenge. The Reserve Bank of India Governor D. Subbarao has recently stated that government data for economic output and prices were neither reliable nor consistent. As in China, this failing arises from a combination of corruption and lack of skills.[39] In 2010 the Central Statistical Organization miscalculated the rise in consumption as 0.3 percent and later corrected it to 3.8 percent, realizing it had overestimated inflation.[40] India's commerce secretary admitted in 2011 that miscalculations and data entry errors led to inflated export figures. Politicians may inflate population data to boost their ethnic group's political representation, as they did in the 2001 census in Nagaland.[41] Unlike in China, India's vibrant free press—including a number of top-notch English language papers, magazines, and journals—does contribute somewhat to fact checking and accountability. Still, the vast size of the country makes it difficult for any news outlet to track all government economic reports. And the majority of news outfits do not rank quality journalism as their top goal.

Another caution concerns the concepts of "center" and "local," which have very different meanings in each country. On paper, China is a far more centralized system, yet local authorities really are very much on their own. It is the appearance of harmony that is far more important than the reality. India's system is far more pluralistic on paper but is in some ways far more centralized in practice. The vibrancy of state and local elections, and of a free press, presents a far more colorful mosaic. Still, in the name of protecting individual rights and carrying forward the rule of law, the center is in many ways more involved in the life of the states and localities. As a result, centrally appointed bureaucratic figures are less accountable to locally elected officials on local matters— from investment policy to infrastructure, from residency permits to marriage licenses to garbage collection. More recently the center of authority has shifted downward dramatically, but those relationships are only now starting to change.

A key reference point is how each central government sees its mission. Both China and India are concerned about balance, especially between local autonomy and central power. In China's case, leaders focus largely on growing the economy. Only recently has GDP monotheism begun to give way to a more complex understanding of what economic growth entails. That means balancing the interests of the inland and coastal areas, the first-tier cities and lower-tier cities, and the various regions, particularly the dynamic southeast and the sparsely populated north and west. In India it is about finding the balance between forward states and backward states, and among the goals of global economic growth, democratic representation, and inclusion of various ethnic groups, religious minorities, and castes. If China has had one false god of economic growth at all costs, India has had to wrestle with the demands of too many gods that have held back sustained growth.

Moreover, in both places, the challenge has been to connect the local to the national to the global. Each is starting to refine its commitment to pluralism and to local control. Each country's capital is trying to balance that commitment with national goals and policies. And finally, each is trying to connect those enterprises to the global economy and global challenges. In neither place has that three-part challenge been easy, nor is the effort anywhere close to being complete.

CHAPTER THREE

CHINA:
PROMISED LANDS, HEARTLANDS, BADLANDS

TODAY'S CHINA IS a crowded three-panel landscape painting. The first panel is a vibrant entrepreneurial coast. The second is a rising, inland region, where most Chinese live and where state-led economic growth dominates. The third is a remote, restive, but resource-rich west. Given this diversity, China's leaders are obsessed with preserving unity—or perhaps more accurately, creating it. Knitting together very different economies, societies, and even political cultures is among the top leadership's hardest jobs. It is particularly hard because many of China's great successes—and also failures—have come from allowing greater local control.

The stock phrase "state-led capitalism" fails to capture this massive project. Across China the government plays an important role. But that role differs from region to region, province to province, and even city to city. From this varied context, leaders in Beijing struggle to weave a unified narrative.

China's coast—with which most of the world is familiar—has become the manufacturing epicenter of the planet. Thanks largely to the coast, in 2012 China became the global leader in world trade, surpassing the United States.[1] Hundreds of millions of Chinese found work in coastal provinces, making inexpensive goods consumed around the world. Partly as a result, nearly half

37

FIGURE 3-1. Sector Share of GDP by Country, 2011

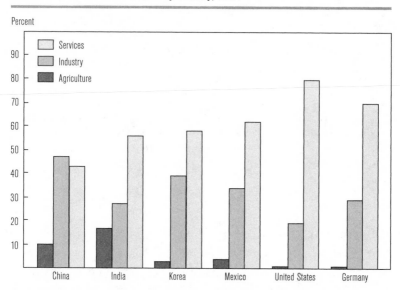

Source: Figure created by author based on 2011 data from Central Intelligence Agency, "CIA World Factbook" (www.cia.gov/library/publications/the-world-factbook/), respective country pages.

of China's economy is in industry—a higher share than in most wealthier countries such as the United States or even Korea, as well as in poorer countries such as India (see figure 3-1).

But coastal China's fast growth is also straining world trade and finance. Many countries assert that China keeps its currency artificially low, making its exports competitive.

Inland China anchors the nation's political stability. Six of ten Chinese live in provinces west of the coast. Keeping the anchor secure requires enormous wealth transfers from the east. Industry is also becoming a bigger part of these economies, but very little of it is exported or even made for consumer goods. Instead, most economic activity in the interior has been in construction and other "fixed assets"—where China also leads the world (figure 3-2). That heavy emphasis on investment is becoming a global concern.

FIGURE 3-2. National Economies by Expenditure Type, 2011

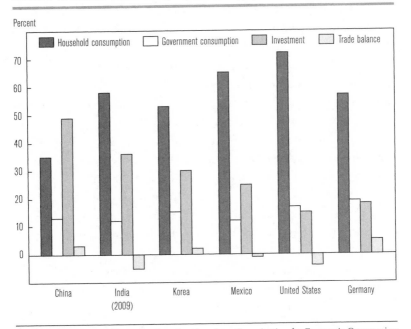

Source: Figure created by author based on data from Organization for Economic Cooperation and Development, "OECD StatExtracts" (http://stats.oecd.org/Index.aspx?DatasetCode=SNA_TABLE1).

Many worry that Chinese local governments have created a real estate and public infrastructure bubble, having spent so wildly that they cannot possibly produce a return on the investment.[2] In an interdependent world economy, a hard landing for China's economy would lead to slumps in other parts of the world that depend on selling raw materials, parts, or finished goods to China.

Finally, China's remote west has produced a resource bonanza for the country. The west has abundant coal, oil, natural gas, and minerals. Mining of an unprecedented scale is helping fuel growth in the interior and coast, and potentially links China's west to a dozen countries in Central Asia. But the road west has not been built without considerable human and environmental tolls. Restive populations in the hinterland have been at the center of major protests and uprisings in each year of China's great rise. And those restive lands border even more troubled neighbors—from Pakistan to Afghanistan to Mongolia.

It is easy to think of China as a monolith—partly because China's insistence that others respect its unity has meant that the country often portrayed itself in a single hue. With that in mind, it is critical to state what should be obvious: different regions have very distinct commercial histories and views of authority. Since Deng Xiaoping's time, implementation of central policy has been left largely to local authorities and adapted to local circumstances. Provinces, cities, and county-level authorities all compete to promote growth. This entails a range of strategies for attracting foreign investment, as well as other activities that—wittingly or unwittingly—affect a wider world.

All of China looks to Beijing for support. Central ministries, banks, state-owned enterprises, and political factions within the Communist Party all are resources to be tapped. In 2012 tax rebates and transfer payments from the central government accounted for 43 percent of local government revenue.[3] Central authorities in Beijing still hold considerable power. But those leaders actually are trying to manage many local Chinas.

The control exerted by the central government across these regions is not always uniform and direct. As often as not, it is steered and funded by local leaders. So any effort by central leaders to adjust trade policy or to rebalance China's economy has a wide array of distinct local consequences. Worse still, their ability to implement any effort is deeply dependent on the cooperation and effectiveness of local leaders. For those reasons, the rest of the world has a major stake in better understanding all three panels of the Chinese landscape.

COASTAL CHINA: PROMISED LANDS

About four in ten Chinese live in a province that borders the Pacific Ocean. These are the provinces that Deng Xiaoping promised would

FIGURE 3-3. China's Urban Population, 2010[a]

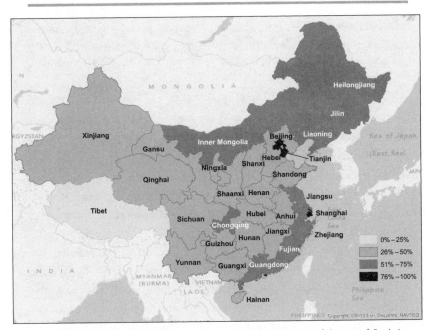

Source: Figure created by author based on data from the National Bureau of Statistics, *China Statistical Yearbook 2011* (Beijing: China Statistics Press, 2011).

a. Expressed as percent of total province population.

bring wealth to China. Those dozen provinces are responsible for nearly two-thirds of China's economy. Four coastal provinces in particular—Guangdong, Shanghai (a municipality with the rank of province), Jiangsu, and Zhejiang—stand head and shoulders above the rest, particularly in generating the export-led revenues that are fueling the rest of China's growth.

In 2011 China led the world in exports, with $1.57 trillion—just ahead of the United States at $1.48 trillion. The big four coastal provinces were responsible for 70 percent of that. With about 250 million people—one-fifth of China's population—these provinces are responsible for about one-third of the economy, and they are among the most urbanized provinces in China (see figure 3-3).

As China's new leaders come to power, the promise of further economic reform has raised expectations on the coast. But exactly which reforms might be pursued is very much an open question. And each province views the reform agenda somewhat differently from the rest.

Guangdong: Pro-Market Reforms Meet Political Reform

In his first trip after becoming the new top leader, Xi Jinping traveled to Shenzhen, in Guangdong province. By visiting China's southern coast and its largest province, Xi sought to highlight that region's importance to the country's recent past and to its immediate future. He was both honoring and mimicking a similar trip by a Chinese leader that had occurred twenty years earlier, when Deng Xiaoping traveled to Shenzhen in 1992 to restart liberalization of China's economy following the Tiananmen Square crackdown.

With over 100 million people, Guangdong is larger than California, Texas, New York, and Florida combined. And to some degree, its distance from the central government has been a blessing. Cantonese is spoken across the province rather than Mandarin. Guangdong was long known for its commercial prowess and also for epitomizing the expression "The mountains are high, and the emperor is far away."[4] Deng's trip to Guangdong—a province once run by Xi Jinping's father—pushed the province to more radically experiment with attracting foreign investment. But to emphasize a new, Beijing-coordinated approach to development, Deng also sped the development of Shenzhen—a centrally planned, Mandarin-speaking special economic zone near Hong Kong.[5]

Deng Xiaoping intentionally focused on coastal development as liberalization's first stage. "The coastal areas, which comprise a vast region with a population of 200 million, should accelerate their opening to the outside world, and we should help them develop rapidly first; afterwards they can promote the development of the interior."[6] The coast's historical access to foreign markets and capital, and the relative ease of transporting goods abroad, made it ripe for development. Guangdong's proximity to Hong Kong and Macau—both of which were still European colonies at the time of the opening—also gave the province access to Cantonese-speaking Chinese who could help connect it to the global economy.

The results of Guangdong's opening have literally changed the world. Americans who cross the Delaware River by train are familiar with the huge glowing letters that adorn a neighboring bridge: "Trenton Makes—The World Takes." Today, that bridge would be more accurate if it spanned the Pearl River in Guangdong. That is the case in Guangzhou, the province's capital, as much as it is in Shenzhen. Each city is home to over 10 million people.

Guangdong's exports have fueled public investment in world-class airports, high-speed trains, glitzy shopping malls, and infinite smartphone options. This region's main concerns for the future are high-end as well: strengthening intellectual property rights and attracting multinationals to the newly built "innovation and technology" industrial parks. The region's governments and businesses also now battle over trade conflicts at the World Trade Organization (WTO) to keep their products dominant in the markets they have developed around the world.

Of the big four export provinces, Guangdong is king, accounting for about one-third of China's total— more than the value of exports from all of Great Britain.[7] Nearly two-thirds of all of Guangdong's goods and services are shipped overseas. The province accounted for about 29 percent of the nation's foreign trade in 2009. Exports made up over 60 percent of Guangdong's GDP.[8]

Many in China pay close attention to the "Guangdong model." About half of its economy is private, both in terms of the number of enterprises and the size of their output.[9] Most products are sold abroad, and many of the private firms are owned by foreigners, with Guangdong's contribution being the land and the workforce but not necessarily the corporate shareholders or upper management.[10] In 2011 Guangdong was the province least oriented toward fixed asset investment, at roughly 33 percent. This is because China had already invested in Guangdong's infrastructure. And as the first province in China to open its economy, Guangdong attracted a flood of foreign direct investment. However, that flood was reduced to a trickle. As Deng predicted—and as his successors have mandated—that investment is now turning inland.

Politics in Guangdong have earned as much attention as its economics. Wang Yang, the provincial party secretary until December 2012, was surprisingly receptive to the voices of ordinary people and civil society groups. He embraced nongovernmental organizations and independent labor organizations—standing at the verge of giving them official recognition. Wang personally negotiated with Honda Motors for wage increases and worker safety improvements and prioritized intellectual property protection so that foreign investors would establish high-value research and development hubs. And in 2011 he sided with a violent peasant uprising in the village of Wukan, prosecuting local party leaders for corruption.

Wang Yang even raised eyebrows by suggesting a new set of public values that sound downright Jeffersonian. "We must shake off the wrong idea that the people owe their welfare and happiness to some dispensation from the party and government."[11]

He did not stop with downgrading the role of the state. With cell phone, Internet, and social media usage rapidly expanding in Guangdong, Wang Yang also seemed to endorse the voice and rights of the people.[12] "People's democratic awareness is increasing significantly in this changing society. . . . When their appeals for rights aren't getting enough attention, that's when mass incidents happen."[13]

Still, when it came to political reforms, the fickleness of local government in China resurfaced within weeks of the country's leadership transition. Wang Yang handed over the reins of power in Guangdong in December 2012. Shortly after that, the *Southern*

Weekly, a privately owned reform-minded paper, was aggressively edited by censors for the first time in many years. The paper's editors appeared to cave under pressure, causing journalists and local residents to protest. After a standoff of several weeks, however, reporters returned to work, under the promise that future restrictions would be loosened. Time will tell whether the province's new leaders lean more toward the locals or toward various competing masters in Beijing.

Shanghai: The Gang and the Global Financial Center

In his rise to power, Xi Jinping probably took his most important step in the spring of 2007 when he became party secretary in Shanghai, the Yangtze River Delta municipality with over 20 million people and the rank of a province. As China's wealthiest city, it rivals Guangdong in economics and Beijing in politics. Perhaps that is why it is so loved by foreigners and feared by many inland Chinese—and why Xi Jinping's appointment was so important.

Xi's assignment to Shanghai was a cleanup operation. The previous autumn, central authorities in Beijing had just slapped down Shanghai's party chief, Chen Liangyu. Under Chen, Shanghai was booming, with annual growth at 12 percent a year.[14] Chen also was growing in political power as the head of the so-called Shanghai Gang. He was increasingly critical of Hu Jintao and Wen Jiabao's macroeconomic policies, which tended to focus on developing inland provinces and the politics of social cohesion.[15] To demonstrate that Hu was in charge, central authorities investigated Chen for corruption, eventually expelling him from the party. Still, the national leaders needed to appoint someone who understood the critical role of the Yangtze River Delta. Eventually they settled on Xi Jinping, the party chief of neighboring Zhejiang province.

Shanghai is the jewel of the Yangtze River Delta, China's most dynamic and globally oriented region, and the financial and commercial center of the country, with ambitions to become a global financial center by 2020. For centuries the region also has been a political counterbalance to Beijing. Nearby Nanjing served from time to time as China's capital. Many of the most important debates during China's economic liberalization have pivoted around how strong and powerful the Yangtze River Delta trio—Shanghai, Jiangsu, and Zhejiang—would grow.

Of all the mainland cities in China, Shanghai is the most worldly and foreigner friendly (not to mention child friendly). In addition to global finance and commerce, Shanghai is home to world-class arts, entertainment, fine dining, fashion, and sports. Our family's three weeks in Shanghai were guided by an American who now runs a series of magazines owned by Singaporeans, targeting high-net-worth individuals. We visited with a global fashion and costume designer, Han Feng, who splits her time between Shanghai and New York. We dined at a Greek restaurant with a Thessalonica-based wine importer, who is starting a vineyard in central China. We went to museums and plays and the ESPN X-Games and Nike Superstore—any of which we could have done in San Francisco or Singapore.

Shanghai is China's version of New York: a managerial and commercial home for businesses that make goods elsewhere in China—and even elsewhere in Asia—with services making up nearly 60 percent of the municipality's outputs.[16] Together, Shanghai and its neighbors, Jiangsu and Zhejiang, export over $700 billion worth of goods and services a year.[17] It is tempting—and not wrong—to think of these three provinces as China's version of New York City's tri-state area—but with almost ten times as many people, four times the exports, and a trade surplus close to $150 billion.

To achieve its goal of becoming a global financial center by 2020, Shanghai will need to accelerate that trend. That will include further reducing the role of the state in business and opening up the political decision-making process to public view. It will also require the central government to reinforce positive steps in the rule of law and to allow China's currency to be more easily exchanged abroad.[18] These are enormous undertakings.

So the question for Shanghai is whether it will continue to move toward a private sector, service-oriented economy or remain anchored in state-led investment. If China's leadership chooses a private sector path for the entire country, then the new Politburo Standing Committee appears to be a Shanghai "dream team." In addition to Xi Jinping, it also includes Yu Zhengsheng, who succeeded Xi as party secretary of Shanghai. At least two other Standing Committee members have strong ties to the region.[19] The resilience of Shanghai-based politicians suggests that inland China knows the importance of this coastal province, even if it bears careful watching.

But if the Standing Committee chooses to advance private sector goals, it may also undercut other infrastructure and investment-oriented businesses based in Shanghai—particularly state-owned enterprises. Construction and manufacturing have not left entirely, and those firms are still largely state owned. The municipality continues to design and build highways and subways, high-speed trains and airports, office buildings and residential housing of various kinds. These state-owned companies directly employ one out of five Shanghainese.[20] A new airport on the east side of town, several new subway lines, and the new financial center development in Pudong—with not one but two buildings over 110 stories tall—have transformed Shanghai's infrastructure, all with a lot of help from the government. Investment now has tapered off, and the construction boom has slowed. If the Communist Party's Standing Committee pursues a private sector approach, it will still need to fill those vacant apartments and offices, as well as find employment for workers in the slowing construction and manufacturing trades.

Jiangsu and the Singapore Sling

Even when the government is behind an enterprise, investing in coastal China is not without its difficulties. Just ask Lee Kuan Yew, former prime minister of Singapore, about his country's experience in Jiangsu province.

47

Deng Xiaoping invited Singapore to invest in Jiangsu's biggest city, Suzhou, just north of Shanghai. Deng admired Lee greatly. Lee was an ethnic Chinese leader who brought the small island nation of Singapore economic wealth and dynamism without sacrificing social order or political control.

The Suzhou Industrial Park was launched as a $20 billion, 20-year, Sino-Singapore joint venture featuring high-tech factories and office buildings and also eventually housing for nearly 1 million people. President Jiang Zemin and Premier Zhu Rongji personally assured Lee Kuan Yew that the project would be a special priority.[21]

Suzhou seemed like an ideal spot for a joint Chinese-Singapore partnership. Jiangsu is China's fastest growing export hub and fifth-largest province, with almost 80 million people—nearly the population of Germany. Jiangsu's two major cities—Suzhou and Nanjing—are homes to factories whose headquarters are in nearby Shanghai. Though smaller than Guangdong in size and exports, Jiangsu is also wealthier, with per capita annual income at about $8,000—almost 20 percent higher than Guangdong's at $6,800.

The province ranks second to Beijing in large companies. But unlike Beijing, many Jiangsu companies are privately owned.[22] And while Guangdong exports 67 percent of its goods and services, Jiangsu exports only 44 percent—with the rest being directed toward consumer goods and local fixed asset investment in machinery, electronics, automobiles, and chemicals.

Despite all this promise, the deal went sour quickly. Local autonomy combined with an opaque political system to undermine the joint venture. The question in Suzhou is not "whither state-led growth?" but rather "which government is in charge?"[23] The Jiangsu provincial government and Suzhou city government, it appears, were never fully on board. They developed a competing Suzhou New District. Jiangsu had been known for policy experimentation; the local bureaucracy was famous for lobbying the central government both for resources and the freedom to experiment. Jiangsu had a patchwork of development zones—twenty-six directed by the center and ninety-nine by the province—designed to compete with—and often undercut—one another.[24] However, the top leadership in Beijing was not necessarily informed about these projects.

By 1999 Singapore had decided to call it quits. "Unless the system can adjust itself to meet the increasing demand on government, its legitimacy will be questioned," Lee Kuan Yew told business leaders in Shanghai. "The most pernicious problem of all is corruption that has become embedded in the administrative culture; hard to eradicate."[25] Local Chinese countered that Singaporeans did not have the patience to understand local customs.

Zhejiang: Alibaba and the Den of Thieves

If Jiangsu is China's hotbed province for government aggressively helping to attract investment, then Zhejiang is China's hothouse for homegrown entrepreneurs. The struggle in Zhejiang is not limiting either government or state-owned enterprises. It is getting reliable capital into the hands of capitalists.

The arena for this struggle is Hangzhou, a beautiful 1,500-year-old lake city that is among China's most revered urban settings. "Just as there is paradise in heaven, on earth there are Hangzhou and Suzhou."

Hangzhou is also a merchant's paradise. In addition to important large companies, thousands of sophisticated small and medium-size enterprises call the city home. Incomes are high, both in the city and in the surrounding countryside. If you want to import anything from solar chargers to sweeteners, from wicker furniture to wax candles, from maternity clothing to medical devices, come to Hangzhou.

Connecting all these firms to their customers is Alibaba. Named after the Muslim merchant who outwits the forty thieves to gain the secret treasure, this trading services company has become a metaphor for private Chinese capitalism. Founded by Jack Ma, the company connects small-scale Chinese manufacturers with domestic and foreign suppliers and distributors. Alibaba will find you a manufacturer and help arrange the logistics. The company's main website is a cross between eBay and Amazon, connecting one small business to another. If you want to sell three-color spandex underwear, and you are willing to buy at least 1,000 units, it will show you five manufacturers.[26]

That entrepreneurial spirit has led *Forbes* to rank Hangzhou as first among Chinese cities in providing a business-friendly environment. The private sector contributes more than 60 percent to Zhejiang's economy, and three out of four workers are privately employed.[27] In 2010 Zhejiang had 180 out of the top 500 private enterprises in China, compared to Jiangsu with 130 and Guangdong with only 13. Because businesses in Zhejiang and Jiangsu are larger and more diversified, they have a competitive advantage over Guangdong.[28] And the province has been among the least dependent of all provinces on fixed asset investment.[29]

In theory China's recent 2012 slowdown should have been good for the private sector here. The slowing of stimulus spending should have benefited firms that did not rely on government support. But, in fact, the opposite has been true: China's efforts to cool off growth have meant that state-owned banks are slowing down their lending. Private sector banks are not large or developed enough to step in and service the market for smaller enterprises. Moreover, private firms that lack government support have been particularly hard hit by slowing global exports.

This definitely has been the case in Zhejiang, especially for the province's small and medium-size enterprises. The export slowdown also has made it even harder for them to get access to financing. Even before the slowdown, large state-owned enterprises in Beijing, Shanghai, and Jiangsu had an advantage in borrowing from state-owned banks. Those same banks have been notoriously cautious in lending to small firms. Independent firms' internal operations tend to be underdeveloped. They often lack the transparency or connections needed to get credit—or both. As a result, a number of smaller firms have sought the help of larger firms to guarantee

BOX 3-1. A Very Special Administrative Region: Hong Kong

Just off the coast of Guangdong province lie two "special administrative regions" that are anomalies in China. While they belong to the People's Republic of China, they are allowed to have their own governments, elect their own leaders and legislators, enact their own laws, print their own money, and levy their own taxes and tariffs. English dominates Hong Kong; both Portuguese and English are widely spoken in Macau.

Hong Kong at first felt familiar. In this vibrant, exciting city, we were pleasantly surprised by the strong presence of mountains, ocean, parks, and periodic blue skies—an Asian version of San Francisco. A visit to Hong Kong Disneyland was a huge hit with the kids.

A leading businessman from nearby Shenzhen made a day trip all the way to Hong Kong to take us to dinner. For him, Hong Kong was the promised land. He told us how much he admired the transparency of Hong Kong's government and its businesses. A local cab driver told us how much he feared the government corruption and corporate criminality on the mainland, especially the corrosive effect it might have on Hong Kong.

But by the end of our stay, we were also left with the uneasy feeling that we'd seen the future—and it was made largely of steel and concrete. Much of the city is connected by large underground shopping malls, walkways, and escalators; restaurants, hotels, grocery stores, and luxury shops all share space in giant, interconnected buildings. One could live for days without ever having to step foot outside. At times it felt like something from the movie *WALL-E*—especially as we realized that this was to be many countries' way to deal with increased crowding, warming, and pollution.

—Kristen Suokko

their credit. By doing so, big firms enable small firms to secure loans from state-owned banks. Other small firms have avoided these complicated schemes and gone directly to informal lenders.

What had once been a credit challenge for Zhejiang's small and medium-size enterprises may now be a credit crisis. With exports down, those small and medium-size enterprises that were able to find financing are now racking up higher nonperforming loans.

Banks cannot collect on loans made to credit-bundling firms. Private banks now are unwilling to lend to even healthy small businesses.[30]

The central government has been quick to act. In March 2012, Wen Jiabao visited Zhejiang's other major city, Wenzhou, to encourage private banks to lend to small businesses. Central authorities also allowed local authorities to attempt a financial reform pilot project to allow greater access to foreign capital.[31] Still, nonperforming loans in Wenzhou hit 3 percent in August 2012. One national bank based in southern China had a nonperforming loan rate of over 9 percent. Television and newspaper media reported on a number of suicides and disappearances of entrepreneurs unable to pay their debts.

Like Alibaba, Zhejiang's entrepreneurs see the rest of China as thieves to be outsmarted. Yet at a time when leaders are struggling with whether to make the nation's economy even more private sector friendly, Zhejiang poses a policy dilemma. Local authorities can apply the policy here that the central government has urged elsewhere: tighten credit to prevent unhealthy speculation. More likely, local authorities will try to help Zhejiang keep its secret treasure by further easing financing for the right kinds of businesses—small and medium-size enterprises in the private sector, particularly those serving domestic consumer markets. That ideal narrow outcome may be elusive in practice.

The Promised Lands' Three Major Global Challenges

China's major coastal provinces—Guangdong and the Yangtze River Delta trio—provide a spectrum of models for economic growth. Each differently mixes public and private industry, manufacturing and services, and imports and exports. That diversity has helped create China's most prosperous region. But it also generates great competition between government entities—as exemplified by Jiangsu's dueling enterprise zones. Indeed, the central government has tried to regain control of the agenda by proposing regional development plans, with a goal of better utilizing resources and promoting coordination among local jurisdictions.[32]

Some common global themes and priorities emerge from the effort to make the coast more competitive globally. First there is the challenge of how to make private firms more competitive. The initial wave of growth came from using low-cost labor to assemble parts and applying technology designed elsewhere. Now firms must focus on producing goods and services higher up the value chain. State-owned companies have survived in China's protected domestic economy, but those firms right now cannot compete in advanced industries with foreign firms. In the high-value-added sectors, a more entrepreneurial and innovative model is needed if China is to become globally competitive.[33] Many argue that this will involve getting state-owned enterprises to become leaner and less reliant on government subsidies.[34]

Meanwhile, local governments are feeling the strain of less support from central authorities. Where once they could depend on Beijing to help them invest in roads and bridges, currently more central transfers are applied toward inland areas—meaning not only less support from Beijing but also higher taxes within the provinces.

The coast also will have to adjust to greater trade scrutiny. This could actually help China address the challenge of making its firms more competitive. However, this will not be easy. Jiangsu province provides a telling example. It is the epicenter of China's solar manufacturing industry, with over 600 firms in the supply chain for developing solar panels for export—with the help of considerable subsidies. As of this writing, these firms are facing a global glut, thanks especially to falling purchase subsidies and tax breaks in the United States and Europe, and also to decreasing natural gas prices. Given the more intense competition, American and European solar producers are now blaming their own hard times on unfair Chinese practices. Their governments have now leveled a series of WTO complaints against China for dumping these products on global markets. So Jiangsu—a province that has benefited handsomely from China's entry into the WTO—now may have to comply with a negative ruling.[35] This may be in Jiangsu's own best interest, but that will not make compliance any easier politically.

Protecting intellectual property is among the most critical elements of coastal China's trade agenda—particularly if the region hopes to move up the value chain. For many years, the region was known as a home of piracy—particularly in Guangdong, where manufacturing firms famously produced knockoffs of Western goods almost as quickly as industrial plans were faxed to people building a new factory. As a result, Guangdong province in particular has had a hard time getting investment in the information technology industry. [36] Local technology companies often are working on second- or third-generation products. New intellectual property is pirated so quickly in China that many technology innovators choose to avoid doing first-generation design and manufacturing on the mainland. So local governments are now pushing to establish a higher level of intellectual property protection to attract a higher level foreign capital—though their ability to implement and enforce such protections and follow through on that rhetoric is still doubted by many foreign firms.[37]

Finally, coastal China has the biggest stakes in getting China to modernize its financial system. Access to capital is a huge challenge for private sector companies. Since capital controls are set in Beijing—and not subject to international exchange rates—private industry tends to wait in line behind state-owned enterprises. Financial sector reform poses some of the hardest choices for coastal China. On the one hand, a freer currency would allow private sector firms greater access to international capital. On the other hand, a freer capital regime would eliminate some of the competitive advantages Chinese companies already enjoy, both from an artificially low exchange rate and from privileged access to state financing.[38]

INLAND CHINA: HEARTLANDS

In 1988 Deng Xiaoping saw the future: "When the coastal areas have developed to a certain extent, they will be required to give still more help to the interior. Then, the development of the interior provinces will be of overriding importance, and the coastal areas will in turn have to subordinate themselves to it."[39]

That subordination is happening now.

Nearly 800 million people—or about six out of ten Chinese—live in inland provinces. Yet they are responsible only for one-third of China's economy. Half of those people are found in four provinces that make up a central economic region, adjacent to the provinces on the coast. These provinces—Anhui, Henan, Hubei, and Hunan—are the historic agricultural heartland of China. The other half of this inland population resides beyond this area, in the deep interior.

Nearly every inland province is still more rural than urban. Inland GDP per capita is still below $4,000 year. Mao, Deng, and many of their revolutionary counterparts hailed from the interior.

Today these vast provinces are struggling to grow their economies and create more jobs. They are desperate to grow their cities and turn them into manufacturing centers, looking to attract low-end industries that are being priced out operating in coastal provinces.

Beijing is greasing the wheels. When I mentioned to a driver in Shanghai that I had just flown in from Beijing, his response was typical: "Did you see my money in Beijing? Where have they spent it now?" The answer is, somewhere inland. Fiscal transfers aim to address the huge income gap between China's coast and interior—a gap that is still growing. In 2000 the average person living on China's coast made $845 a year more than his or her counterpart in the west. By 2009 that number had grown to $3,074.[40] More than 60 percent of the financial expenditure in the central and western regions came from central government transfer payments.[41] Between 2003 and 2007, almost 90 percent of central government transfers were used to support the central and western regions.[42] While many coastal Chinese resent the transfers, others see them as a necessary rebalancing after decades of preferences for the coast.

The world has a stake in this great cash transfer. The development of China's heartland is critical for political stability. The economic boom of the last thirty years was fueled by hundreds of millions of inland workers making their way to coastal factories. The effort to build self-sustaining interior economies is now what keeps China's leaders up at night. Or it should be.

Fiscal transfers and other preferential policies are only investments. They do not, by themselves, create sustainable business models. In fact, many now wonder whether those investments were financially sound and whether the environmental and other social costs are worth the price. If sustained economic activity cannot be developed in China's interior, China and the rest of the world could suffer. Sustainability may depend on greater transparency than inland leaders are capable of tolerating.

In this vast expanse of China, many provinces could help tell this story. It is worth focusing just on the provinces that make up the Western Economic Triangle of Sichuan, Shaanxi, and Chongqing provinces, over 1,000 miles from the coast. For at least the last sixty years, as far as Beijing has been concerned, they have been among the most critical of all inland provinces—a refuge during China's civil war and World War II, and also the edge of Han civilization as China faced its far west interior. These provinces lie on the western edge of China's interior.[43] In a recent survey of foreign businesses operating in China, their three capital cities (Chengdu, Xi'an, and Chongqing) ranked as the most likely next destinations for foreign investment.[44] The provinces are home to about 160 million people, roughly equal to the population of the Yangtze River Delta trio.

Field of Dreams or Real Estate Fantasy?

China's inland west is trying to adopt the same strategy that propelled China's coastal east: "Build it and they will come." It's right out of the movie *Field of Dreams,* where an Iowa farmer built a baseball diamond in his corn field, miraculously attracting baseball players across time and space to come play. Just when the family wondered how it could afford to live without using that field for corn, a stream of fans started flooding into the field, demonstrating their love of the game (and presumably saving the farm).

If China's coast is struggling to make a transition to a more outwardly oriented set of norms and practices, inland regions are simply trying to replicate the growth strategy that first propelled the coast toward higher productivity and wealth. Traveling west in China feels like traveling back in time. Inland regions are fighting hard to attract investment while reluctantly loosening the helpful and visible hand of government. So far, growth has been stimulated by a combination of direct government spending and lending by state-owned banks.

Coastal provinces once grew the same way. Major public investment was combined with liberalization to help lure export-oriented manufacturing. That same strategy is now being adopted inland. Nearly 70 percent of all inland economic activity is focused on building airports, roads, office buildings and apartments, power plants, factories, and equipment. On the coast, by contrast, that number is around 40 percent. Inland China is banking on the fact that urbanization and rising incomes will make its investments pay off and stimulate the economy. Those funds are spread across twenty-some provinces in the center and west of the country.

The name "Western Triangle" is telling. The provinces' three capital cities—Chengdu, Xi'an, and Chongqing—technically are still east of China's "midfield stripe," but they are the western edge of populated China.[45] Imagine that Chengdu is St. Louis, except that there is no coastal California-Oregon-Washington on China's western border. Instead, the lands west of Chengdu are high desert and vast mountains. Though more than half of China's area lies west of the Western Triangle, more than 90 percent of China's people live east. It is also the western edge of a monolithically *Han* China, with the country's eastern provinces being over 96 percent Han Chinese.

Upon landing in Xi'an and Chengdu, my family's first impressions were that we had arrived in more spread-out versions of an east coast Chinese metropolis. Modern high-speed expressways and ring roads eased us into glass- and steel-dominated downtowns. The skylines, while not quite so tall and crowded as in Shanghai, still have plenty of forty- and fifty-story buildings. Luxury stores dot the main squares, as do billboards hawking the wares of the global economy. The random "Fartier" knockoff advertisement elicited giggles from our daughters in the back seat.

But looking beneath the surface, the economies are dwarves when compared to the coastal giants. Sichuan province's GDP is the largest of the three. The provincial economy is only slightly smaller than Shanghai's, but Sichuan covers eighty times more land than Shanghai and has four times as many people. On average, a person from Sichuan has one-quarter the earnings of his or her counterpart in Shanghai. The combined GDP of the Western Triangle was about $670 billion in 2011—about 40 percent of the $1.6 trillion total in the Yangtze River Delta.

All three provinces are quite rural. Chongqing—a province-level municipality—is technically the world's largest city. But only half of its inhabitants are urban. It was carved out of Sichuan province, which is still 60 percent rural, and Shaanxi is only slightly more urban. While agriculture generally is about 5 percent of the output in Guangdong and the Yangtze River Delta provinces, it is double that in the Western Triangle.

As with Western Europe in the nineteenth and early twentieth centuries, the development strategy here is premised on making these places more urban and less rural. In China that comes with a strong push from the central government.

"In China, urbanization is both a result and a driving force of the fast developing economy," says Aimin Chen about the Chengdu model.[46] Dr. Chen is an urban economist trained at Penn State, who moved back to China after a career in American academia to become vice rector at Sichuan University. Over a bowl of spicy *dan dan* noodles in one of Chengdu's courtyard tea houses, she explained to me how Chinese policymakers have moved from gradualism to promoting central cities and now to promoting a hub-and-spoke system around a few major cities. This is particularly true in the Western Triangle, where local governments are building both central cities and smaller hubs to draw workers from the countryside. Planners hope that infrastructure and real estate investment will create economic activity. That, in turn, should lure manufacturing and service sector jobs.

The central government directs much of its support toward these efforts. This was especially true of the 2008–9 stimulus program. "In the second quarter of 2009, in contrast to the eastern regions of Guangdong (7.1%), Zhejiang (6.3%), and Shanghai (5.6%), the growth of GDP in Chongqing, Sichuan, and Shaanxi was consistently impressive, at 12.6%, 13.5%, and 11.8%, respectively."[47] Figure 3-4 shows how certain inland provinces are far more dependent on government spending.

Direct stimulus funding combined with loans from state-owned banks focus on fixed asset investment, in particular. In 2009 Xi'an spent $37 billion on fixed asset investment, about 92 percent of GDP.[48] In the same year, Chengdu spent $59 billion, about 89 percent of GDP, and Chongqing spent $78 billion, roughly 81 percent of GDP.[49] By contrast, Shanghai and Beijing only spent 35 percent and 40 percent, respectively, on fixed asset investment in 2009.[50] (The entire United States spends around 15 percent annually, on average.) Figures 3-5 and 3-6 illustrate graphically and geographically these different investment strategies.

Most public funds went into highways, roads, bridges, and airports. Some of these appear to be important investments. For

FIGURE 3-4. Government Expenditure-to-GDP Ratio, 2009

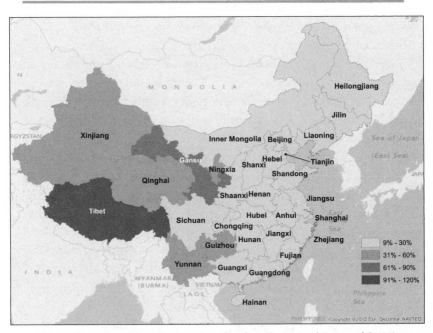

Source: Figure created by author based on data from the National Bureau of Statistics, *China Statistical Yearbook 2011* (Beijing: China Statistics Press, 2011).

instance, all three cities have extraordinary traffic jams. As a result, all are developing badly needed subway systems. As of January 2013, each had one operational subway line, with two or three other lines in construction or planning. Still, local governments also said they would try to induce higher consumption—both of publicly provided social services, such as health care and education, and also of basic consumer goods from the private sector. Yet critical social investments received the short end of funding.[51]

The focus on fixed asset investment in this region is not only on public infrastructure but also on private construction of housing, office complexes, and entertainment facilities. Those may or may not pay off. Across all of China, local governments have amassed

FIGURE 3-5. Fixed Asset Investment-to-GDP Ratio, 2009

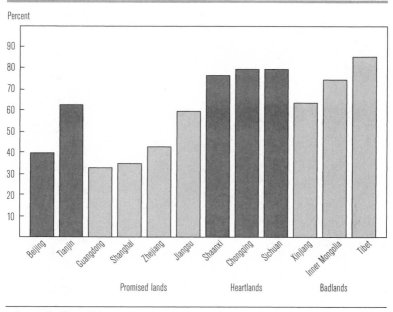

Percent

Promised lands   Heartlands   Badlands

Source: See figure 3-4.

as much as $1.7 trillion in debt through loans to private real estate developments. The Chinese government itself estimates that as many as one-third of those loans will not be repaid, while Standard Chartered Bank puts the estimate as high as $1.4 trillion.[52] Given that the fiscal constraints on provincial governments are rather weak, there is little to stop local authorities from outspending their mandates.[53]

In the optimistic scenario, all this investment will pay off. All of the empty apartment housing and office buildings may lay empty for a while, but incomes and urbanization will increase, and those buildings ultimately will be full of new tenants.[54]

More ominously, a December 2010 report from HSBC stated that "investors already have begun to examine local governments' fiscal condition as concerns grow about the post-stimulus

FIGURE 3-6. Provincial Fixed Asset Investment-to-GDP Ratio, 2009

Source: See figure 3-4.

overhang."[55] That applies both to commercial efforts as well as to many public work projects—from roads to subways to sewer systems—that do not appear to have sufficient user fees or other revenue streams to sustain their long-term operating costs. Loans from state-owned banks to finance these investments may not be repaid, forcing the central government to cover the costs. Even the normally staid HSBC is a bit worried. "It's the lack of transparency and the potential knock-on impact of local government debt that is the greater concern."[56]

Indeed, the frail health of local banks, real estate development, and nonperforming loans might actually counterbalance the country's current account and trade surpluses. And even if China's central government still holds considerable assets, such as foreign

---

BOX 3-2. Heartland China: A Study in Contrasts

China, like India, is a study in contrasts: the worldly cities of the coast, the industrial belts, and the agrarian, sometimes idyllic areas like the rural village of Yangshuo, in Guangxi province, where we hiked and swam and biked our hearts out. Our final stop was Chengdu, where all of the contrasts, aspirations, and issues of China are in full view.

Chengdu, like many parts of the country, has a strong natural presence—the magical Qing Cheng Mountain is just an hour away. Chengdu also offers lovely teahouses, delicious Szechuan food, and proximity to Tibet. We tried our hands at making *dan dan* noodles under the watchful eyes of students at a local culinary institute and held baby pandas at the impressive panda research center.

But we also experienced some of the worst pollution and lowest "sunshine totals" of our time in China—the results of Chengdu's desire to become an economic powerhouse coupled with its unfortunate geography. Compared to other Chinese cities of its size (16 million), Chengdu has a relatively low carbon footprint thanks to natural gas and enormous hydropower dams fed by the headwaters of the Yangtze River. But there was still plenty of evidence of coal plants and car emissions. Sometimes we feared that our apartment building was on fire when we smelled the soot through our heat and air conditioning system. And we had to laugh when someone in the United States asked if we had seen the solar eclipse that May.

—*Kristen Suokko*

---

currency and U.S. Treasury notes, it may be difficult to liquidate some of these assets while still holding on to their current market value. That would depend, of course, on the need for cash to bail out the local governments and state-owned banks. The challenge is that no one really knows their health, given the opacity of local financial systems. Local state-owned banks and businesses are simply not subject to the external supervision needed to get a true picture of the economy's balance sheet.[57]

Yet the economy of the Western Triangle is only one element of its global importance. Political stability in this key part of China remains vital to the country's future. Each of the Western Triangle's three provinces is experimenting with local control—and all are experiencing different outcomes.

Xi'an: From Underground Antiquities to Aerospace Future

A unified China was forged from Xi'an in 221 BC. The Emperor Qin attacked and conquered feuding warlords from his Xi'an base. To eternally mark his accomplishment and protect him in the afterlife, Qin had thousands of terra-cotta warriors buried in an underground mausoleum even before his own death. That was sometime between the height of Pericles' Athens and Julius Caesar's Rome. Today, as Europe is debating whether to keep Athens and Rome in their union, China's national government considers it a top priority to develop Xi'an.

Xi'an is not only the epicenter of ancient China, it is also the capital of Shaanxi province, the gateway to China's west—and therefore also the fortress entrance *from* the west. The Silk Road across the western high plains into Central Asia begins here. Other than the terra-cotta warriors and ancient central walled city, the other two most visited tourist sites are a Buddhist tower and a Muslim bazaar. The non-Han diversity speaks volumes about Xi'an's strategic importance to Beijing and why the capital has spent so lavishly on public and private development there.

Today's leaders of Xi'an city and Shaanxi province know that government-led growth will only go so far. They know that the local coal economy will provide power and revenue but also that it will pollute the air and water. They know that they need to attract private investment—domestic and foreign—if they are going to fill the many empty office parks and condominium developments that dot the center and outskirts of this ancient city.

So the city has focused on electronics manufacturing, civilian aviation, and service outsourcing for software.[58] Samsung is building a $7 billion flash memory chip plant, and Ericsson and others are developing service centers there.[59] With the central government's permission, Xi'an is striving to become a center for private civilian aviation business.[60]

Still, product manufacturing in the Western Triangle lags far behind the coast, particularly when it comes to exports. In Shaanxi province, for instance, exports were only about $6 billion in 2010, or 4 percent of the province's $150 billion economy—a tiny percentage of a tiny economy, compared to the coastal economies with similar size populations. The province ran a trade deficit in 2008 and has barely cracked the export-led growth model. In fact, the move into high-tech is fraught with contradictions and dead ends. As pioneers in the aerospace business have begun to discover, they must first create a base of engineers, pilots, aviation safety experts, and other technicians. All of that is very complicated when China's military retains jealous control over nearly all of China's airspace.[61]

The Chongqing Model—and Bo Xilai

State-driven development is an economic strategy with global implications. In Chongqing it also had a political component that was more overt than anywhere else in China. Or at least it did under Bo Xilai.

Under Bo's leadership, Chongqing became a counterpoint to Guangdong. As a municipality with provincial standing, it has 30 million people—a bit less than Canada, though packed into a territory roughly the size of South Carolina.[62] While Bo grew Chongqing's economy and addressed social issues, he also made global headlines in 2012 for a sordid and sensational scandal. Bo had been party secretary there for five years and also a member of the nation's Politburo. Like Wang Yang, he was a rumored candidate for the high altar of the Standing Committee—that was until March 2012, when he was removed from office and the Politburo for "serious disciplinary violations."

Under Bo's guidance, the municipality led China in growth in 2011 at a whopping 16.4 percent, fueled by state-owned companies and public spending.[63] His "Chongqing model" emphasized shared prosperity and communitarian values, socialist egalitarianism, and a benevolent state. Bo also was actively constructing a high-tech "new city" for offices and manufacturing plants and had successfully attracted Hewlett Packard and Acer to Chongqing. It was a start, as Chongqing only had $7 billion in exports in 2011, amounting to only 6 percent of its economy.

Since low wages were one of Chongqing's few competitive advantages, Bo Xilai did not seek to raise workers' salaries. Instead, he used public funds to invest in affordable housing, with plans during his tenure for 800,000 apartments costing $16 billion.[64] As elsewhere, much of Chongqing's growth was state led and financed by state-owned banks. In this case, Chongqing was investing in housing to attract workers not just from the province-municipality's countryside but also to draw Chongqing natives back from the factories in Guangdong, Jiangsu, and Zhejiang. By allowing country natives to receive all the benefits of being city residents—such as access to schools and hospitals—Chongqing officials hoped to increase the urban population to 70 percent of the province. The only catch was that these migrants had to give up their rural residency and with that their claims to ancestral homes and farms. Citizens would become even more dependent on the state, which remained a great concern to many. And farmers feared that they would have no land to fall back on during economic hard times.[65]

Bo Xilai combined his growth model with an unmistakably top-down political philosophy. He and his nationally famous police chief, Wang Lijun, ran a throwback police state. They targeted street-level crime, such as gambling and prostitution, as well as corrupt provincial and local officials who had developed illicit relationships with local state-owned and private businesses. These prosecutions were popular, netting nearly 5,000 criminal arrests. But they also seemed politically motivated, rolling back significant advances in the rule of law in China. For almost two decades, Chinese judges and lawyers had become trained in core practices of jurisprudence, including how to handle evidence and witness testimony, and perhaps most important, judges were gradually exerting some independence from their political masters on most routine cases. Yet Bo Xilai and Wang Lijiun seem to have wiped all that away in short order. For a great number of cases, a "three chiefs conference"—the chief of police, chief justice, and chief prosecutor—would determine the outcome before taking the case to trial.[66]

Bo also promoted patriotic, Mao-era songs. His campaign became known as "Stamp Black, Sing Red"—with the "black" referring to crime and the "red" referring to a restoration of communist ideology. Bo seemed to say, look to the state—and to *me*—for happiness. But as China enters its first downturn in over a decade, one of the key questions facing central leaders is whether they can afford economically *and* politically to follow Bo's approach of province-directed, investment-heavy, debt-fed development.

Of course, Bo Xilai was himself disgraced. Just as his style of leadership was unusually public and media friendly, so was his downfall. His wife, Gu Kailai, was convicted of murdering a British businessman. When his top cop, Wang Lijun, presented Bo Xilai with evidence of the murder, Bo demoted him. Seeking protection, Wang Lijun fled to the U.S. consulate 200 miles away in Chengdu.

In the words of my Brookings colleague Cheng Li, the Bo Xilai case is the "most serious political crisis since the 1989 Tiananmen incident."[67] The murder of a foreigner and subsequent cover-up became an international drama. A former police chief seeking safety in the American consulate was both an act of sedition and a sign how far China still needs to travel to establish the rule of law. For some Chinese leaders, the scandal may make them more cautious and unwilling to explore new strategies. While China's senior leaders seem to agree that Bo and his wife crossed a line in abusing their power, many still share his view that the Communist Party leadership should not be questioned in providing growth and stability. Period. For Bo's supporters, an unbridled private sector, nongovernmental organizations, peasants' rights, independent courts—or even separating the state from Communist Party control—are too much *pluribus*, too soon.

Sichuan Province: Pandas, iPads, and Bookworms

Of the three Western Triangle provinces, the leader seems to be Sichuan—the home of China's revered Panda Breeding Center. The current mayor of Chengdu, Ge Honglin, has hustled to attract manufacturing investment. Initially, his city seemed to benefit from the shift of very basic manufacturing into the region. Garment firms began to relocate from Guangdong and Zhejiang, in the face of rising costs for land, labor, and environmental protection.[68]

But Ge Honglin wanted Sichuan to avoid being stuck on the lowest rung of development. He became known to outside visitors as a hard-charging, ever-present entrepreneur, promoting a "Smart Chengdu" agenda based on computer manufacturing and software and Internet services. The city is billing itself as the Silicon Valley of China. Lenovo and Dell have set up facilities there. In the case of Lenovo, the company and the city together made a $100 million investment. Foxconn makes nearly half of all Apple iPads here—a fact that the city highlights in all its promotional material. Both because of Chengdu's southwestern location and its emphasis on high-tech development, it received government approval to establish direct flights to Bangalore, India.

With Chengdu in the lead, Sichuan province has inched ahead of its Western Triangle neighbors. The province exports significantly more than either Shaanxi or Chongqing at $18 billion or 7 percent of the massive province's economy—a statistic befitting its reputation as the inland manufacturing powerhouse. More Shanghai-based businesses are planning to set up shop in Chengdu than in any other inland city.[69]

Ge Honglin convinced *Fortune* magazine to host its annual Global Forum in Chengdu in 2013. He is trying to show off his close cooperation—indeed, collaboration—with Western investors to provide them with what they need to succeed in China. That includes quarterly meetings with the local American Chamber of Commerce. The province and city regularly buy multipage advertising inserts in the *New York Times* and *Washington Post,* boasting the region's considerable strides.

Ge himself is an import, having come to Chengdu from the Yangtze River Delta. Born in Jiangsu, he rose up through the Shanghai provincial government's steel industry research division. That included a stint in Beijing where he earned a doctorate in engineering, which entailed two years of research at the University of Windsor in Canada. After a decade of learning Shanghai's state-owned steel businesses and earning a place on that province's Standing Committee, he was drawn to Chengdu.

He has brought along Shanghai-style entrepreneurialism and openness to foreigners. So aggressive is the mayor in attracting Western investors, he is known to bring foreign executives to Chengdu's favorite hangout of Western expatriates: The Bookworm, a restaurant-bookstore owned by a former Irish journalist. The offerings of the bookstore include a number of titles currently officially banned in China. Yet when the mayor waltzes in with a potential new investor, he proudly takes them directly to those shelves. He is keen to demonstrate not only that Chengdu is open for business but also that it is a tolerant place where expatriates can live in considerable freedom.

But no one should think that expats are the only bookworms in Chengdu. The city boasts some of China's great universities, including both Sichuan University and the Southwestern University of Finance and Economics. Those centers of excellence have worked with the local government to market Sichuan province as a technology manufacturing center with connectivity to other high-tech hubs.

Ge Honglin was asked how Chengdu was able to sustain its growth even with the slowdown of the world economy and the cooling off of exports. "Chengdu has stressed balanced urban and rural development to narrow the gap between the city and the countryside. It has stressed development of high-end indus-tries, changed the mode of economic development and sped up the adjustment of the industrial structure."[70] In addition, the high-tech district in southern Chengdu is the future home of the world's larg-est freestanding building: the New Century Global Center will be an all-in-one shopping and entertainment mecca that will include a quarter mile of indoor "coastline," including a fisherman's wharf and hot springs.[71]

However, Chengdu faces the same question as Chongqing and Xi'an: can it attract enough business to help pay off the major con-struction investment? How many Western companies will invest in inland China? How many workers will they employ, and will it be enough to fill the apartments and shopping malls?[72]

Certainly the construction boom has attracted millions of low-skill workers to these cities. But often these workers are just sub-stituting the barracks-style apartments in Chengdu for similar ones that they had occupied in Guangdong. Furthermore, the wages here are no better, nor are the working conditions. Foxconn's Chengdu plant famously employs almost 200,000 workers, but it also has been the site of suicides and riots protesting work conditions. Those events prompted a systemwide review by Foxconn and Apple, which entailed bringing in the Fair Labor Association to audit working conditions and which led to some improvements. While Chinese real estate investors are betting on ever-rising wages and employment, the manufacturing firms face the challenge of keeping wages low enough so that they remain globally competitive.[73]

To make it easier for people to move from farms to factories, Sichuan and Chengdu are in the process of dismantling the prov-ince's *hukou* (household registration) system. Chengdu already extends all social security programs to all migrant workers. In 2012 the province and city together began to eliminate the division between rural and urban hukou. Implementation has been slow, however. Provincial officials are carefully monitoring an emerg-ing power struggle. On the one hand, local officials in Chengdu's suburban and semirural districts want to develop farmland into commercial properties. On the other hand, farmers want to retain their land rights—or at least benefit from the fair market value of their ancestral lands.[74]

That confrontation between developers and farm holders is not just about property values. There is a social cost across China's heartland in this wrestling for real estate. Collusion between developers and local governments has helped fuel local investment, but it also has angered local residents. Forced demolitions of families' homes have sparked thousands of protests, albeit usually small and isolated ones. Internal instability arising from public anger remains Chinese leaders' greatest fear and could have profound global implications.[75]

Li Chungcheng, the deputy party secretary of Sichuan province, was recently arrested on corruption for the brazen way he confiscated land from farmers. He had become known as Li Chaicheng—or "Li destroys the city"—for being so quick to confiscate farmland or to destroy homes and apartments to facilitate new construction.[76] A similar story circulated over a thousand miles away in Shanxi province, where the mayor of Datong, Geng Yanbo, has been nicknamed "Geng Chaichai"—"Geng destroys and destroys"—and also "Geng Yizhi"—"Geng points his finger and it disappears."

Developers or local governments often hire thugs to scare people into selling their homes. With limited compensation for their reclaimed homes and land, people have resorted to extreme measures. At the most extreme, this can include self-immolation, burying oneself alive in the demolition site, or entering into a suicide pact with neighbors. In one case, a farmer created homemade rockets to fight off land developers and won a record amount of compensation because of the media attention.[77]

Whether Chengdu—as well as Chongqing, Xi'an, Wuhan, Harbin, Kunming, Nanning, and Zhengzhou—can pull off economic self-transformation is perhaps the most critical question facing

China's development model, which faces the challenge of balancing social and economic costs and risks. Local governments in the heartland face additional challenges of identifying reliable revenue streams to fund social services, not to mention coordinating their policies with one another. If they can overcome some of these obstacles, China's interior will continue to develop. But if failure in a few of these areas leads to a vicious cycle, the bedrock of national stability may begin to shake.[78]

THE FAR WEST EMPIRE: BADLANDS

From a Chinese perspective, the most heroic jobs involve bringing growth and peace to the vast landscapes west and north of Xi'an, Chengdu, and Chongqing. The Great Wall was built over 2,000 years ago to defend against warriors from these territories. The Middle Kingdom has struggled for centuries to exclude the nomadic people that traversed the inland deserts, high plains, and mountainous terrains. On occasion the nomads from the badlands won—and some of China's most noteworthy dynasties came from these non-Han Chinese territories.

Non-Han minorities today make up more than a fifth of the 360 million people in the twelve western territories, more than double the national percentage. The further west one travels, the greater the number of citizens of non-Han heritage. Those populations often spill across borders, sharing ethnic ties with many of China's thirteen sovereign neighbors: Afghanistan, Bhutan, India, Kazakhstan, Kyrgyzstan, Laos, Mongolia, Myanmar, Nepal, Pakistan, Russia, Tajikistan, and Vietnam. Considering the neighborhood's habitual instability, China is always on the watch for the trouble these populations might bring.

Modern China has rejected the old Great Wall strategy. The three largest territories west of China's midfield line—Xinjiang, Inner Mongolia, and Tibet—are officially called "autonomous regions." In practice, they are the exact opposite. The central government not only appoints party secretaries but also watches constantly for any separatist itch.

The current strategy might be termed "build and populate." More central government money (per capita) is spent building in Tibet than in any other region or province; the amount is five times higher than for Shanghai, seven times higher than for Chongqing, and sixteen times higher than for Guangdong.[79] Far from letting these provinces "liberalize," China's Ministry of Finance is blunt: western province governments could not function without major central support.[80] More than half of all investment in Tibet comes directly from central government coffers. Likewise, 30 percent of Xinjiang's fiscal revenue comes from Beijing and other provinces.[81]

Just as President Eisenhower, a former general, made it a national priority to build the U.S. interstate highway system, so have China's leaders emphasized constructing roads and airports in the west, making it easier for the army to access these remote and restive places. And most of that building is being done by Han Chinese from the heartland. Just as inland provinces sent hundreds of millions of workers to export-driven manufacturing jobs on the coast, they now are sending millions west to work in construction and security. The Chinese are quick to point out that the Han conquest of their far west resembles America's own westward expansion by settlers of European descent a century and a half ago—except that the Han version is far more humane.

The "go west" policy is deeply popular in Han China. Most view the far west with deep-seated nationalism, a desire for territorial unity, and protectiveness about national security and sovereignty. Even the most globalized, liberal Chinese hope to keep a tight grip on Xinjiang and Tibet, especially in the face of ongoing separatist movements. Ironically, discussions of China's west almost always revive the history of China's east, where European powers tried to carve up the Pearl River, Yangtze River, and Yellow River deltas.

Of course, this Chinese policy has elicited protests in Tibet, Xinjiang, and Inner Mongolia, including massive riots in 2008, 2009, and 2011, respectively. The government's policy in each case was a version of the U.S. surge in Afghanistan and Iraq: send in more resources and manpower. For a rising national political leader, a tour of duty in the badlands of Tibet, Xinjiang, or Inner Mongolia can launch a career. Serving in China's "wild west" has been the ultimate proving ground for a would-be leader's patriotism, personal sacrifice, and effectiveness.

Xinjiang's Young Turks: Quite a Riot

In July 2009, the city of Urumqi—the capital of massive Xinjiang province—burst onto the global scene. The local Uyghur population rioted, attacking not only police and government buildings but also ethnic Han Chinese civilians. Official reports estimated that about 200 people died, and another 1,700 were injured—though Uyghur exiles claimed that the death toll was significantly higher. The proximate cause, ironically enough, was tensions between Han and Uyghur workers over 2,000 miles away in a Guangdong factory, demonstrating that ethnic tensions flow from the coast to the interior and back, just as do people and money.

The riots dominated television news in China as well as internationally. President Hu Jintao cut short his visit to the G7 summit in Italy—in the midst of the response to the global financial crisis—to restore order.

Xinjiang covers one-sixth of China—the largest province by territory. It borders seven countries and has almost 22 million inhabitants representing thirteen ethnic groups. Most residents are still rural, but the province is quickly urbanizing thanks to the Han Chinese settlers who now constitute about 40 percent of the total population. Their numbers nearly match those of the native Uyghurs—Turkic Muslims who have dominated the region for millennia. Xinjiang slipped in and out of Chinese control in recent centuries. After the Communist Party's victory in the civil war, Mao reestablished Xinjiang as a province in 1949.[82]

Beijing has been pouring cash and people into the region. The capital city, Urumqi, is now predominantly Han Chinese.[83] The national leadership clearly hopes this will assuage Uyghur violence and secessionism, though it is unclear whether this policy is having the opposite effect of deepening resentment against the advance of the Han.

As with much of China, the infrastructure spending has emphasized connectivity. Seven new expressways and eleven new rail lines are being planned or built.[84] The goal has been to link Xinjiang not only to central China but also to Central Asia and Europe. The vision is for a modern Silk Road, with international passenger and freight rail, satellite communications, optical fiber cable, electric power lines, natural gas pipelines, and civilian aviation links.[85] New Xinjiang airports alone will entail more than $4 billion in new investment.[86] Government spending is nearly 80 percent of Xinjiang's economy, amounting to over $50 billion in 2010 and nearly $100 billion in 2011. The province regularly exceeds its growth targets.[87]

The Chinese government is not just giving to Xinjiang; it is also taking from it. It is especially taking Xinjiang's energy resources. Coal is king in China, supplying 80 percent of all national energy needs. Xinjiang is second only to Inner Mongolia as China's largest coal producer. It is set to take the top spot, as the province is home to nearly 40 percent of Chinese coal reserves.[88] The province also accounts for 13 percent of China's crude oil and 29 percent of its natural gas, with even more in reserve. And while Xinjiang still relies heavily on fiscal transfers, oil and gas production helps balance the books, accounting for nearly 30 percent of the province's economic output and about half of its heavy industry.[89]

Xinjiang is also China's main connection to Pakistan, Afghanistan, Tajikistan, Kyrgyzstan, and Kazakhstan. Potential gas imports from Central Asia or the Persian Gulf would pass through the province. Chinese firms have invested heavily in natural gas exploration and pipelines in Turkmenistan and in roads and tunnels in Tajikistan.

More important, Chinese and Pakistani leaders have long envisioned pipeline and rail routes across Pakistan that would link China to the Indian Ocean and the Persian Gulf. Today, it takes two to three weeks for Chinese oil tankers to reach the Gulf. But when high-speed rail and roads are completed, cargo transport from eastern China to the new Chinese-built Pakistani naval bases at Gwadar, Pasni, and Ormara, just east of the Gulf, can be completed in less than forty-eight hours.[90] To that end, China has helped to design and finance the strategic Gwadar deepwater port in Balochistan, Pakistan. In addition, Chinese companies have secured the rights to oil blocks and what is believed to be the world's second-largest undeveloped copper deposit in Afghanistan.[91]

All of these efforts bring together a focused national commitment to settling Xinjiang, with a more inchoate and loosely coordinated effort to exploit natural resource wealth beyond China's borders. Chinese leaders are wary of Muslim insurgency in these bordering nations, particularly Pakistan—which could, in turn, spread to minority groups in Xinjiang. So the central government is supportive of investment in those nations—especially if it helps promote stability—while recognizing that the top priority remains within China's own borders.[92]

Tibet: From Tears to Modernity

A year before Xinjiang's riots, Tibet had some of its own. In March 2008, protests sought to commemorate the 1959 failed Tibetan uprising that led to the exile of the Dalai Lama. Protesters particularly targeted the media spotlight of the Beijing Olympics. Outside China, media focused on Tibetan independence and the return of the Dalai Lama. Inside Tibet, however, protesters targeted the influx of Han Chinese, the dilution of Tibetan culture, and the growing inequality between Han immigrants and native Tibetans. Seasonal Han migrants were having an easier time finding jobs in construction and other areas than were ethnic Tibetans.[93] The Chinese central authorities clamped down hard, aggressively shutting down peaceful demonstrations. The protests exploded into riots, targeting Han and other non-Tibetan Chinese.[94]

Tibet, of course, is far better known but also far less populated than Xinjiang. This vast territory is the size of Texas, yet has only about 3 million inhabitants. There are another 1.3 million Tibetans scattered across neighboring Sichuan.[95] Since the People's Liberation Army "liberated" Tibet from its native kings and Buddhist priests in the early 1950s, Tibetans around the world have been calling for a "Free Tibet."

Within China, the view of Tibet is nuanced. Buddhist statues are still revered across China, and Tibet is seen as the epicenter of Chinese Buddhism. Still, many of China's most important political leaders cut their teeth in Tibet trying to keep it "autonomous" but still very much part of China. Most famously, Hu Jintao served as Tibet's party secretary in the late 1980s, and as such he orchestrated the government response to Tibetan riots in 1989. Hu's crackdown on protest preceded the Tiananmen Square shutdown later that year and earned him great praise within Communist Party circles.

Tibet is still among the poorest of Chinese provinces. According to the UN, it had the lowest human development index of China's regions in 2005. Per capita income is only two-thirds that of Xinjiang, one-third that of Inner Mongolia, and not even a quarter of Beijing's.[96] Incomes are much higher in the capital city of Lhasa—which has one-fifth of the province's population—but those higher incomes tend to go to the migrant Han Chinese. While ethnic Tibetans are still the majority in Tibet as a whole, Han Chinese now outnumber them in Lhasa.[97]

In 2012 the central government pledged to foster "leapfrog development" and "lasting peace and stability" in Tibet. The goal is to raise per capita net income close to the national average by 2020.[98] Already Tibet receives the greatest share of fiscal transfers in the country at $1,329 per capita—a stark contrast to Guang-dong, where the central government sends about $82 per capita.[99] Backed by central resources, Tibet's government plans to invest about $47 billion between 2011 and 2015 on hundreds of social and economic development projects. That comes to about another $1,200 per person over that five-year period, or about double the amount spent in the previous five years.

As elsewhere, authorities plan to spend on infrastructure, envi-ronmental protection, housing, health care, social security, and vocational training. One-third of the new investment targets rural areas: new roads, homes, and irrigation systems; tap water; electric-ity; and gas. It also will pay for health care and social welfare ser-vices. More than $4 billion will go toward developing indigenous industries for tourism, mining, agriculture, and livestock breeding; $2 billion will go toward protecting wetlands and pastures, soil erosion reduction programs, and urban sewage treatment.[100]

In Tibet—as in other sparsely populated, economically less developed provinces—the central transfer payments are more than ten times the amount of funds generated from local enterprises and tax collection.[101] Still, judging by the riots, the challenge for the central authorities is not just to produce relatively high GDP num-bers but also to convince Tibetans that this march to modernity will allow them to maintain some degree of their cultural heritage and political autonomy.[102]

The Not-So-Wild West: Inner Mongolia

Protests came to Inner Mongolia in May 2011, and the authorities in Beijing paid attention. Like Xinjiang and Tibet, Inner Mongolia is a natural resources treasure chest. And as in Xinjiang and Tibet, Inner Mongolia's native populations resent the Han presence and that the province's natural resource wealth seems to benefit the new arrivals more than the traditional residents. Unlike the other western provinces, however, Inner Mongolia's native population is far less restive. The region is both more prosperous and more deeply integrated into Han China—a product of proximity and shared past. It is significant that Mongols had ruled China in earlier centuries.

Nonetheless, Inner Mongolian rural herdsmen resent that traditional grasslands have given way quickly to coal mines. In 2011, seeking to block the ubiquitous coal trucks, one herder was run over and killed. Waves of peaceful protests demanded protection of herders' property, protection of the grasslands, and punishment of those responsible for the incident. Students joined the protests—a lightning rod in post-Tiananmen China.[103] Authorities even seemed to fear that local Han Chinese workers might join, seeking higher wages in one of China's newly wealthy provinces.

A rising star in Chinese politics stepped forward. Party Secretary Hu Chunhua initially followed the martial law script he had learned as a junior official in Tibet. Paramilitary forces were sent in to seal off town squares and schools—even though the protests were peaceful and not directed at Han civilians.

Yet "Little Hu"—as he was popularly known to distinguish him from former president Hu Jintao—also took a page from Wang Yang's more liberal style of leadership. He met with protesters and acceded to many of their demands. "If the interests of the masses are not well protected, development cannot be sustained."[104] The truck driver was convicted and executed, the county party chief was dismissed, and a former party chief was sentenced to prison for bribes. The local mine was shut down, and an increase in social and environmental spending was promised.[105] The State Council issued a statement on improving living conditions in Inner Mongolia, and officials announced $308 million to promote Mongolian culture and $200 million for student subsidies.[106]

Inner Mongolia has been majority Han Chinese since the early twentieth century, with the Han outnumbering Mongolians by two to one as early as the 1940s.[107] Its economy has made a steady, speedy transition from grains and nomadic livestock to extraction of the region's vast coal and mineral wealth. It now supplies a billion tons of coal a year—one quarter of all of China's production and equal to the entire national coal output a decade ago. And that is just scratching the surface, since Inner Mongolia has at least a 300-year supply of coal, which is about a quarter of the world's total coal reserves. Inner Mongolia is also the main supplier of rare earth minerals and uranium, and potentially natural gas. Such resource riches have led to considerable investment. From 2001 to 2011, Inner Mongolia grew the fastest of all provinces, averaging 17 percent GDP growth annually.[108] In 2011 the province had a GDP of $220 billion—about the same as Chile's, with about 50 percent more people. That is very wealthy for China's far west—more than double Xinjiang's GDP for a population of roughly the same size. Inner Mongolia's GDP per capita of $7,004 in 2011 was even higher than Guangdong's ($6,618).[109]

But it would be a mistake to think that all of that wealth is shared evenly. Perhaps even more than in other parts of China, income inequality is on the rise. The city of Ordos has the highest number of Rolls-Royces, Ferraris, Jaguars, and Mercedes-Benzes per capita in China.[110] However, Inner Mongolia's happiness index—the ratio between the average output of a province per person and the average take-home salary per person—was at the bottom of the list, worse than in Tibet and Xinjiang.[111] Following the protests in June 2011, central leaders pledged to increase the income of urban and rural residents to the national average by 2020.[112]

Real estate speculation is also a huge problem. In addition to its fancy cars, Ordos is probably China's most famous "ghost town." Developers have had to cut property prices by as much as 70 percent given that there are few buyers and almost no residents.[113]

Under the Twelfth Five-Year Plan, the projected annual GDP growth for Inner Mongolia is 12 percent a year. Who reaps the gains of this growth remains to be seen. Some herders resent the government's relocation policies that try to force them into manufacturing and urban jobs. Furthermore, Mongolians face job discrimination not just on tribal lands but also especially in urban areas.[114] The challenge for the government here is taming the mining and construction boom. While that energy has fueled coastal China, it has only marginally improved Mongolian livelihoods.

Despite these challenges, recent gains were enough for Hu Chunhua to be considered a success. Only fifty years old, he has since been promoted to party secretary of Guangdong and has joined the central Politburo. Many believe he will become a member of the elite group of seven senior leaders on the Standing Committee in 2017, when a handful of current Standing Committee members retire. His youth and stature make him a candidate for China's premier in ten years when Xi Jinping retires.[115]

Moving the West Forward

Given the nearly universal support for China's "go west" strategy among the Han Chinese, the region will continue to draw Beijing's attention for years to come, including as the bridge to Central Asia and even the Persian Gulf. Beijing will keep a close eye on restive minorities, not only as sources of tension in their own right but also because of their potential connection with kinsmen across the wider, even more turbulent region. China truly sees itself as a stabilizing force in the region, by literally paving its way west to provide access to landlocked regions and by helping to grow the local economies and integrate them with neighboring nations. If that effort is to be sustainable—or at least less turbulent—China will need to better address local concerns about cultural and environmental protection. Of course, there will always be a limit to how much autonomy Beijing will give to these regions.

For the near term, implementing the go west strategy will mean considerable investment by the central government in those places, particularly in infrastructure. But unlike in China's central interior, these regions generate an immediate payoff: a mining and natural resource bonanza. That alone will keep central authorities committed to the region. So while far west China seems furthest removed from the coastal provinces that have made China a global player, in fact, this region is fueling China's forward march into a brave new world. One can expect central authorities to remain committed to that process, regardless of their perspectives on the rest of China's global future.

CHINA'S REGIONS, INSIDE OUT

The three regions and ten provinces briefly described above constitute China's better half. That is, taken together, they are half of China's economy, and they still only comprise about 500 million people or about one-third of the nation. Even within that better half, one can see at least three approaches to economic and political life. Each approach comes with a very different view of the world beyond China's borders.

The export-oriented coast is indeed a rising competitor with the rest of the world. Its thirst for foreign markets and natural resources is well known. This is the part of China that is potentially entangling the country in a number of global hotspots. But it also mostly has been a major force for stability, both in bringing prosperity to the rest of China and in deepening trade and financial ties with Japan, Korea, and Taiwan, whose companies have invested heavily in this region.

That is not to understate the challenges facing the coastal provinces. The region's ascent has begun to slow and level off, with labor and other social costs now rising. Internally, the coast is now being asked to help finance inland development—a fact well known within China. When developed countries ask China to play by global trade rules, it is most likely these provinces that will be affected. Abiding by global rules will mean reducing the role of state-owned enterprises, making corporate and bank finance more transparent, and providing protection for the environment and intellectual property. Some companies and individuals in these regions might want to do this for their own self-interest, particularly if it helps attract foreign investment and technology. Still, these changes are hard to undertake in any society, given the vested interests involved. But the provinces of the coast are now navigating rising costs and broader distributional demands, so their compliance may be slower than foreigners might like.

Bringing prosperity to China's interior—home to 800 million people—will be critical to the country's stability. Yet the middle of China is underappreciated outside the Middle Kingdom. This part of China takes up much of the leadership's time and energy—and money.

One dimension of this governance challenge has begun to attract foreign attention: China's considerable infrastructure investment. In the optimistic case, that investment has been a short-term stabilizing domestic force in Chinese politics. It also has been a major lubricant for the global economy. The enormous effort to build roads, airports, subways, sewers, power plants, and other public infrastructure will now link these lower-cost interior manufacturing centers to global markets, and also link global goods and services to nearly a billion new consumers. For that best-case scenario to come true, both domestic and foreign companies will need to relocate beyond easier access points on China's coast. Foreign firms will need to choose China's interior over low-cost competitors elsewhere in Asia, Africa, and Latin America. Inland consumers will also need to step up their spending, despite the fact that they have considerably less buying power than do their coastal Chinese counterparts. Foreign retailers will need to readjust their expectations and their products.

The middling and worst-case scenarios for inland China could have troubling consequences for global politics and economics. Those scenarios start with the social dislocations and environmental impacts that already have marked this region's rapid growth—such as choking pollution, inhumane living conditions, politically toxic fights over land and property rights, and rampant crime and corruption. All of these issues already spark protest on a daily basis, and the new Chinese government rightly fears that any one of them could trigger broader protests that sweep across the interior, challenging the regime.[116]

But the scenarios turn worse if the enormous "private" investment in this region meets an unhappy ending. Local governments have become real estate developers and investors, relying on those revenues to fund a range of government services. They also may have created an uncontrollable real estate bubble—well beyond the control of central authorities who bemoan their "implementation incapacity" when attempting to enforce national policy at the local level.[117] If the rows of empty office towers and apartment buildings remain unfilled, at some point a bailout will be needed for the state-owned banks that have subsidized all this private construction. Either central coffers will be able to cover this, or the country will need to begin printing trillions of dollars worth of additional Chinese currency, potentially destabilizing global markets.

The nations of the world have largely worried that the Chinese currency is undervalued, meaning that Chinese goods and services are artificially inexpensive for foreigners. However, China's currency may actually be overvalued. If China has to start printing even more money to pay for overleveraged banks, the value of the yuan could actually fall further, leading to even greater dumping of Chinese goods on foreign markets. This would make it even less likely that China will be able to start the consumer spending—including importing goods and services—that nearly everyone agrees is in the country's and the world's common interest.

Other forces shaping the interior, such as the massive countryside-to-city migration, land acquisition, crime and corruption, and environmental destruction, also are beginning to gain attention. Sometimes local experiments to address those issues work; other times they do not, but the consequences are only felt locally. But on occasion, local experiments gain national attention, as they did with Bo Xilai's "Stamp Black, Sing Red" campaign. And when the divergence from Beijing is big enough, they then garner national and international attention—as they did in the case of Bo's ultimate disgrace.

Finally, developments in the far west are creating a third Chinese world view. For centuries China viewed the various non-Han minorities in these regions as foreigners to be excluded or, at best, managed. Now the country is trying to assimilate these peoples and develop their resources. Neighboring Central Asian states—while still viewed as potential adversaries—are also seen as possible economic partners. Some hold needed natural resources; others are land routes for acquiring needed oil and gas or for transporting Chinese goods to European and Middle Eastern markets. All are seen as potential customers. Yet given the unstable lands involved—both outside and within China's borders—this region of China remains a wild zone of empire where China's potential future leaders will be put to the test.

CHAPTER FOUR

INDIA:
FORWARD STATES, BACKWARD STATES,
AND SWING STATES

INDIA, LIKE CHINA, now has both spectacularly wealthy urban centers and also hundreds of millions who live in rural poverty. India's coast, like China's, now features states that are global trade and investment hubs. Its hinterlands, like China's, struggle to generate sustained economic growth, to responsibly steward natural resources, and to develop effective and transparent governance.

India's economic successes are real. As markets opened, Indians and others began to invest in the country's businesses. Some high-profile exports have captured global imaginations, particularly in technology and services. Trade has grown dramatically, jumping by nearly 20 percent each year for the past decade. Exports totaled almost $187 billion in 2010.[1]

Still, it is obvious to most visitors of both countries that India lags far behind China, both in economic output and infrastructure.[2] After leaving India and traveling to China, my eight-year-old daughter quipped, "Daddy, this looks more like America."

Reform efforts in India started a decade after China's. But where China chose GDP monotheism, India's leaders wanted greater economic growth but did not want to ignore other gods of progress. Whether in New Delhi or in state capitals, most Indian leaders also have remained committed to democratic governance as well as maintaining a multiethnic, multilingual, multireligious, and multi-caste society.[3]

Just as India is renowned for its multiple religions—including a few polytheistic ones—it also worships at least three core political values: multiculturalism, democracy, and economic growth. The priority given to these values varies dramatically from state to state. Prosperity has lagged in India's so-called backward states. Politics have been dominated by social tensions, and democracy has not led to economic growth. Growth-oriented policies often have taken a back seat to the divisive politics of poor versus rich, farm versus city, Hindu versus Muslim, one caste versus another. In what we might call the forward states, economic growth has become a higher priority, although these states also must manage social tensions arising from religion, caste, and language. As in China, history, geography, and poor governance have conspired to determine which states are forward, which are backward, and which are swinging in one direction or the other.

The diversity of India's economic performance is exemplified by India's seven most important states, which I refer to here as India's G-7. To a large degree, those states rule India. About 730 million people live there—just shy of the industrialized G-7's current 746 million. At current population growth rates, India's G-7 will likely have more people than the industrial G-7 in the next decade. These states make up over 50 percent of India's GDP—about $800 billion. If India returns to 7 percent economic growth, they will help lead India past several developed G-7 nations.

In selecting India's seven most *important* states, I did not use a single indicator of whether a state was either the country's most populous, most wealthy, or most productive. Rather, all three combined determine a state's importance. Population is critical, since influence in the national parliament depends on how many parliamentary votes a party controls. As regional and state-based parties continue to grow, so also grows their power in parliament.

TABLE 4-1. India's G-7

Units as indicated

State	Chief minister	Popu-lation (millions)	Rural popu-lation (percent)	GDP per capita (dollars)[a]	GDP (billions of dollars)[a]	Average GDP growth 2005–12 (percent)[b]
Uttar Pradesh	Akhilesh Yadav	200	78	627	128	7.01
Maharashtra	Prithviraj Chavan	112	55	2,113	224	11.09[c]
Bihar	Nitish Kumar	104	89	489	46	11.32
West Bengal	Mamata Banerjee	91	68	1,165	96	7.24
Andhra Pradesh	N. Kiran Kumar Reddy	85	67	1,492	123	8.91
Tamil Nadu	J. Jayalalithaa	72	52	1,753	119	10.11
Gujarat	Narendra Modi	60	57	1,567	104	10.28[c]

Sources: Table created by author based on data from Registrar General and Census Commissioner, "Census of India 2011: Provisional Population Totals" (http://censusindia.gov.in/2011census/censusinfodashboard/index.html). GDP data are from Directorate of Economics and Statistics of the respective state governments and the Central Statistics Office; see "Statement: Per Capita Net State Domestic Product at Current Prices" (http://pib.nic.in/archieve/others/2012/nov/d2012112201.pdf) and "Gross State Domestic Product at Current Prices" (http://mospi.nic.in/Mospi_New/upload/State_wise_SDP_2004-05_14mar12.pdf).

a. GDP is for fiscal year 2011–12 nominal GDP. GDP and GDP per capita figures were converted to dollars based on current prices, at the exchange rate of 1 U.S. dollar to 47.94 Indian rupees.

b. At constant 2004–05 prices.

c. Excludes 2011–12 GDP growth.

Yet some states are more important than their population alone would indicate. A few highly productive, fast-growing states are changing India.[4] Based on my criteria, Table 4-1 lists India's most important seven states—each of which I visited—and their current chief ministers.

Each of the seven chief ministers listed is a major force in India. Open any newspaper or magazine on a given day in India—in any city—and you are likely to see at least three of them and sometimes all seven. Unlike the leaders of the industrial G-7, they never meet as a distinct body. The group includes forward states, backward states, and swing states. Understanding how they increasingly are in charge of their own destinies is key to understanding how economic policy is being made—or not made, or even *un*made—in India.

Politics in each of these places shapes India's national and international outlook. The forward states are at the frontlines of attracting global investment and shaping the global economy, across a range of goods and services—from manufacturing to high-tech services to pharmaceuticals. They are contributing a surge in wealth and a growing consumer class. But they also contribute to a rising nationalism that could shape Indian democracy in the future. While the forward states have made progress on governance, much dysfunction still remains.

The backward states in this group, by contrast, are the heart of a rural India that still struggles with global engagement. Many Indians in these states fear that global markets will upend fragile, subsistence livelihoods. Still, a few enlightened leaders in those places are starting to discover governing techniques to advance development goals—from providing basic law and order to adopting modern technology.

Finally, the swing states are trying to harness their globally connected cities and use them to develop their predominantly rural populations. Figure 4-1 shows how India's G-7 states vary in the make-up of their economies, with backward states being the most agricultural and forward states having the most manufacturing.

Modern India may "worship" three gods—growth, democracy, and multiculturalism—but how it does so differs from place to place. The result is an India that is often hard to follow, the same way observers often struggle to follow the European Union as a single entity. In a global era, that diversity is both India's great strength and also a constraining weakness.

FIGURE 4-1. Sector GDP of India's G-7 States and the Capital Region, Fiscal Year 2011-12

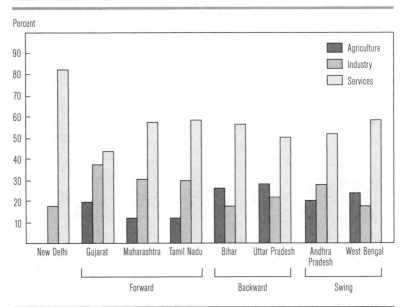

Source: Figure created by author based on data from the Ministry of Statistics and Program Implementation, "(GSDP) Gross State Domestic Product (NSDP) Net State Domestic Product (2004–05 Series)," February 27, 2013 (http://mospi.nic.in/Mospi_New/upload/SDPmain_04-05.htm).

FORWARD STATES: THREE EMERGING GIANTS

Maharashtra, Gujarat, and Tamil Nadu are the most forward of India's states. All three hug India's coast—two on the west, one on the southeast. Each has at least one relatively modern, globally focused city. Each has its own long history of foreign trade and commerce. All three are about half-urbanized. Manufacturing and professional services as a share of GDP are the highest in the country.

Each state has a slightly different regional focus. By proximity, Maharashtra and Gujarat face west to Iran and the Middle East, and northwest to Europe. Oil from refineries in Gujarat and manufactured goods from Maharashtra flow outward, as does a diaspora that works in Gulf State oil fields and in London high finance. Gujarat also keeps a wary eye focused on neighboring Pakistan. By contrast, Tamil Nadu exports south and east to Singapore, Thailand, Indonesia, and the rest of Southeast Asia—not only for trade reasons but because of the considerable Tamil diaspora in those places. And it looks warily at neighboring Sri Lanka, separated by a narrow strait, with a protective eye monitoring the island's Tamil minority.

In global trade talks, farmers from these Indian states once joined forces with India's predominantly rural states. Together they acted like other least-developed countries. They wanted to protect their economies from rich-country products but also wanted unimpeded access for their exports to those same markets. Now India's industrial states feel more confident in competing on a level playing field with other manufacturing nations. Notably, information technology and biotech businesses located in a few forward states now seek the highest available intellectual property protection. Leaders in these states worry about India's trade balance and fluctuations in the rupee. They are now more likely to push New Delhi to make it easier for foreigners to invest. In a federal system where it is still difficult to sell goods across state lines—more difficult in many ways than selling to Europe—they also increasingly want India to have a single, common market.

Maharashtra: Magnificent yet Mired

Prithviraj Chavan should be a celebrated world leader. As chief minister of India's wealthiest state—and one with nearly as many people as Japan—he is at the center of business, arts, entertainment, and culture on India's golden coast. Yet Chavan's job of keeping Maharashtra at the front of the pack in India is a daily fight—not only against his enemies but also against his friends. He must wake up each morning wondering what he did to deserve his thankless job.

Maharashtra stretches along the middle of the country's western coast, facing the Arabian Sea, looking toward the Persian Gulf and the east coast of Africa—just as California dominates America's

Pacific coast and looks to Asia. To Maharashtra's north is Gujarat, and to its south is the small wealthy state of Goa. Maharashtra also sprawls eastward, across the spine of the subcontinent, connecting it to other major Indian states such as Chhattisgarh, Andhra Pradesh, Madhya Pradesh, and Karnataka.

With over 110 million people, Maharashtra is home to one-tenth of all Indians—and highly productive ones at that, generating 15 percent of the country's output. It is also India's most urbanized state, with half of its people in cities. It is a home to manufacturing, but more important, it dominates financial and corporate management.[5]

Scores of Indian companies headquarter in Mumbai, Maharashtra's state capital and also India's largest, most cosmopolitan, and most complicated city. Mumbai, also known as the "Maximum City," houses the main stock exchanges as well as capital and commodity exchanges.[6] It is also an all-in-one media, entertainment, and trade hub, with a scenic beachfront and active nightlife. Morning walks along Mumbai's magnificent three-mile Marine Drive take you past white sand beaches, waterfront cafes, cricket stadiums, and wedding parks. Mumbai is New York, Los Angeles, and Miami rolled into one. Only New Delhi comes close in importance—and is not nearly as much fun.

Thanks to Mumbai, Maharashtra accounts for about one-third of all foreign direct investment to India. In absolute terms, however, foreign investment is rather small, at about $10 billion a year—about the same amount of foreign direct investment as in Shanghai (which has one-fifth the number of people) and about half of that received by Guangdong province, which has a similar size population.[7] And despite its relative wealth within India, Mumbai faces critical shortages. With 12 million people in the city and 30 million in the metro region, it is constantly in need of better roads and sewers, and more water and power. It is estimated that half of Mumbai's residents live in its enormous and teeming slum neighborhoods such as Dharavi, made famous in the film *Slumdog Millionaire,* or Annawadi, the focus of Katherine Boo's *Beyond the Beautiful Forevers.*[8]

BOX 4-1. Mumbai: Indian Mosaic

Mornings on Mumbai's Marine Drive: runners in Nike gear, barefoot Jains, burka-clad women watching their husbands exercise, sari-clad women with earbuds and iPods, yogis and meditators, turbaned Sikhs, pigeons and dogs.

Across the huge boulevard are some of the most expensive hotels, restaurants, and apartments in the city. Uniformed children climb into their cars to go to their private schools. A family of seven sleeps on the sidewalk and tries to sell flowers to passing motorists.

Then there is Dharavi. Parts are like turn-of-the-century New York—industrious and active but also messy, toxic, dangerous—and others resemble poor rural villages from another era. It is easy to see why residents resent the designation "slum," as it is clear that there is rhythm and community and striving here just as anywhere else. Perhaps Dharavi is best described in this piece by our daughter Annika (age 10).

—*Kristen Suokko*

A Day in Dharavi

I wake up. I have rolled off my uncomfortable potato sack. I put on my sari and let my great-grandmother do my hair, pulling and tugging. I gingerly step over my three aunts, seven uncles, mother, father, four brothers, three sisters, and great-grandfather.

As I walk into the pottery shop where I work, I say a quick prayer to Shiva. I make 3 pots in ten minutes. In the seven hours I work before lunch, I make 126 pots.

At lunch I quickly stuff a samosa into my mouth and run off to pray. I pray to Brahma, Shiva, Vishnu, and Ganesh. I pray for my family and my life. I lose track of time.

As I run back, I see a petite white girl with a bow in her blond hair. I reach out to touch her face, and she jumps back in disgust. I wonder what I did wrong.

I get back to the shop and go behind it. I lift my garments. I crouch over the hole and do my business. I splash water on my hands and go back to work.

I make 347 pots in the day and collect my salary of 694 rupees. I sneak one pot into my pocket and bring it home. I fill it with water. My mother collects a butchered lamb from a friend, and we cook it over the gas stove. We eat in silence, savoring our food. We say one last prayer and strip for bed. I think about my day. I have a good life.

—*Annika Antholis*

The lack of investment and lack of infrastructure are related, of course. Prithviraj Chavan understands this well, having studied engineering at Berkeley and served as India's minister of both atomic affairs and parliamentary affairs. But he has not found a way to rise above the political infighting to make the investments Mumbai needs to truly take off. Chavan was *appointed* to his post in 2011. His party, the Congress Party, is still the strongest in the state, but it tends to lack leaders who distinguish themselves in the public's mind. So the party's national leader, Sonia Gandhi, picked him to lead the state. Such an appointment would be standard practice in China; in democratic India, it is an anomaly.

Chavan's two main rivals each head up the state's two inwardly focused political machines, and they taunt Chavan, calling him Sonia's pawn. His first rival is the political party Shiv Sena, which continues to control the Municipal Corporation of Greater Mumbai after once again winning local elections in late February 2012. As a result, Chavan's state government and the Shiv Sena's municipal government continue to battle one another over education, infrastructure, and public housing.

Shiv Sena was built by party boss Bal Thackeray in the 1970s to defend the local Marathi-speaking Mumbaikars from migrants—an effort that has kept Mumbai from living up to its global promise. For nearly forty years, until his death in November 2012, Thackeray fought for local control in decisionmaking, administration, taxation, and even the declaration of holidays.[9] Shiv Sena's power base lies in Mumbai's expansive slums.[10] These districts are not beggar-filled warrens but rather beehives of small manufacturers and local service providers.

Slums like Dharavi are a volatile mix of longtime residents and more recent immigrants from other states. While many residents wait for permanent housing, most cobble together makeshift plumbing and electricity—not to mention satellite dishes and slum schools with computer rooms. Thackeray's machine serves "native" residents but not migrants. He criticized each successive wave of ethnic and religious minorities—starting with South Indians in the 1970s and 1980s, then Muslims in the 1990s, and immigrants from Bihar and Uttar Pradesh in recent times.

In contrast, Chavan and the Congress Party promote a more tolerant and inclusive Mumbai and Maharashtra, not just for job-seeking Indian migrants but also for foreign investors. A few new neighborhoods, such as Bandra Kurla in the city's north, feature wide, clean boulevards, office towers, and shopping malls, similar to the streets of Beijing. They lack the character, charm, and pedestrian-friendly feel of lower Mumbai, but they have been magnets for multinationals and others looking to take the Maximum City to a new, global future.

The Congress Party's battles with Shiv Sena have been a major roadblock to developing Mumbai's completely inadequate infrastructure. The spectacular Sea Link Bridge is a case study in how the quagmire of political infighting slows down public investments that could benefit the entire city. Sea Link is a three-mile highway across Mahim Bay, designed to connect northern suburbs like Bandra Kurla to older financial districts at Mumbai's southern tip. By avoiding the snarled and teeming middle of Mumbai, Sea Link promised to cut an hour of travel time from the airport to downtown. Yet thanks to protests at every turn by local Shiv Sena affiliates and partners, the project was seven years behind schedule and came in at twice the initial cost, at $291 million. Currently the road still deposits drivers back into Mumbai less than halfway to downtown. Similar delays have plagued the completion of modern subways and rail systems.[11]

Both in Mumbai and in other parts of Maharashtra, the Congress Party also competes at the polls against the breakaway Nationalist Congress Party (NCP). Thanks to proportional representation, multiparty government is endemic in Indian politics. This means that on election day, the two national parties—Congress and the Bharatiya Janata Party (BJP)—compete against not only one another but also against smaller, regional parties. But since neither

Congress nor the BJP is likely to win an outright majority, each must forge coalitions with some of its rivals. As the columnist M. J. Akbar explained to me, "The Congress Party is destined to fight an endless battle to defeat its friends." In Maharashtra the NCP is the Congress Party's biggest "frenemy."

In Maharashtra's state legislature, the Congress Party controls 82 seats (21 percent) and forms a coalition with the NCP, which controls 62 seats (16 percent), as well as with a number of smaller parties. That frenemy relationship extends to the nation's capital, where the Congress Party also needs the NCP's 9 votes to form a governing coalition of 262 votes in India's parliament. But the two parties barely cooperate.

The NCP's boss is Sharad Pawar. Pawar himself has served as chief minister multiple times and is a protectionist sugar magnate from Maharashtra's second biggest city, Pune, an auto manufacturing powerhouse of 8 million people. In the national parliament, Pawar leveraged the NCP's 9 votes to gain the post of agriculture minister. His goal: to slow India's liberalization of farming—much to the chagrin of domestic and foreign investors. In Maharashtra's state assembly, he holds even greater sway. The NCP has enough votes to appoint Chavan's deputy chief minister, whose portfolio includes state finances. That gives the NCP an effective veto over anything Chavan and the Congress Party want to do. So while Prithviraj Chavan might fight to invest in Mumbai infrastructure or to reform the power or water sector, Sharad Pawar will fight to make sure that agricultural interests are not ignored.

The net of these countervailing forces is stalemate. The balance of power between the Shiv Sena, the Congress Party, and the NCP keeps in check both rural and urban forces. It also sustains gridlock between manufacturing, agriculture, and service sectors of the economy. Efforts to move any one sector forward usually involve accommodating other sectors.

The international implications are fairly clear. In the eyes of many foreign investors, at least, Maharashtra has not stepped forward as it needs to—both for itself and for India. Rather than becoming a truly global financial, commercial, and manufacturing center, the state is held back by infighting and the need to balance competing interests. Prithviraj Chavan has been unable to maneuver around both the Shiv Sena and his own coalition partners to fully realize Mumbai's global future.

Gujarat's Narendra Modi: Running and Gunning

Meet India's most admired and most feared politician: Narendra Modi, chief minister of Gujarat.[12] The state of Gujarat, to Maharashtra's north and west, constantly reminds its more famous neighbor of what is possible in a well-run state that lacks an effective political opposition. In fact, if India were governed by GDP monotheism, Narendra Modi would be party secretary. Under his guidance, Gujarat has been India's fastest growing state. As a result, he is by far the most popular politician from his BJP party.

Modi combines the pragmatic and efficient spirit of Gujarat's entrepreneurs with charismatic and potentially destructive, divisive, and bellicose Hindu nationalism. That mix has real global implications.

Before visiting Gujarat, I had heard about Modi—from all sides—all across India. "India's most effective public official." "If given five years, he would transform India's economy." Just as important, he also was described with the strongest condemnation. "He cannot be forgiven for the riots." "Gujarat borders on a cult of personality." As I have learned, there is almost no way to start a conversation about Modi without angering someone in India.

I spent ninety minutes with Modi at his chief minister's residence in the capital, Gandhinagar. In person, he is a policy maven—introverted and precise but also passionate about the most technical of subjects. On a wide range of issues, his Gujarat is pushing, not following, New Delhi and India.

That is certainly the case in economic growth, where much of Gujarat's development has come from manufacturing. In Modi's words, "In Gujarat, we are good at making things."[13] In the last decade, manufacturing nearly tripled in Gujarat, jumping from about $10 billion in 2003 to $29 billion in 2009.[14]

Modi launched "Vibrant Gujarat" in 2003—a trade-oriented confab to market the state to Indian and foreign investors. He established simple rules: "We will not pay any incentives and will not accept any bribes. But I will provide single window facilitation, quality power and water, and will honor my commitments." One Gujarati businessman told me that he had been suspicious back then and had doubted that any companies would ever actually invest. But they did. According to state published reports, pledged investments have grown from 76 MOUs amounting to $14 billion in 2003 to nearly 8,000 MOUs signed in 2011 for $450 billion.[15]

These foreign investors include Ford, Colgate-Palmolive, Procter and Gamble, Nestlé, Hitachi, Hyundai, and Peugeot Citroën. But more striking is that India's leading corporations have set up shop in Gujarat, choosing it above other Indian states. In particular, Reliance, Tata, and Bajaj Auto have made Gujarat a hub—if not a major hub—of their domestic manufacturing enterprises.

Modi also targeted rural development. "If it does not work in the villages, it will not work in the city." His eyes light up when discussing infrastructure, agricultural colleges, solar energy, and climate change. "I prioritized four things," he said, holding up his four fingers, and then pulling each one down in turn: "Water, electric power, connectivity, and distance education."

Modi expanded water and power resources to both the city and the countryside and invested heavily in the development of manufacturing in Gujarat, in particular the petrochemical and automotive industries. When another state—West Bengal—was slow to make way for Tata Motors to build a factory for its Nano minicar, Modi sent a short text to Ratan Tata, the chairman of Tata Group: "Welcome to Gujarat."[16] Fourteen months later, cars started rolling off the assembly line in Sanand.

As a result of such aggressive promotional strategies, foreign investment is expanding in Gujarat, making its economy the fourth largest in the country, behind Delhi, Maharashtra, and Karnataka but ahead of larger states such as Tamil Nadu, Andhra Pradesh, and West Bengal.[17]

However, in the social realm, Modi's efforts on behalf of Gujarat's poorest have not always been as successful. Despite efforts to improve rural education, roads, and connectivity, several indexes of human development have fallen on his watch. Gujarat's poorest citizens have fallen behind far more backward states when it comes to rural employment as well as child hunger and malnutrition. Furthermore, in Gujurat three out of ten girls still cannot read or write.[18]

Modi's political power is not just built on his economic advances. It also has to do with his version of Hindu nationalism. Modi is among the most vocal proponents of *Hindutva*—an appeal to "Hindu civilization"—similar to the emphasis on "Western Civilization" or "Judeo-Christian values" at the center of American conservatism.

Yet beyond simply advocating for Hindutva, Modi's power to inspire and to polarize is built on the belief that he is willing to back up his words with actions. A single incident has branded Modi in that regard: Gujarat's 2002 Hindu-Muslim riots. On February 27, 2002, fifty-eight Hindus were burned alive in a train car, in what appeared to have been an orchestrated attack by a Muslim mob in the Gujarat town of Godhra. Adding to the emotional toll of the massacre, the Hindus were returning from a pilgrimage. The next day, Modi called for a day of mourning— which many Hindu mourners took as an invitation to riot. Gujarat exploded, with the death toll reaching a thousand people, mostly Muslims. Unlike previous riots in India, these burst live onto the nation's television screens. As a result, the riots are the single event for which Modi is known by nearly all Indians—and that may always be the case.

When I met with Modi, he raised the riots without prompting. In his telling, the inability to stop or slow the riots was a rookie error. "I had never run anything before, I had never run for elected office, and I was just installed in my position the day before," he said. "And then the Godhra train incident happened."[19] Numerous eyewitnesses feel that Modi was either complicit or at least indifferent to Muslim suffering. Accusations persist that he empowered and perhaps even guided goon squads to terrorize Muslim neighborhoods; directed the police to allow attacks on Muslims; sought to cover up the worst of the crimes, including by murdering corroborating witnesses; or failed to prosecute Hindu nationalists. No formal charges were ever pressed against Modi. A lengthy special investigation produced a confidential report, but India's Supreme Court recently turned the whole matter back to the local courts of Gujarat.

The U.S. government found enough reason for concern that in 2005 the State Department revoked Modi's visa. It cited a provision that bars any government official who "directly carried out, at any time, particularly severe violations of religious freedom."[20]

Many think Modi should show greater contrition.[21] When I met with him, he danced around accepting responsibility. He suggested that he has missed opportunities to lead: "I have made mistakes, and my government has made mistakes. What is important is that we recognize them, evaluate what we have done, and then fix them." He has called for intercommunal healing, leading a state-wide fast for "peace, unity, and harmony" and expressing "pain . . . for the families who had suffered."[22]

Still, Modi has never apologized. Opponents fear a slick charm offensive in an effort to soften his image in advance of the national parliamentary elections in 2014, which could make him prime minister.

Whether guilty or innocent, he remains hugely popular in Gujarat. In December 2012, he won a reelection mandate in the state's legislative assembly, winning 115 of 182 seats.[23] Modi's party—the Hindu nationalist BJP—lost only two seats, allowing him to govern the state with little opposition and no rival in sight.

That has led to enormous debate within the country as to whether the BJP will put him forward as their candidate for prime minister in 2014. Other than the Congress Party—the party of Mahatma Gandhi, Nehru, and Nehru's family—the BJP is the only other truly nationwide party in India.[24] The Congress Party is social democratic leaning and secular whereas the BJP is free market leaning and Hindu. Narendra Modi is both economically and culturally devout, which makes his worldview all the more important for other global leaders to understand and take seriously.

I asked Modi about the growing involvement—and even coordination—of state chief ministers on issues of foreign and security policy. The biggest flashpoint in the spring of 2012 was a proposal by the central government to establish a national counterterrorism center (often referred to as NCTC). This is a loaded issue in a country that still fears terror attacks, particularly from Muslim minorities, who make up nearly 20 percent of the population. Several chief ministers protested that the central government was usurping what had previously been state rights.

Modi started cautiously, "Foreign policy belongs to the center," clearly aware that any comment by a chief minister on foreign policy would be seen as going beyond a state's authority. But he went on to say that the "center and states both have equities" and that "the center simply needs to do a better job of consulting." When it came to Iran, he declined to discuss the particulars of that country's nuclear ambitions or its oil trade with India (though much of that oil is processed in Gujarat). But he did say that one should not discriminate between state sponsors of terror. "One policy should fit all." Modi's comments were fascinating yet elliptical. Cutting off Iranian oil would be a major policy shift for India—apparently acceding to U.S. leadership and pressure. But Modi also could have been poking at the United States for supporting Pakistan, despite the latter's backing of Islamic extremist groups, while at the same time the U.S. was trying to isolate Iran.

Modi made clear that he considers Pakistan to be a state sponsor of terror. "They provided shelter for Bin Laden, and they continue to support terror." Modi's tenure in Gujarat—including the riots—is closely watched next door in Pakistan, making his growing popularity in India a potential flash point in bilateral relations.

Modi felt most comfortable talking about economic diplomacy, including his own trade missions to China, Europe, and Japan. He seems to be enjoying the global platform Gujarat's economic boom has provided for him. He has written Prime Minister Manmohan Singh to ask whether the states can have their own representatives at key embassies overseas. Modi expressed great interest in the fact that dozens of American states often have their own offices in countries as far afield as Germany, China, and Brazil, independent of U.S. embassies.[25]

Perhaps because of his economic diplomacy, Modi did not demonstrate the deep suspicion many Indian nationalists feel toward China. "China is good at making things. Gujarat is also good at making things. We can compete with China or cooperate with them." In my conversation with him, Modi avoided discussing China itself as a direct threat. Instead, he questioned Chinese counterparts in their support of Pakistan, which he believes undermines China's commitment to global counterterrorism norms. "They listened to me and were polite. I do not think it will change the way they behave."

Modi may never be able to move past his role in the 2002 riots. Despite his popularity, his party is not likely to win enough seats in 2014 for them to govern alone. Many potential coalition partners—and even some within the BJP—fear or even detest Modi; they do not like what Modi has done and are uncertain how he would behave as prime minister. The BJP seems inclined to put him forward as the party's candidate for prime minister. But he is, and will continue to be, the most dynamic and turbulent force in India's national politics—and perhaps its foreign affairs.

Tamil Nadu: A View to the East

If Maharashtra looks to Arabia, and Gujarat looks over its shoulder at Pakistan, then Tamil Nadu looks to Southeast Asia. Sitting on the southernmost tip of the subcontinent, the region has maintained deep trading relations with Singapore, Malaysia, Indonesia, Thailand, Vietnam, and Myanmar. Tamil Nadu also connects that region to the western Indian Ocean and its monsoon-buffeted trade routes to Africa and the Middle East.

After Maharashtra and Gujarat, Tamil Nadu is India's third most important manufacturing state. It is one of India's two most important high-tech producers and exporters, and is among the most globally focused states. It also often feels like a nation unto itself.

If Tamil Nadu—or Tamil Land—were its own country, it would be the nineteenth largest in the world, its population of 72 million people ranking it just behind Turkey and just ahead of Thailand and Iran. Urbanized and urbane, Tamil Nadu has an 80 percent literacy rate—quite high by Indian standards. More people in Chennai speak English than Hindi. One of out of five people here is Christian, and the local Catholic and Syrian Orthodox communities date back to the first century. The Apostle Thomas is said to have been martyred in Chennai in AD 72.

Also martyred on the outskirts of Chennai was Rajiv Gandhi. In 1991 he was killed by Tamil extremists who were angry that as prime minister he had refused to side with the Tamil minority across the narrow strait in Sri Lanka.

Even as India's economy has grown, Tamil Nadu is often forgotten by the Western press. Its capital city, Chennai, is generally ignored. A city of a mere 9 million people, it is overshadowed by high politics in New Delhi, high finance in Mumbai, high technology in Bangalore and Hyderabad, and high poverty in Kolkata. Still, Tamil Nadu is a slow and steady industrial power within India—fourth in GDP and per capita GDP. The state hosts Ford, Hyundai, Nissan, and Renault, which all make cars for India's growing domestic market. High-tech giants Infosys and Cognizant have major operations here, selling all over the world. In the last decade, the state has experienced over $130 billion in investment, both in manufacturing and in software services. The region also has leveraged its strong universities, port, and quality of life to attract $5 billion in foreign investment, particularly in manufacturing. Having created an automotive manufacturing hub, the state has now shifted its focus to the assembly of hand-held electronics.

Manufacturing makes up one-fifth of Tamil Nadu's economy, a slightly lower proportion than in Maharashtra and Gujarat.[26] Despite fertile land and an abundance of water, agriculture constitutes only 12 percent of the state's economy.

The Port of Chennai is one of India's most important, with cars, tobacco, footwear, and cotton heading to Southeast Asia and around the world. Tamil Nadu exports more than twice as much per capita than the average Indian state. Yet most of what the state makes is consumed by Indians.[27]

As in Maharashtra, services are an enormous portion of the economy—nearly 60 percent. But where Maharashtra specializes in management and finance, Tamil Nadu is a high-tech hub.

When American software engineers design the latest applications or programs to run everything from a Kindle to an airplane's control systems, they technically are "designed in America." Yet in many cases, the basic designs are sent to South India. While the designers (many of whom are South Indian émigrés) sleep in the Bay Area, programmers in Chennai and Bangalore write, rewrite, and test the thousands of lines of code needed to bring programs to life. When our daughter Kyri's Kindle broke in Chennai, I searched for a replacement on the Internet under "Chennai Kindle." I found articles describing how the Kindle was designed in Chennai, but at the time, it was impossible to buy or fix one locally since Amazon had not yet opened its Indian sales and service operation. By the end of 2012 that, too, had changed.

Chennai is by far the world's single greatest conduit to the United States for highly skilled workers. Half of all U.S.-issued visas for high-tech workers go to Indians—particularly the H-1B, which allows a firm to transfer a foreign-based employee into the United States. Half of that half—that is, 25 percent of the global total—go to workers from five South Indian provinces that together make up less than one-seventh of India's population.[28] In 2012 South India sent twice as many high-tech workers to the United States as did all of China.[29] All those visas were issued in Chennai.

Fourteen U.S. visa officers here, including former lawyers, engineers, and tech professionals, are on the frontlines of globalization. Each visa officer interviews over 100 South Indians a day. The process does not cost the American taxpayer a dime; it actually turns a profit.[30]

Depending on how you view the global economy, U.S. visa officers stationed in Chennai are either sentries or synergists. In one view, they are protecting American workers in a "flat world" where computer chips and container ships make jobs magically disappear. In the other view, they are helping to build live human bridges that span borders and connect "hills" of innovation. In reality, they are both.

When they do their job well, U.S. visa officers clear the way for Indians who bring high-tech dynamism to the U.S. economy. One South Indian entrepreneur made the case to me quite succinctly: "We are accustomed to talking about trading goods and the movement of capital. But there is a new world of trade—the ability of our ideas and our services and our people to move about the planet." This gentleman—who chose to remain anonymous—should know. Born in Chennai, he received his master's and doctoral degrees in the United States in aerospace engineering and spent seventeen years in Michigan working for the research unit of an American automotive company.

Now he is back in Chennai, working on various joint ventures with Western companies in the realm of advanced technology manufacturing. He also sits on the global technology advisory council of a major American manufacturer, where he preaches the importance of innovation in products and processes.

Since Tamil Nadu always has considered itself far from Delhi, party politics here have remained a largely local affair. The two local parties are built around personalities and patronage. They are only barely distinct from one another in ideology, unlike the two nationwide parties—the socialist-secular Congress Party and the nationalist-Hindu BJP. Those two national parties hold very little sway in Tamil Nadu. Figure 4-2 shows the control of state legislative assemblies by the major national and regional political parties.

The Congress Party still competes and wins across India, and the BJP controls some important states. But it is worth pointing out that indigenous regional parties now control four of India's G-7: Uttar Pradesh, Bihar, West Bengal, and Tamil Nadu. Those parties sometimes align with Congress, sometimes with the BJP, and sometimes remain nonaligned.

The Tamil Nadu state government is currently controlled by the All India Anna Dravida Munnetra Kazhagam (AIADMK) political party, led by the current chief minister, J. Jayalalithaa, a famous actress who combines Ronald Reagan's on-screen charisma with Huey Long's populism and patronage. Her personal and political history is rich with steamy and salacious connections. Her face graces not only the front pages of local language newspapers but also billboards and advertisements all over the city.

Jayalalithaa rode the wave of public outrage following an enormous scandal involving the rigged auction of the country's 2G telecommunications spectrum. Her predecessor, Chief Minister Muthuvel Karunanidhi, was tainted by the "2G scandal"—particularly because the main culprits were top officials from his Dravida Munnetra Kazhagam (DMK) party. (The Congress Party in Delhi was also rocked by the scandal, appearing to tolerate the corruption of a key coalition partner.)

Jayalalithaa swept into power and has focused on sweeping out all vestiges of DMK rule. She took pleasure not only in defeating Karunanidhi but also in undoing his extravagance. She shut down a modernist $200 million new state government headquarters in Chennai. The entire government and all legislative assembly members moved back to Fort St. George—the old, faded colonial-era government compound along the waterfront. The lavish new complex is being converted into a public hospital and a medical

FIGURE 4-2. Ruling Political Parties in India's State Legislative Assemblies, 2013

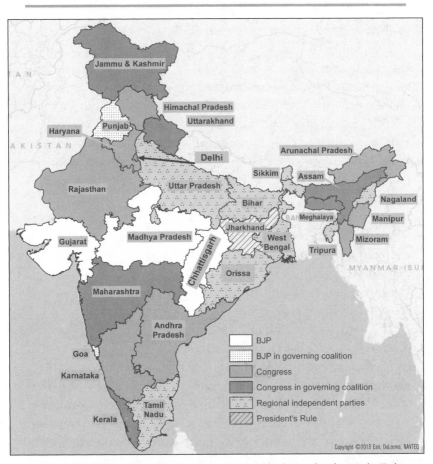

Source: Figure created by author based on state assembly election data from *India Today,*
The Hindu, Times of India, NDTV, Zee News, Indian Express, IBN Live, MSN, Rediff, Seekers
Find, and *News Bullet,* updated May 2013.

school. In a single act, Jayalalithaa provided health services and
higher educational opportunities for the people and also demolished Karunanidhi's monument to himself. Back in Delhi, the Congress Party has gotten the message: Jayalalithaa should not be
taken lightly.

If Jayalalithaa's grandstanding were all theatrics, it might be bad for Tamil Nadu. But, in fact, she seems committed to making a difference. She consistently targets the huge deficits run by Karunanidhi and has begun to tackle subsidies that were draining public coffers. She surprised many in 2011 by actually raising bus and milk prices. She has committed to increases in education spending, including providing laptops for all students in tenth through twelfth grade. Senior Indian Administrative Service officers in the state once clung to their formulaic adherence to rules set by New Delhi. They now are beginning to work with her, understanding that she is serious about controlling the reins of state power.

Jayalalithaa's next step appears to be tackling Tamil Nadu's huge infrastructure deficits that have slowed its otherwise impressive decade of growth. But the question is whether Tamil Nadu can keep up with Maharashtra and Gujarat. "Many investors are playing arbitrage with the big three states . . . and Tamil Nadu is starting to lose," one investor told me privately. And that is where the state's infrastructure gap comes in.

The need for better roads, sewers, water, ports, and electricity is apparent to all. Jayalalithaa targeted all of those challenges in a comprehensive plan called "Vision 2023," released in March 2012 and outlining over $30 billion in public investment each year over a decade. It envisioned making Tamil Nadu a top destination for business in Asia. Its residents would be as wealthy, on average, as people in China's coastal provinces are today, and poverty in the state would largely be eliminated. The plan targets not only roads, highways, and public transportation but also education, health, and rural development. During our three weeks living in Chennai in January 2012, Jayalalithaa announced several initiatives, including a new bus rapid transit system and a new "outer ring road" to divert the incessant stream of trucks that clog the city center.[31]

The challenge here—and elsewhere in India—will be mobilizing local government administrators. The contrast with China could not be greater. In China unelected city and district-level authorities are encouraged to focus on service delivery and entrepreneurship. In India there may be nearly 3 million local elected officials across the country, but most lack any control over either revenue or authority to fully take on tasks as simple as collecting garbage or filling pot holes. State-level political leaders and nationally appointed bureaucrats are involved in each of these decisions, leading to gridlock.

"India is in transition," says Raj Cherubal, director of Chennai Connect, an urban planning think tank. "We are an upside down country, with almost no local control. But we are starting to turn things around." So when Jayalalithaa announced her infrastructure plans, she made a point of emphasizing local control and sidelining Indian Administrative Service officers who get in the way. "Even the illiterate know that you can no longer just blame Delhi," said Raj Cherubal.[32]

By any account, Maharashtra, Gujarat, and Tamil Nadu are India's three leading states. The 250 million people that live in those three states make up a fifth of India's population but nearly one-third of its GDP. They differ dramatically from one another—in language, culture, politics, and economics. But all three share productivity, entrepreneurialism, relative affluence, literacy, urbanism, and a general openness. In an Indian context, they are forward in nearly every sense. If they can continue reforming their economies and can keep political infighting to a respectable minimum, India's future looks bright.

BACKWARD STATES: TURNING AROUND?

If India only had forward-leaning states, it might be a larger and more complicated version of Thailand or Indonesia. But the northern rural "Hindi belt" of backward states makes India what it is—home to more subsistence poor people than any country on earth.

Two north Indian states alone, Uttar Pradesh and Bihar, have over 300 million people. Over 80 percent of those people live in rural poverty. That is more poor people than the total population of the three forward states combined. Leaders in this part of India usually do not talk about the global economy. While Uttar Pradesh and Bihar once had some of India's most productive textile factories, most have been shuttered.

Yet in a modern global era, even India's backward states are now looking upward and outward. Their ambitions are not terribly high by global standards, and their success will depend on doing some very old-fashioned things, such as focusing on security, education, roads, and electrical power. But in that regard, they are showing signs of improvement. How well they complete the journey to modernity will help determine how well the rest of the country moves forward toward a global future.

Bihar: Nitish Kumar, Man from Hope

Bihar is India's most recent success story. Its chief minister, Nitish Kumar, has made it hip to be square, bringing a nerdlike focus to social and economic performance.

Bihar's basic statistics are not so hopeful. The state has more than 103 million people—thirty-five times the population of Arkansas, living on 75 percent of that U.S. state's land area.[33] Nine out of ten live in the countryside, making Bihar one of the most rural states in India. Its biggest city, Patna, has only 5 million people. The state is twice as crowded as New Jersey, but ten times larger. Bihar is also a land-locked, caste-divided, and crime-ridden state.

In Nitish Kumar's first five years in office—from 2005 to 2009—Bihar's economy grew at 11 percent on average.[34] The state reported over 16.7 percent growth in 2011–12.[35] Of course, Bihar was starting from a low base.[36] The average Bihari earned about $200 a year—less than $1 a day.[37] Even after a decade of economic progress, average incomes in Bihar are less than half of the Indian average—and over half of Bihar lives in poverty.[38]

When Nitish (as he is commonly referred to) took office, only about three in ten girls could read or write.[39] His predecessors had mastered the art of caste-based politics, focusing on intercaste rivalries and divisions, similar to America's own history of ethnic politics. Caste-based politics featured innuendo, code words, and slights (both real and perceived). Petty tyrants colluded with crime rackets to oppress local minorities and rival castes.[40] The most prominent and profitable industry was kidnapping.

Bihar's biggest exports were people—especially those with any wealth, education, or aspirations. Doctors and teachers flooded out of the state. So too did young men, in search of construction jobs in Maharashtra or Tamil Nadu. Bihar's greatest revenues were remittances. Elsewhere in India, such as in Mumbai, politicians would run nativist campaigns against the influx of Bihari immigrants.

With help from the central government, Nitish first attacked Bihar's lawlessness. "The thieves had AK-47s. Our police had old guns from the British colonial days. The thieves had the latest SUVs. Our police vehicles would break down. Five police officers would get out of the car, and push to get it started. Then it would make a big sound as the engine kicked in. Every criminal nearby could hear it."[41]

The central government agreed to support a policy of "state building"—that is, it supplied Nitish's administration with money and military muscle, despite the fact that his party (Janata Dal United) is in opposition to the Congress Party. Nitish worked with police and prosecutors to emphasize not just arrests but open and expeditious trials. Prosecutors convinced witnesses to testify, and Nitish personally vouched for their safety. "What was important was to send a signal that [their] government was competent." Bihar's trial and conviction rates went from being among the worst in India to right near the top. Seven years later, over 70,000 criminals are behind bars. India's most crime-ridden, corrupt, and economically weak state is now one of the best governed and perhaps the most effective in fighting corruption.[42]

Nitish also used central government resources to pave roads to many of Bihar's 200,000 villages and settlements, making it easier for children to get to school. He provided free midday school meals, uniforms, and bicycles to increase attendance. More important, he

111

hired 150,000 new teachers, 50 percent more than neighboring Uttar Pradesh, a state twice as large. He placed special emphasis on girls' education, cutting female illiteracy from 70 percent to below 50 percent.[43] That accomplishment was not only the greatest such achievement in India, it also helped him forge a caste-neutral constituency of women.

The extraordinary results speak for themselves: by 2012 the average Bihari's income more than doubled to about $500 a year.[44] Much of that came from public investment in schools, roads, and law enforcement. And those investments were largely financed by New Delhi, with two-thirds of those funds coming from central transfers, grants, and loans.[45] Figure 4-3 shows the share of each state's economy that is attributable to government spending, with the poorer state governments spending more as a proportion of GDP than the wealthier state governments.

The biggest private sector gains came in manufacturing and food processing, which increased the industrial component from about 10 percent of the economy in 2000 to about 17 percent a decade later. Marked gains were also found in construction, tourism, and infrastructure.[46]

Enormous challenges and constraints remain for Bihar. Only one in five enterprises is connected to the electrical grid. The payments from those firms that do get electricity do not cover the state's costs for power. When power is free or heavily subsidized, you get what you pay for: unreliable and low-quality electricity. And in a place so densely populated, acquiring land for new factories or other industries is extremely difficult and expensive. Moreover, the lack of a skilled labor force, inadequate banking services, and poor infrastructure all pose challenges to investors.

Nitish's brand of politics, of delivering public goods to the poor, has led many in India to hope that he might head the opposition to the Congress Party in the 2014 parliamentary elections. While the BJP is the largest opposition party, it is unlikely that by itself it

FIGURE 4-3. Government Expenditure-to-GDP Ratio by State, Fiscal Year 2010–11

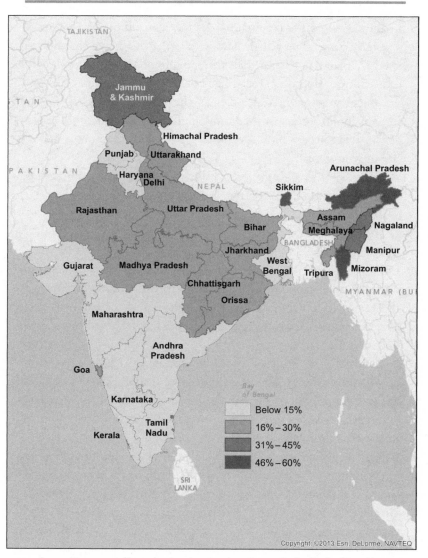

Source: Figure created by author based on data from Reserve Bank of India, "State Finances: A Study of Budgets of 2011–2012," March 2012 (www.rbi.org.in/scripts/AnnualPublications. aspx?head=State+Finances+%3a+A+Study+of+Budgets).

could amass enough votes to win an outright majority in parliament. And if Narendra Modi becomes the BJP's leader, his communalism might alienate other regional parties that depend on Muslim votes.

Many hope that Nitish Kumar could head up a coalition of smaller, regional parties that are committed to a new politics of economic development. Just as a certain former governor of Arkansas once ran a campaign on "It's the economy, stupid," many Indians look to Nitish's results-oriented message that could appeal across religion, caste, and clan. In short, they see him as India's "Man from Hope."

At the very least, his approach is catching on next door in massive, 200 million–strong Uttar Pradesh.

Uttar Pradesh: Symbolism, Socialism, and the World's Fourth-Largest Democracy

In March 2012, Akhilesh Yadav and his Socialist Party (Samajwadi Party) won a surprise landslide victory in Uttar Pradesh. That was the same week Vladimir Putin was returned to power in Russia. The election in Uttar Pradesh was larger, freer, and fairer. The outcome was far less certain.

By itself Uttar Pradesh would be the world's fifth-biggest country—behind China, the rest of India, the United States, and Indonesia. It has more people than Russia, Brazil, Japan, or Mexico.

In fact, Uttar Pradesh's election was the most significant in India in the lead-up to the upcoming 2014 national parliamentary elections. Local politics here are a bellwether for national politics. Uttar Pradesh's representatives take up one in six seats in India's national parliament. When India's governing party does well in Uttar Pradesh, members of parliament feel compelled to stay with the governing coalition. When opposition parties do well, it can spell more gridlock in New Delhi. Yadav's Socialist Party is a regional party, and it has remained unaligned with either major bloc—itself a symbolic statement.

Uttar Pradesh is a touchstone for determining how India views itself. Its cultural riches are abundant. The state has the holy Ganges River, the holy city of Varanasi, and the Taj Mahal. But despite its treasures and diversity, poverty in Uttar Pradesh is endemic and grinding. It may constitute one-fifth of India's population, but it contributes less than one-tenth of India's GDP.

Factories that once made shoes or saris in Kanpur and Lucknow are now shuttered, reflecting deficits in technology, infrastructure, marketing, and the ability of small firms to scale up. Nearly two-thirds of the state is rural, and the average person lives on less than $2 a day. The question for Uttar Pradesh is not how to catch up to the economic powerhouses of Maharashtra, Tamil Nadu, and Gujarat. Rather, it aspires to be a middle-tier state such as Andhra Pradesh or West Bengal. Like next-door Bihar, ambitious people in Uttar Pradesh move elsewhere in India. Their remittances are an important source of income back home.

If Uttar Pradesh's first challenge is economic, then its second is social. Poverty here is superimposed upon one of the most deeply engrained caste systems in all of India. And like caste, religious conflict here remains barely below the surface. The city of Ayodhya has become a symbol across India of Muslim-Hindu tensions. In 1992 a Hindu rally turned into a riot that completely demolished a sixteenth-century mosque, which was thought to have been built at the birthplace of the Hindu deity Lord Rama. The 2002 Gujarat riots were sparked when fifty-eight Hindus were killed on a train returning from a pilgrimage to Ayodhya.

For five years—from 2007 to 2012—Uttar Pradesh was run by Kumari Mayawati, who came from what was historically regarded as the lowest caste, the Dalits (known in the West as "untouchables"). Mayawati aspired to represent those who have been "vanquished, trampled upon and forced to languish in all spheres of life."[47] This referred not only to Dalits but other backward castes (literally called "OBCs") and religious minorities.

Her 2007 landslide victory promised to transform the state. For the first time, Dalits had their own chief minister. It is hard to overstate the psychological impact on a population that had suffered generations of both abuse and neglect. Her 2007 election was as meaningful to lower castes in Uttar Pradesh as was Barack Obama's to African Americans—if not more so. In the words of Ashutosh Varshney, Mayawati had an "opportunity to combine the politics of dignity . . . and the politics of economic development."[48]

She went on a spending spree, building hundreds of statues (including of her) across the state as a symbol of the rise of the untouchable class. Like Nitish Kumar in neighboring Bihar, she also built roads and hired teachers—though not nearly as many as he did, for a population twice as large as Bihar's. During her five years in office, Uttar Pradesh posted 7 percent economic growth, which was still below India's average. That growth was extremely uneven, with only six of the state's seventy-one districts accounting for 25 percent of the growth between 2000 and 2009.[49]

Many have argued that Mayawati's rule was a necessary moment for Uttar Pradesh. Dalits needed to have their day in the sun. But Mayawati's subsequent defeat does not mean that identity politics are dead. The dignity of the Dalits has been established, and they are now an electoral force that can no longer be taken lightly.

Yet symbolic politics without economic development ran out of steam. Akhilesh Yadav reminded voters that under Mayawati the state had not advanced on the UN's human development index. In addition, she was regularly accused of corruption. Therefore her decisive defeat was not a surprise.

Akhilesh's father founded the Socialist Party in Uttar Pradesh and was a former chief minister of the state. In many ways, the elder Yadav built the Socialist Party as one of the original regional parties, focusing on the decline of India's northern industrial base under Congress Party rule. But the Socialist Party was also notoriously corrupt and was beaten badly by Mayawati's breakaway faction.

Akhilesh Yadav has promised a generational overhaul. His campaign was relentlessly positive. He borrowed from Nitish Kumar in neighboring Bihar, focusing on a simple message of economic development. While his father was anti-technology, Akhilesh promised to give every student a laptop. He ran his campaign through Facebook, Twitter, and call centers, targeting the cell phones that have become increasingly common in Uttar Pradesh's villages. His appeal was less to caste and more to farmers directly and to aspiring urban youth.

Akhilesh also reached out to Muslims. Unlike the Congress Party, he did not promise offices to Muslim leaders. Instead, he simply convinced them that development will lift all boats. His message: how you feed yourself is as important as how you see yourself. He started expelling party goons left and right, sending the message that resources would go toward public ends, not toward party officials. Unlike the Congress Party's Rahul Gandhi—who is a national figure in a national party—Akhilesh's vision was largely confined to Uttar Pradesh. In India's cultural heart, he argued that economic development must come first. Now he must deliver, in India's largest and most corrupt state.

Left behind in the election were India's two biggest parties—the Congress Party and the BJP. Congress's defeat was particularly significant because Rahul Gandhi himself was personally auditioning to be the face of the Congress Party with national elections just two years away. Rahul is the Harvard-educated son of the current Congress Party chief, Sonia Gandhi. Rahul's father (Rajiv), grandmother (Indira), and great-grandfather (Nehru) all had been prime ministers. Someday he could become the first successive fourth-generation prime minister in *any* modern democracy. But the world's fourth-largest democracy—Uttar Pradesh—told Rahul that he still had some work left to do.

SWING STATES: WHICH WAY DO THEY GO?

Straddling the extremes are India's swing states: Andhra Pradesh (population more than 84 million) and West Bengal (population

117

over 91 million).[50] Each has more people than Germany but is as poor, per capita, as Nicaragua. Chief ministers in these states have learned the hard way that the rural poor may not be ready for a full-speed-ahead embrace of globalization. Globally focused cities such as Hyderabad have prospered in recent years, but politicians who have promoted a global perspective have not necessarily benefited. Over two-thirds of voters in these states still live in the countryside, and they have made their voices heard when they have felt ignored. Still, some leaders have shown that persistence can pay off. Successfully balancing upward and global aspirations with the needs of the poor can help swing these states forward.

Andhra Pradesh: Reddy or Not, Here It Comes

Andhra Pradesh and its gleaming capital Hyderabad together illustrate both how to move forward in India and the hurdles that obstruct that path. Led by a succession of two very effective leaders—Chandrababu Naidu and Y. S. R Reddy—Andhra Pradesh demonstrated that it was a challenge to simultaneously modernize and mobilize the poor. Democracy and the cultural divides in Andhra Pradesh are as difficult to master as in any Indian state. But under the right leaders, it can be done.

Hyderabad vaulted onto the world stage in the late 1990s, led by a charismatic leader, Chandrababu Naidu, who headed his own regional political party. Elected in the early 1990s, just after liberalization, he seized the agenda of economic development and reform.

Naidu famously cornered Bill Gates at the U.S. ambassador's house, asking for 10 minutes. Armed with a laptop and a PowerPoint presentation, he used the next 40 minutes to convince Microsoft to invest in Hyderabad. He promised and delivered investment in infrastructure, especially airports, highways, and schools that are now among the most impressive in all of India. Western information technology (IT) companies flooded into Hyderabad. For every public rupee spent, more than two rupees of private investment fueled this growth.[51]

BOX 4-2. India's Optical Illusion

Early in our trip, an acquaintance said, "No one has a right to be bored in India." The founder of several successful nonprofits, she was referring to India's vast opportunities—to do good, to be entrepreneurial, to learn new things. After almost three months there, we understand only a tiny fraction of what is possible.

We saw so much: tropical, laid-back Chennai in the south; fast-paced Mumbai in the west; buttoned-up (by Indian standards) Delhi in the north; colorful Rajasthan and spiritual Rishikesh; rural and urban, hip and hippie, poor and prominent. But India is so diverse, so vast, and so ancient that years of living there still would not do it justice.

The country thrives on diversity. The sounds say it all: the constant cacophony of Hindi music, Muslim calls to prayer, honking horns, hawkers, construction, and conversation. And yet—even with plenty of prejudices and conflict—the majority of Indians live peacefully and tolerantly with their ethnically and religiously different neighbors.

India is also striking in its resilience. Another acquaintance commented, not entirely positively, on Indians' ability to shrug off seeming catastrophes, whether accidents or natural disasters or terrorist attacks. It is a feature noticeable even among our drivers, whose calm in the midst of punishing, lawless traffic was universal. Is it indifference? Self-protection? Or something deeply spiritual? We do not feel that we were there long enough to really understand.

One friend aptly compared India to the optical illusion of the old woman and the young girl. On the surface it shows you one thing—dirt, poverty, and colorful chaos. But look at it another way, and it is something else entirely—beautiful, rich, and boundless. We were fortunate to have the chance to taste all those things, even just a bit.

—Kristen Suokko

With the help of the World Bank, he also pursued structural reforms. Most prominent was the power sector, where rates were set artificially low and where only about 40 percent of electricity use was metered by the state's power company. The rest was given away. As a result, revenues were insufficient to upgrade either power supply or transmission. Naidu raised rates and applied meters, and his actions brought about more reliable and higher quality power.[52]

The results were impressive. Economic growth has been above average for nearly fifteen years; industry and services have risen considerably, at the expense of agriculture.[53] Hyderabad's IT industry, in particular, began to catch up to Tamil Nadu, Karnataka, and Maharashtra. A drive into central Hyderabad from the airport shows off campus parks for a host of Western companies—the likes of Microsoft and Google, Deloitte and Accenture, and GE and IBM.

In making this shift, Naidu saw himself as the CEO of the state. That involved not only attracting businesses but also overhauling Andhra Pradesh's bureaucracy. Naidu passed the "Industrial Single Window Clearance Act," providing investors with streamlined approvals and clearances.

Naidu helped Andhra Pradesh move from being one of India's poorest and most agricultural states to being squarely in the middle. For a while, he seemed to have won the support of both Hyderabad's educated middle class and the rural masses in the countryside. He handily won reelection in 1999. He doubled down on his success, regularly attending the annual World Economic Forum in Davos to tell the success story of Hyderabad and attract even more international businesses. But as Hyderabad continued to take off in the early 2000s, Naidu's political stock elsewhere in Andhra Pradesh fell. By 2004 he was defeated in a landslide. His party's coalition won only one in six seats. The steep and fast fall had many causes, but the rural poor were a critical factor.

While Hyderabad's $75 billion annual output constitutes 60 percent of the state's economy, 90 percent of the voters live in the rest of the state that produces the other 40 percent of the economy. Hyderabad has fewer than 7 million people, less than 10 percent of the state's population of 86 million. Even when all other towns and cities are counted, two-thirds of the state's population is still rural, with six in ten workers employed in agriculture. Although farming in Andhra Pradesh is more productive than India's average, it still contributes less than a quarter of the state's economy. So while the state ranks twelfth in per capita GDP and third in total economy, it falls below the Indian average on the UN's Human Development Indicators.[54]

Farmers, in particular, felt ignored during Naidu's second term. Many farmers rioted in 2000 when Naidu raised electricity rates yet again. He also was slow to respond to flooding after a particularly heavy monsoon. And when monsoons turned to droughts a few years later, a rash of farmer suicides broke out across the state.

The rural-urban divide was superimposed on complex identity politics. The region around Hyderabad is known as Telangana, and its residents consider themselves the modern heirs to an ancient Telangana kingdom—one that never ceded power to the British. Telangana increasingly resents that it funds nearly 75 percent of the state government, even though it has only 40 percent of the population. Many there have called for a separate, new Indian state—presumably including Hyderabad. Of course, that would reduce the rest of the state to a rural and poor stub.

But frictions within Andhra Pradesh were not the only drag on Naidu's popularity. In his first two victories, he had made coalition partners with a rising BJP. Initially, this helped considerably in Andhra Pradesh, which is over 80 percent Hindu. But Hyderabad also proudly boasts some of the greatest forts of Mughal (i.e., Muslim) rule and a successful and well-integrated Muslim merchant class. After the 2002 Gujarat riots, Naidu's party suddenly lost almost all Muslim support.

Thus in 2004 Chandababu Naidu lost to the Congress Party's Y. S. R. Reddy—a pediatrician and devout Christian with a message about serving the poor. Reddy's campaign began with a low-key walk from village to village in this massive state. He promised greater attention to social welfare, particularly for rural Andhra Pradesh.

Once elected, Reddy focused on a massive irrigation expansion project, old age pensions, and employment programs in villages. Most important, perhaps, he did not kill the Hyderabad goose that laid the golden egg. Naidu had set Hyderabad and other urban centers on a path of growth, and that continued under Reddy. Industry grew by 7 percent and services grew by 10 percent. One indication of the durability of Naidu's reforms was that electricity output grew 8 percent under his successor's management. But while Reddy continued with Naidu's economic reforms, he went slower on the Telangana secession issue, deferring to a drawn-out process that put the issue on the back burner.

Y. S. R. Reddy easily won reelection in May 2009. It was a sign that, in a largely rural state, one could pay attention to the needs of the rural poor and also still grow a global city. Calls arose for him to assume a role in national politics as a Congress Party leader who could seamlessly walk from an Andhra Pradesh village into a Hyderabad boardroom.

Less than six months after his triumphant reelection, however, Reddy was killed in a helicopter crash. He was so popular and his death so unfathomable that local Telegu-language TV channels reported that over 120 people either died of shock or committed suicide upon the news.

After a caretaker chief minister held office for less than a year, the Congress Party appointed Nalan Kiran Kumar Reddy as Y. S. R.'s replacement. Of no immediate relation to Y. S. R. Reddy, the fact that he is a Reddy was not immaterial. In Andhra Pradesh, the upper-caste surname "Reddy" traces its roots back at least to a thirteenth-century dynasty and connotes education and managerial skills—similar to being a Vanderbilt, DuPont, or Carnegie. Marrying into the name is said to enhance a dowry considerably. With Y. S. R.'s death, the name became Kennedyesque. Many suspect that Nalan Reddy—a former state legislator and college cricket star—was chosen by Congress Party leaders to forestall an insurgency by Y. S. R. Reddy's son, who had established a new "Y. S. R. Congress Party" dedicated to his father's legacy.

The combined Naidu-Reddy legacy was to move Andhra Pradesh forward by allowing industrialization while still taking care of the needs of the rural poor. It is a delicate balance, and it is uncertain that it can continue to be mastered successfully. Over the last fifteen years, since Naidu's first election, Andhra Pradesh has performed above average in growth, especially in industrial output. But leaders of all major parties in Andhra Pradesh now seem to embrace the importance of balancing such growth with attention to social equity.[55]

Swinging Backward: West Bengal

West Bengal was once a shining star in India, but now it seems determined to walk away from the global economy, and perhaps modernity. The state's capital city Kolkata (formerly Calcutta) was the capital of British India before 1911 but is now synonymous with over three decades of mismanagement by the world's longest-serving elected Communist Party. The communists have been replaced, but the new boss in town—Mamata Banerjee—has helped scuttle some of the most prominent investment and cross-border agreements in India today. Whether she will find a way to balance growth and social welfare remains critical to India's northeast and to the Ganges River Delta.

In the early years of independence, Kolkata was India's east coast counterbalance to Mumbai—if not its superior. The city had some of India's finest universities and newspapers, and the state held a quarter of India's industrial capital stock in 1950. Even a decade later, the state produced 13 percent of India's manufacturing output. Yet by 2000 that proportion had been halved.[56] For the last decade, at a time when India was rediscovering manufacturing, West Bengal's industrial output increased at only half the rate of states like Andhra Pradesh, Tamil Nadu, and Gujarat.[57]

State-level leaders contributed significantly to this decline. For thirty-four years, from 1977 until 2011, the elected communists slowly eroded the state's industrial base, stalled and undermined investment, and drove manufacturers to other, rising states. West Bengal habitually ran huge deficits. This is illustrated in figure 4-4,

FIGURE 4-4. State Debt-to-GDP Percentage, Fiscal Year 2009–10

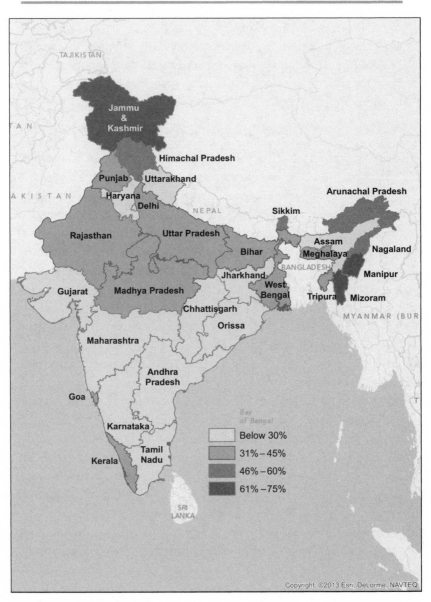

Source: See figure 4-3.

which shows each state's budget deficit as a percentage of state GDP. So while economic growth in West Bengal has been high in recent years—compared, say, to Andhra Pradesh—it also is among the states with the highest government debt-to-GDP ratio. The communists regularly turned to the Congress Party for fiscal salvation, and forged a tense coalition in the national parliament.

Having witnessed a decade of growth elsewhere in India, the communists began to change their approach in the early 2000s. They courted investment from a range of companies. Software developers such as Wipro, Infosys, and Cognizant began to take advantage of Kolkata's several top-tier universities. Perhaps most visibly, the state courted investment from Tata Motors, which planned to build its revolutionary new Nano—an affordable $2,000 minicar—in a new plant outside Kolkata.

The Nano plant would soon become legendary in India, not for what it would make but for where it would be built. As states compete for investment, land acquisition for development is critical—and also politically explosive. For investors an effective process for land acquisition is a sign of administrative efficiency. But two out of three Indians still live in a densely populated countryside, and for these small landholders, land is everything. If a politician allows the wrong kind of land acquisition deals to go through, the invisible hand of the market can suddenly meet the millions of very visible hands filling Indian ballot boxes. In this case, local farmers used that power as a weapon of the weak.[58]

With the Nano plant, the West Bengal communists played the game badly. To acquire land for the Tata factory, they applied the not-so-invisible hand of eminent domain for private development—a legal tool that is a staple of Chinese economic development and has gained controversial traction elsewhere in Asia. (It is even occasionally used in the United States.) This approach provided a political opening to the left of the Communist Party—one seized by a populist Congress Party stalwart, Mamata Banerjee. She led a grassroots, West Bengal breakaway faction of the Congress Party (the All India Trinamool Congress). Banerjee argued that more farmers would be moved from the land than would be employed in the factory. Her protest effectively stalled construction on the plant.

After two years of delay, in 2008 Tata Motors decided to move the plant to Gujarat.[59] While industry saw this as a victory for Narendra Modi, Banerjee and her supporters saw this as her crowning achievement. She became a hero and won a sweeping statewide victory two years later, unseating the Communist Party after three decades of rule. Her party now controlled nineteen seats in the national parliament, without which the current Congress Party–led government could not form a majority.

Like Narendra Modi, Banerjee is difficult to stereotype. She is by all accounts personally ethical and committed to her job, as she sees it. She and her finance team appear focused on cleaning up a state that had become one of the most poorly run and corrupt in India. She also brings a passionate attention to rural poverty. And she has devoted considerable time and attention to resolving West Bengal's own set of intraregional issues, including Maoist rebellions, the status of West Bengal's 25 percent Muslim minority, and the economic and tourist development of Darjeeling—the spectacular and prosperous tea-growing hill region in the state's north.

However, investors have come to fear her. For Banerjee populist opposition to global corporations is a badge of honor. She refuses to attend business conclaves and initially refused to meet with foreign ambassadors promoting industry. In a move to generate revenues, she has imposed import duties on the goods from other states. She has been reluctant to make land concessions to technology giant Infosys, slowing construction of a facility that would have employed up to 10,000 new IT workers.

Perhaps most important, she began to upend national politics, flexing her local muscle in a way that has come to signify the new, rising state-level leader. She has slowed government efforts to reform fuel subsidies. More brashly, she demonstrated her maverick tendencies with a last-minute cancellation of her participation in a trip to neighboring Bangladesh with Prime Minister Singh. The trip was designed to celebrate a water-sharing agreement between India and Bangladesh, which was then washed away when Banerjee exercised the constitutional right, given to state leaders, to veto water agreements.

Banerjee is probably most famous for opposing a new national foreign investment law. In late 2011, she threatened to withdraw Trinamool from the nation's governing coalition over new rules that allow foreign retail giants, such as Walmart, to own a majority stake in supermarkets and department stores. For over a year, Prime Minister Singh's government acceded to her demand, stalling implementation of the law. But with his popularity flagging, the prime minister finally called Banerjee's bluff, making clear he intended to move forward. Banerjee called for a no-confidence vote—and lost.[60] Akhilesh Yadav's Socialist Party from Uttar Pradesh broke its nonalliance and lent grudging support to the prime minister, allowing him to pass the measure.[61]

These two swing states, West Bengal and Andhra Pradesh, will serve as benchmarks for all of India. Wealthier states will need their consistent support for modernization if there is going to be a nationwide consensus in parliament. The push for modernizing domestic infrastructure and greater global integration almost always comes from the industrialized states such as Maharashtra, Gujarat, and Tamil Nadu. Swing states such as Andhra Pradesh and West Bengal have reacted cautiously to the push for global integration, wanting to take advantage of the benefits of modernity but also not wanting to be seen as having abandoned the poor in the countryside.

Meanwhile, poorer states such as Bihar and Uttar Pradesh will look to states such as West Bengal and Andhra Pradesh to see if global integration can lead to wider benefits. Already, many migrant workers from the backward states flock to India's middle-income and upper-income states in search of construction jobs and industrial work. If that work ends up being sustainable, it may encourage the backward states to pursue an industrial future of their own—if for no other reason than to bring their emigrants home.

INDIA'S REGIONS, INSIDE OUT

India's three goals of growth, democracy, and multicultural balance are pursued in all three categories of its major states. Yet the way they are balanced in each group is often radically different—particularly when it comes to India's efforts to embrace the global economy.

As in China, a great deal of this effort can be captured in how well each group links itself to foreign markets and international investment. Infrastructure, urbanization, transparency, and political stability are the most critical lubricants for hastening engagement with the global economy. India has trailed China in greasing the wheels of its internal machine, but a number of states are coming to see the importance of those global priorities. They are acting accordingly.

As in China, all of India's states are now wrestling with internal challenges that are byproducts of the global economy—such as internal migration, access to land, and maintenance of air and water quality. India also struggles with a national bureaucracy that is still more centralized and less experimental than in China. Local Indian Administrative Service bureaucrats are appointed by New Delhi, all the way down to the district level. The process of using the levers of the state to seize the global economy has been much slower than in China. That is partly because of the country's deep internal commitment to a more methodical—if not lumbering and infuriating—political process. India allows both bureaucrats and individual stakeholders to slow national level economic activity that may benefit a greater number of people. This does not mean that India should eschew the reality and principle of pluralism and adopt GDP monotheism. But it does mean that a few key strategic decisions are critical for India to grow its economy so that it can support the plethora of bottom-up goals.

India's forward states have been at the forefront of this global engagement. As in China, they all had the advantage of being coastal states, with long traditions of trading and foreign commerce. They also have had higher literacy rates and cities that have long welcomed engagement with a wider world. Still, they have struggled with internal political challenges that have kept their infrastructure well behind that of foreign competitors and prevented them from experiencing the export-driven growth seen not only in China but also across Southeast Asia. Thus it remains an open question as to whether these states can continue to acquire manufacturing jobs to employ not only people from their own countryside but also the many millions of migrants that have come to them from the backward states.

Moreover, there is the potential for these forward states to pose a real challenge to Indian foreign policy. The rising middle classes in these states tend to be more assertive and nationalistic than in other parts of India. Thus they may advocate their own regional foreign policy interests over more tempered foreign policy run out of New Delhi—whether it is Gujarat's fixation on Muslim Pakistan or Tamil Nadu's fixation on Sinhalese Sri Lanka. It is telling that in 2012 Sonia Gandhi gave in to pressure from Tamil Nadu members of her coalition to support a UN Security Council resolution against Sri Lanka. Without their support, her governing coalition might have fallen. For a woman whose husband had been killed for not backing Tamil demands, this must have been a difficult decision to swallow.

A successful industrial India may be a more nationalistic one—and that problem would be a luxurious one for India. For the time being, it will still have to come up with a sustainable solution for the half-billion of its people living in abject rural poverty. Most of these people are concentrated in a few landlocked, backward states. There are promising signs on this front, especially in recent governance gains in Bihar and in the election outcomes in the country's biggest state, Uttar Pradesh. If economic development can continue apace in the most caste-biased of states, it not only would relieve considerable poverty but also could diminish a huge obstacle to the rest of the country's global engagement. But that, too, will come with a cost, as considerable state spending will be needed on infrastructure, schools, police, and education. And, in the initial phases, those revenues will have to come from outside these economically challenged states, continuing to strain national accounts.

Perhaps the most important places to watch, in this regard, are the swing states—states such as Andhra Pradesh and West Bengal, with rapidly urbanizing and globalizing cores. They are to India what the Western Triangle and similar places are to China: places fighting against the tide to catch up to industrialized rivals, who still feel the burden of bringing a huge number of rural poor into modern urban life. Because of India's democratic system—and politicians constantly vying for the votes of the rural poor—these places will have the biggest struggles in attracting both Indian and foreign investment, reforming power subsidies, acquiring land for industrial development, and investing in high-end projects, such as export processing zones. Such efforts will all seem like luxuries to rural voters. These are the places where the inside of India will have its most important engagements with the outside world.

The rise of effective state-level leaders in all three kinds of states may actually portend well for India's national government. India's prime ministers have come predominantly from the Hindi belt. Their experience has tended to be in national ministries, managing the odd coalitions needed to stitch together over a billion people. The central government now has an opportunity to embrace the input of experienced local leaders when making national policy. In so doing, New Delhi is likely to get a more direct feel for what is making India work. That applies to attracting foreign investment, strengthening interstate commerce, or improving infrastructure.

Some local-to-national input may come from a relatively new development: trading off the support of one regional leader for another within a governing coalition. When Uttar Pradesh's

Akhilesh Yadav decided to back the Congress Party and his Socialist Party replaced Mamata Banerjee's Trinamool Congress in the
governing coalition, he sent a signal that state-based leaders are
willing to band together to support pro-growth policies. This development would appear to strengthen the hand of the central government and allow it to play one regional party off against another.
What is unknown is what states like Uttar Pradesh might extract
in return for their support.

Finally, local leaders may soon rise to run India. In the United
States, the vast majority of twentieth-century presidents have served
as governors. Chinese national leaders increasingly have taken a
turn at local and provincial government. That experience is largely
alien to India, but its day may be coming. Promoting leaders who
have run nation-size states could have real advantages—assuming that they can look past parochial interests. They could bring
directly to New Delhi the pragmatism and entrepreneurial spirit
found in the states and their leaders.

CHAPTER FIVE

POWER POLITICS, INSIDE OUT

SINCE HU JINTAO and Manmohan Singh took power in the early 2000s, China and India have regularly pledged greater cooperation with the United States and Europe on finding reliable, affordable, and sustainable sources of energy. One could predict that their regular summit meetings with industrial powers would touch on energy cooperation. China and India, along with their U.S. and European counterparts, have participated enthusiastically in a series of clean energy ministerial meetings.

Ten years and two American presidents later, those efforts have not been entirely wasted. But American and European energy relations with both emerging giants remain unsettled at best and troubled at worst.

What the big four do on energy is massively important. Taken together, the United States, European Union, China, and India constitute two-thirds of global energy demand. They also produce two-thirds of the world's greenhouse gas emissions and possess two-thirds of existing nuclear power plants.[1]

These aggregate numbers are critical and give good reason to keep focused on these four continental unions. But, once again, the aggregate numbers mask where much of the action really is taking place. States, provinces, and localities are often key movers on energy issues. Whether it is drilling for oil and gas, mining coal, or promoting renewable energy, local laws and local political support help to determine success or failure.

Where energy resources are located and also where they are needed are major factors that influence national energy policies. Depending on their abundance or dearth of resources, some Indian states and Chinese provinces often have more in common with one another across borders than they do with other provinces or states within their own country. Energy-rich regions all struggle with how to turn underground resources into sustainable jobs. Places that have succeeded in energy-intensive manufacturing often struggle with how to get access to more fuel as well as with how to control pollution.

When it comes to establishing national policies on fighting climate change, different regions face off against one another. It is a dance familiar to Americans, who are used to the political tango between climate-conscious states like California and New York, on the one hand, and pro–fossil fuel states like West Virginia and Texas, on the other.

CHINA: EVERY BREATH YOU TAKE

Energy policy ranks high on China's policy priority list. This shift in priorities can be seen in the latest five-year plans. The most recent—which will guide the Xi Jinping government through 2015—emphasizes a whole new set of strategic and emerging industries focusing on energy conservation and environmental protection, next-generation information technology, biotech, high-end manufacturing, new energy, new materials, and clean energy vehicles. These new industries replace old favorites such as aviation, shipping, telecommunications, and more traditional fossil fuel energy production. The goal of these changes is a 16 percent reduction in energy intensity—that is, to use one-sixth less energy in producing each additional unit of economic output. This is largely an effort to improve energy efficiency, but China also plans to put greater emphasis on nonfossil fuels as well.[2]

It is not concern about changes in the global atmosphere that has moved clean energy up the priority list; it is local air pollution. China's thirst for energy is quite literally choking the country. To breathe the air is to breathe coal. My daughter Annika called it straight: "India is dirty. China is *polluted*."

In our three months in China, the only mainland city where I would consider running outside was coastal Shanghai. Recent readings of air pollution meters in Beijing have rated the air well past dangerous—literally off the charts of what was once thought to be the maximum.[3] In January 2013, the "airpocalypse" affected 800 million people.[4] It was caused not only by emissions from coal-fired plants but also by millions of cars and trucks. In the first two days of the airpocalypse, over 10,000 face masks were purchased in Beijing through the online shopping site Taobao.[5] Many expatriates do not last more than a year or two in the city. They are choosing to leave because of the pollution and its health impacts on their families.[6]

Only by inhaling the extraordinary urban air pollution across a half-dozen Chinese cities, in all parts of the country, can one fully understand the true physical limits of GDP monotheism. Several corporate executives told us privately that while they love the challenge of doing business in China, they and their families can live for only two or three years, at most, in Beijing. The simple reason: air pollution. All of this has meant a tug-of-war between national and local officials over how to improve air quality and energy efficiency.

It is not as easy as turning off a switch. In two decades, China has become the world's biggest energy consumer and also its fastest growing. Coal provides 70 percent of all power to the country; oil provides another 20 percent, and the rest comes from gas, nuclear, hydroelectric, and other, renewable sources.[7] Much like the United States, China's energy largely is domestically generated. But as China's demand has grown, it has increasingly had to go abroad to get new resources. The unquenchable thirst for energy resources has dramatically changed the global demand for energy—literally shaking global markets—with serious consequences for the global atmosphere.

And then there is the complicated game of central and local jockeying around natural resources. Much like the United States, the coastal regions consume energy more productively and efficiently than the rest of the country, and are the first to take on mandatory efforts to curb greenhouse gases. The inland parts of the country that are trying to catch up economically are less likely to pursue cleaner production methods. In fact, for many inland provinces, economic growth is tied to the worst energy practices.

Coal Is Still King in China—and the King Is Moving West

Most coal burned in China is mined in China.[8] Coal is produced in nearly every Chinese province, although the vast territories to the north and west—principally Inner Mongolia, Shanxi, and Shaanxi—now produce nearly two-thirds of all domestic Chinese coal.[9] Xinjiang and Ningxia are also fast-growing coal producers and will likely catch up in overall production in the coming years. These provinces have a strongly vested interest in keeping coal as king. More than half of the coal is used for home and office power and heating; most of the rest goes into heavy industry. The steel and construction industries alone accounted for 30 percent of China's coal usage in 2011.

Of course, since most of China's economy is located on the coast, most of the energy consumption also happens on the coast. Guangdong relies on coal for 52 percent of its energy; in Shanghai that proportion is 54 percent, and in Jiangsu, 64 percent.[10] Likewise, the Western Triangle provinces of Sichuan, Chongqing, and Shaanxi are all heavily dependent on coal.[11] Of all the major provinces, only in Beijing does coal account for less than 50 percent of energy consumption.[12] While all of these numbers are below the national average of 70 percent, coal still is the main fuel of choice.

China's coal industry is a unique version of state-driven capitalism. There are several large-scale producers, but the top ten companies only produce 20 percent of all coal.[13] Most coal extraction operations are locally owned and managed—even if "local" means that many are owned by provincial governments, especially in the poorer, inland provinces. That means that these coal companies are a power source, in more ways than one. The central government is trying hard to consolidate them, but that is not nearly as easy as it sounds. In the last few years, the central government has had to shut down thousands of illegal coal mines.[14]

Coal is a singularly important driver of China's economy—economically empowering the north and west while electrically powering the east and south.[15] The owners of coal mines not only supply China's power, their extravagance helps support the luxury car dealerships and retailers of fashion brands. One organizer of a luxury goods expo in Beijing explained that he expressly invited guests from the third-tier cities Taiyuan and Tangshan because both places have many wealthy individuals from the energy sector who have high purchasing power. At least 30 percent of Beijing's high-end items are sold to the coal and oil bosses from Shenyang, Dalian, Taiyuan, and Tangshan.[16] Ordinarily, the hordes of mainland Chinese tourists in Hong Kong and Macau are reviled by locals; but any coal boss from the inland province of Shanxi is always welcome in Hong Kong's luxury stores and Macau's casinos.

Absent a major technological or regulatory breakthrough, coal is likely to remain the most important source of energy in China for the foreseeable future—even if its consumption is clearly unsustainable. And this is not just because of local air pollution problems. China's heavy reliance on coal to meet its energy needs is a global concern: the country has become the world's leading producer of greenhouse gases. It currently pumps into the atmosphere 8 billion metric tons (or gigatons) of CO_2 each year—over 25 percent of the world total, and rising. To put this in context, most scientists agree that the entire planet needs to cut *total* greenhouse gas emissions to about 15 gigatons of CO_2-equivalent by 2050.[17] If industrial countries meet their ambitious pledges to cut emissions by over 80 percent in the next four decades to stave off a climate catastrophe, China would likely still need to cut its emissions in half, from 8 to 4 gigatons. Even if China's economy were to stop growing, that would be a considerable undertaking. So given China's expected economic growth, it is hard to imagine how emissions could be cut unless China's coal economy is reduced dramatically or its carbon emissions are captured and stored.[18]

Local and Global Reasons to Shift to Gas and Oil

In May 2012, I interviewed the head of the Sichuan Energy Private Finance Corporation—a state-owned bank. As I began to describe my project, he stopped me to ask a question of his own: "How can Sichuan get natural gas fracking technology from the United States?" On the day in question, at high noon, my family and I could not see more than one block from the window of our thirtieth floor apartment window in Chengdu.

The energy executive's question spoke to one of the most important shifts in China's energy economy: the transition from coal to natural gas. That shift is, in part, a result of concerns about local air pollution and climate change. It also is an acknowledgment by the central government that it has lost control of the coal economy.

Use of natural gas—the cleanest of the fossil fuels—is expanding rapidly. As with oil, China has domestic supplies, largely in the north and west. The greatest domestic sources are Xinjiang and Qinghai provinces in the far west, and Sichuan and Shanxi provinces in the center-west. Many Chinese provinces are actively exploring fracking technology to uncover domestic riches.

These efforts, however, have met major challenges. Nearly all of China's shale gas deposits are located much deeper below the surface than in the United States, posing an underground hurdle to their nascent efforts. Perhaps more important, much of China lacks a critical ingredient in the fracking recipe: water. China's northwest—which is potentially rich in shale gas—is arid, and what little water exists is already polluted and in high demand. China's other shale-rich province is Sichuan, in the southwest, where water is abundant. This agricultural heartland province is home to the headwaters of the Yangtze River. Yet that resource is also a constraint, because both provincial and national officials are cautious about the environmental consequences of using this critical water supply for gas drilling. Finally, the government has had a hard time finding engineers with the detailed know-how for drilling and deploying fracking technology.[19]

As a result, the central government is also evaluating new technologies that extract natural gas from traditional coal fields, such as exploiting coal bed methane and producing syngas from coal. These have the potential to convert China's coal resources in Shaanxi, Inner Mongolia, and Xinjiang provinces into more environmentally sustainable energy.[20]

Since both of these natural gas strategies are in their early stages, China remains a net gas importer. China's gas imports increased by 20 percent in 2012 and are expected to increase another 24 percent in 2013.[21] It gets most of its liquefied natural gas from Australia, Qatar, and Indonesia. Turkmenistan provides the majority of piped imports. Kazakhstan and Uzbekistan are also growing sources. China is nearing completion of pipelines from Myanmar and potentially is building one from Russia down the road.[22] Currently, natural gas constitutes only 4 percent of China's energy mix, but the government expects that proportion to rise to 10 percent by 2020.[23] To develop and secure those sources, China is spending billions of dollars on drilling, pumping, piping, and shipping businesses.

The rising use of oil is as important. Since oil is largely used as a transportation fuel, it is not much of a substitute for coal. It already is a larger source of energy consumption in China than is natural gas, as the country rapidly is becoming more mobile. While many Chinese leaders speak glowingly of electric vehicles, right now those cars still largely plug into a coal-fired grid. Given this state of affairs, oil- and gas-powered vehicles may actually be cleaner options.

Like the United States, China was once self-sufficient in oil and even exported it. But in just two decades, China went from being a net exporter to being the world's second-largest net importer, thanks to the dramatic increase in fuel demand from millions of new cars, trucks, and trains. China now consumes over 9.8 million barrels per day, but it only produces around 44 percent of that, so it imports about 5.5 million barrels per day.[24] That amount is expected to grow. Thus China is not just in need of foreign oil, it is now deeply dependent upon it. Saudi Arabia and Angola are its largest suppliers, at 20 percent and 12 percent, respectively. Its other oil suppliers are a who's who of politically complicated countries: Iran provides 9 percent; Russia, 7 percent; Sudan, 5 percent; and Venezuela, 4 percent.[25] China has quickly become the number one oil importer from Sudan, Angola, and Iran.[26]

The oil and gas corporate scene is much different from that for coal. Both sectors are largely run and managed by a few large, state-owned companies that compete with one another. The two most prominent are Sinopec and PetroChina. That makes it easier for the central government to control them and to apply national taxes. These companies remain responsible for domestic exploration, drilling, and transportation across the country—mostly using pipelines from west and north to east and south.

The western provinces are critical to the oil industry. The government hopes to make Xinjiang the largest domestic producer and storage base for oil by 2015. Moreover, state-owned PetroChina and China National Petroleum Corporation are building pipelines from Central Asian neighbors like Kazakhstan through Xinjiang, on to Chongqing, and eventually to the east coast.

But energy-thirsty eastern provinces are not just waiting around for overland pipelines. They look to the Pacific Ocean and beyond for energy. China's unquenched thirst for oil and gas has already led it into conflicts with Japan, Vietnam, and the Philippines over territorial claims to islands in the South China Sea, which happen to be surrounded by an oil-rich sea bed. The corporate champion is China National Offshore Oil Corporation (CNOOC), which is largely responsible for international development and acquisition. Today, much of CNOOC's supplies come by sea from the Middle East and Africa, traveling around India and through the Strait of Malacca. And if U.S. and Canadian oil and gas exploration continues apace, North America may soon be shipping directly to China.[27]

Chinese international energy companies also often try to acquire foreign companies. Quite famously, in 2005 CNOOC was denied in its effort to take over Unocal, with many in the U.S. Congress worried about unfair trade practices and national security risks. Regardless, Chinese energy firms have set their sights on resources stretching from Canada's tar sands to offshore operations near Angola and Nigeria.

Renewables: Not Where They Need to Be

Given the human and environmental hazards of coal and the national insecurity that has come with dependence on oil and gas imports, it should come as no surprise that China has been trying to expand production of renewable and other low-carbon energy sources—especially hydropower, wind, solar, and nuclear. However, each of those low-carbon energy sources is found in a different region of China. With the exception of hydropower, the supply does not meet demand—quantitatively and geographically.

Let us start with the exception: hydropower. China is already the world's largest producer in total (though not in percentage terms), with hydropower supplying 6 percent of the country's energy while wind and other renewable sources make up less than 1 percent of consumption. Much of the hydropower is generated a thousand miles inland in the western and central headwaters out of the Himalayan and Tibetan plateaus. Sichuan and Yunnan provinces in particular account for 24 percent of hydropower development.[28] Not far behind them is Hubei province, home of the massive Three Gorges Dam.

Of course, there is good news and bad news in China's hydropower story. The good news is that it is being generated in the poorer inland provinces, precisely where China wants to drive greater economic growth. The bad news is that the breakneck construction of dams has been done with little regard for local environmental concerns and even geological stability. Many still believe that the 2008 Sichuan earthquake was caused, in part, by the Zipingpu Dam nearby. The weight of 320 million tons of water near a major fault line is suspected of precipitating the earthquake.[29] In Tibet, Sichuan, and Yunnan provinces, some of the rivers being dammed flow south into India, Bangladesh, Burma, and Thailand. This creates border tensions—especially since those nations are thinking about building their own dams.

The country's massive solar and wind production build-out is only now starting to be used domestically. Most of that use is in the arid and windy north and west—in Inner Mongolia as well as Gansu, Xinjiang, and Hebei. Wind power has benefited from enormous financial contributions by the central government. In contrast, solar power production has benefited from local and provincial government support and was originally targeted for export markets.[30] In 2010 only 5 percent of photovoltaic modules made in China were used domestically.[31]

Solar and wind each share major drawbacks. They are less easy to deploy at scale, and they cannot be used as the ever-ready base load energy needed in any locality. That means they can only supplement coal or gas or nuclear power. Demand is much lower in coal-rich western provinces where the wind blows strong and steady.[32] In 2010 less than 60 percent of the installed solar power capacity was connected to the grid.[33] As a result, western solar and wind energy generation has yet to make a dent in energy demands in the rest of the country.

Industrial China Has the Whole World's Climate in Its Hands

In the face of all this, China has been wrestling with how to make the shift to cleaner energy sources without cutting off the economic growth that it needs to develop its interior and western regions. That tightrope walk is embodied in how the country has slowly unrolled its climate change policies. In September 2012, China announced an experimental emissions trading system for six provinces and municipalities. Four of those jurisdictions are coastal: Beijing, Tianjin, Shanghai, and Guangdong. Two are in the interior: Hubei and Chongqing. Table 5-1 shows the emissions, population, and GDP statistics for the participating provinces.

Taken together, those places are among the most productive in China, accounting for more than one quarter of China's GDP, even though they are home to less than one-fifth of the population. They are already among the most energy efficient provinces in the country and the least carbon intensive, producing only about one-sixth of the country's CO_2 emissions.

Still, precisely because they are more economically advanced, they are being asked to cut their emissions first. The export powerhouse provinces of Guangdong and the Yangtze River Delta each have been asked to do the most by making an 18 percent reduction in their energy intensity. Chongqing, Sichuan, and Shaanxi, by comparison, only need to improve by 16 percent. And the western provinces only need to improve by 10 percent.[34] So as natural gas imports continue to increase in China, one can expect them to concentrate first along the coast.

Chinese central authorities certainly plan to make nuclear power part of that emissions reduction story. Currently, nuclear power accounts for only about 2 percent of total energy consumption, but this proportion is likely to increase. As of January 2013, China had seventeen operating reactors and twenty-nine reactors under construction, about half of the global nuclear power capacity being built.[35] Operational reactors are all located in the east

TABLE 5-1. Carbon Dioxide Emissions and GDP of Cities-Provinces in the Pilot Emissions Trading System

Units as indicated

City-province	CO_2 emissions (2007)		Population (2010)		GDP (2011)[a]	
	Millions of tons	Percent of national total	Millions	Percent of national total	Billions of dollars	Percent of national total
Guangdong	345	5.7	104	7.8	823	10.2
Hubei	236	3.9	57	4.3	304	3.8
Shanghai	153	2.5	23	1.7	297	3.7
Tianjin	88	1.5	13	1.0	175	2.2
Chongqing	87	1.4	29	2.2	155	1.9
Beijing	80	1.3	20	1.5	252	3.1
Subtotal[b]	989	16.4	246	18.4	2,006	24.9
China total	6,023	. . .	1,339	. . .	7,301	. . .

Source: Table created by author based on data from Jiang Jinhe, "Characteristics of Carbon Emissions in China and the Analysis of Policies for the Development of a Low Carbon Economy [in Chinese]" (Shanghai Municipal Development and Reform Information Network, July 18, 2011) (www.fgw.gov.cn/fgwjsp/zhyj_content.jsp?docid=491402); National Bureau of Statistics of China, "Communiqué of the National Bureau of Statistics of People's Republic of China on Major Figures of the 2010 Population Census," April 29, 2011 (www.stats.gov.cn/english/news andcomingevents/t20110429_402722516.htm). The GDP figures were found under the "National Accounts" annual data from China Statistical Database, "Regional Domestic Product," 2011 (http://219.235.129.58/reportYearQuery.do?id=1300&r=0.29697783476949946 (http://219.235.129.58/welcome.do).

a. GDP converted at 1 U.S. dollar to 6.4615 Chinese yuan.

b. Slight difference between summed versus calculated percent of total due to cumulative rounding effects.

coast provinces of Jiangsu, Zhejiang, and Guangdong, which have the highest energy demand and are the most capable of financing the reactors.

But given the rising consciousness of those on the coast, these provinces also have been the most likely to oppose new reactor construction in recent years. Central authorities suspended nuclear plant approvals in 2011 after the Fukushima nuclear accident, but after safety reviews were done, the government resumed plant approvals in May 2012.[36] Reactors under construction or being planned are dispersed throughout the country, although none are being built in the western provinces.[37] When I asked the head of Sichuan's energy finance corporation about nuclear power, he said that public protest and fear of earthquakes were the single biggest obstacles to developing nuclear power plants in the region.

Two big challenges remain if China is going to shift to cleaner energy. First, the more developed coastal provinces have to follow through on implementation. Chinese provinces regularly underperform their stated outputs on environmental protection. If the wealthier provinces do not reach their goals for implementation, there is little chance that poorer inland and western provinces will do any better. Already Guangdong has asked for forbearance on its 18 percent emissions intensity reductions target, seeking an "appropriately lowered target" for its next five years. The provincial government argued that it was starting "from an already low level of energy consumption . . . making it more difficult, and more costly, to achieve further savings."[38]

Second, the inland provinces continue to have a very high stake in the future production and development of fossil fuels. If Guangdong received an exemption in meeting energy efficiency targets, that would shift the burden of reducing energy intensity westward to poorer inland and far west provinces. "Local governments in China's central and western provinces have argued that the relatively lower energy-intensity in the country's southern and eastern coastal regions, where Guangdong is located, was made possible only because western provinces provided the coast with low-cost energy sources and a cheap labor force."[39] In other words, inland and western provinces have begun to recycle the same arguments made by China for years in international negotiations, that they should have common but differentiated responsibilities. In the short to middle term, there will be no effective regulation either of local air pollution or greenhouse gases in these places. The best prospects for China's interior are breakthrough technologies in natural gas extraction or in capturing carbon and storing it below the surface.

INDIA: THE PRICE IS RIGHT–EXCEPT WHEN IT IS NOT

"Lights out tonight, trouble in the heartland." So begins the first cut from *Darkness on the Edge of Town*, Bruce Springsteen's classic rock album.[40] On the last day of July in 2012, the darkness in India was not only on the edge of town. Darkness spread across India's troubled heartland, stretching from India's lush eastern delta border with Burma to its mountainous and dry western border with Pakistan. Over 600 million people were estimated to have lost power—about half of all India (and nearly one in ten people on the planet). Out of India's twenty-eight states, the outage covered nineteen plus the National Capital Territory of Delhi (see figure 5-1). Three interstate grids had failed: the northern, northeastern, and eastern. Two-thirds of those affected lived in four places: the National Capital Territory of Delhi, Uttar Pradesh, Bihar, and West Bengal.

The blackout shut down factories, traffic lights, trains, and office buildings. Yet what might be more alarming is how much of the region was able to function without public electricity. First of all, a great number of Indians have no public electricity to begin with. For those that do, power shortages and blackouts are so common across the region that many barely noticed. Many have adapted by relying on diesel generators, especially airports, hospitals, and many factories that demand continuous power to remain operational.

Some version of this story happens daily across most of India. Over 1,500 miles from New Delhi, in Chennai, every day at 2 p.m., like clockwork, the lights go off at the Madras Club, our home for about a month. Within thirty seconds, a whooshing sound follows, and then lights magically return.

It took us about a week to figure out what was actually happening. In that part of Chennai, blackouts are scheduled. This was common all across the city—even in R. A. Puram, Chennai's most exclusive district. R. A. Puram hugs the Adyar River and is home

FIGURE 5-1. Indian States That Lost Power in the July 2012 Power Blackout

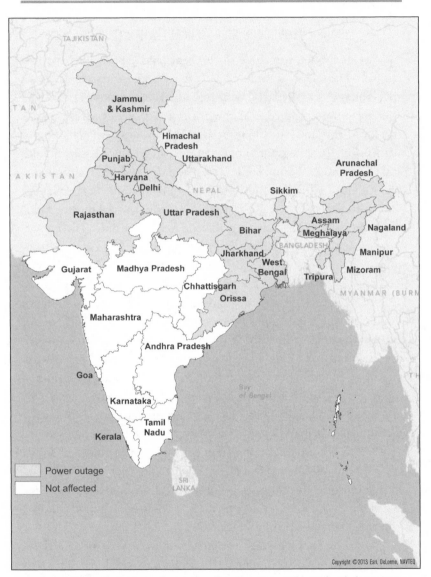

Source: Figure created by author based on data from Helen Pidd, "India Blackouts Leave 700 Million without Power," *The Guardian*, July 31, 2012 (www.guardian.co.uk/world/2012/jul/31/india-blackout-electricity-power-cuts).

to the Madras Club, the U.S. consulate, and South India's wealthiest families. Regardless of income or status, power in R. A. Puram only runs from early morning until 2 p.m.[41] Those who can afford a private generator then simply flip a switch.

Tamil Nadu is much better than most states. It was spared the July 31 blackout as it maintains its own power grid. The same is true of Andhra Pradesh and Maharashtra, which provide electricity to 100 percent and 88 percent of their villages, respectively.[42] In fact, there is only one state in India that is significantly better than those three, where there are no blackouts and 100 percent electrification: Gujarat. There, Narendra Modi successfully tackled energy reform. His secret? He made people actually pay for their power.

It sounds quite simple, but in Indian politics and government, nothing could have been more difficult. During years of socialist rule, India established a range of subsidies and discounts that provided low-cost or free electricity to its enormous rural and poor populations. As a result, a huge number of Indians claim to be rural and poor even if they are neither. Most Indians do not directly pay anywhere near the full cost of electricity.

Much of the blame falls on state governments. Over forty percent of all electricity-generating capacity is owned by state electricity boards; of the remainder, about 30 percent is owned by the central government and the rest by private enterprise.[43] Those figures do not count the enormous number of backup diesel-powered generators that whoosh into action when the power invariably fails. Ineffective pricing and collection fees limit the ability of most state electricity boards to acquire adequate fuel and run power plants. Together with the central governments, the state electricity boards also help build and maintain transmission lines—or not maintain them.

Even in "normal" times, 25 percent of power generated is lost in transmission, thanks to a combination of aging infrastructure and outright theft. India probably needs to invest more than $2 trillion in transmission upgrades alone.[44] And there is the fact that some states still have relatively low rates of village electrification (see figure 5-2). But the money currently collected from end users is insufficient to cover the unit costs of electricity, let alone new capital investment. So any money spent on fuel and transmission comes directly from state and national coffers. That drains resources that could go to schools, roads, or other public investments for which it is even more difficult to collect revenues.

In 2004 Gujarat did what no other Indian state had fully done. It sent officials door to door to see who was poor and who was not. The inspectors started in the countryside, determining who was using power for farming and who was using it for household or industrial purposes. State authorities proceeded in a straightforward and disciplined manner. Moreover, the state also separated transmission—including collection of fees—from production of power. Those two steps allowed for the state-managed transmission company to effectively charge and collect fees. It also allowed private power companies to charge and collect a fair price for the energy that they were supplying to the grid.

Gujarat's farmers were willing to pay as soon as they realized that power would be more reliable. "Once farmers had power, they wanted to buy electric appliances," Chief Minister Modi explained to me. "Now we have high-quality power all day, every day, in every village."[45]

Andhra Pradesh, Tamil Nadu, and Maharashtra are trying to follow suit. Each has learned that getting prices right on electricity is critical to its industrial futures. In the last ten years, each raised electricity prices, despite political opposition. Chandrababu Naidu did it in Andhra Pradesh in 2000, which helped contribute to his defeat. Jayalalithaa did it in Tamil Nadu in 2012 and seems to be surviving. These states also have tried to cut down on energy theft and false claims of rural poverty, and as a result, they now provide electricity to 90 percent or more of their populations (see figure 5-2). Each provides more power each day than in previous years.

FIGURE 5-2. Village Electrification in India by State, 2010

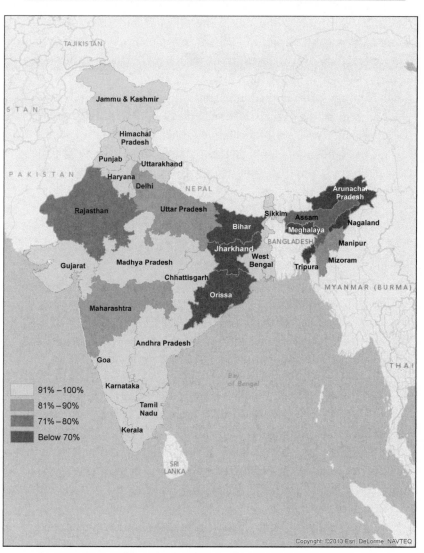

Source: Figure created by author based on data from Directorate of Economics and Statistics, Planning Department, *Economic Survey of Maharashtra, 2009–2010* (Mumbai: Government of Maharashtra, 2010).

But until prices are fully right in those places, power will fail, and diesel generators will need to swoosh into action.

Aside from power shortages, the chronic underinvestment in electric power infrastructure in India has generated an additional side effect: an overinvestment in diesel fuel. Diesel generators are far less efficient per unit of energy than a coal-fired power plant, and they also contribute significantly to local air pollution. Although diesel fuel receives some subsidies, prices are beginning to reflect the true costs of a relatively open market, now incorporating basic costs of importing, refining, and delivering the fuel to customers.[46] While it is more expensive, it is still worth buying when the lights go out.

A Growing Reliance: India's Oil and Gas Revolution

The most discussed building in Mumbai is probably the twenty-seven-story home of Mukesh Ambani, India's wealthiest man and the head of Reliance Industries. Ambani's personal wealth is estimated at just under $25 billion, about a billion for each floor of his Mumbai home. So much has been written about Ambani and Reliance that it tends to obscure perhaps the most important part of his family and industry story. The family became one of the first to make the most important energy linkage in India in the last six decades. The Ambanis recognized that liberalization of the import, refining, and distribution of petroleum, diesel, and natural gas could fulfill an unmet demand for power.

Mukesh Ambani's father, Dhirubhai, had already built a small textile empire and was among the first to experiment in making polyester threads and other petroleum-based synthetic materials. From that experience, he learned the hard science and business of converting crude oil into a marketable commodity. Once energy refining and distribution were partially liberalized in the early 1990s, Dhirubhai saw that he could build a bigger empire from refining and distributing petroleum and diesel.

Mukesh took that vision to the next level at the beginning of India's explosive growth in the late 1990s and 2000s, turning his father's growing conglomerate into India's largest company, whose taxes alone provide 5 percent of all national government revenues. The fact that the Ambani family was located in Maharashtra and had its roots in Gujarat was not insignificant. These two neighboring states have a long trading relationship with the Middle East, so getting the crude imports for the refineries was easy. Then Gujarat's reform of the power sector took the enterprise to a whole new level, providing huge demand for its product. Reliance Industries built an enormous refining facility outside Ahmadabad.

The successful combination of Gujarat energy reform and Ambani's investment there has benefited all of India, especially industrial India. But the business itself is built largely in the west of the country, in Gujarat and Maharashtra. Though India still lacks integrated oil or gas pipelines, the coastal locations of these facilities make transport relatively easy to other developed or developing states that lie along the coast, such as Tamil Nadu, Andhra Pradesh, and West Bengal. Reliance companies also bring real technology and value-added manufacturing to a commodity imported largely from the Middle East. The refining boom, in turn, has also fueled the dramatic growth of India's automotive industry—not just cars but also trucks, three-wheeled auto rickshaws (called "tuk-tuks"), scooters, and motorcycles.

Likewise, natural gas has become a critical fuel and could be a game changer for the country. Already natural gas is being used in the auto industry. Perhaps the most dramatic environmental improvement in India over the last decade has been in New Delhi's air quality. In the mid-1990s, New Delhi's air had become a foul soup of wood smoke, kerosene, diesel, and coal exhaust. The Delhi state government and the central government had passed rules limiting different emissions, but they had never enforced them. India's supreme court forced the government to implement a comprehensive set of rules and to monitor compliance. Among other actions, all public transport vehicles and all taxis (including three-wheel auto rickshaws) were ordered to switch to natural gas from 1998 to 2002.[47] New Delhi's air quality improved dramatically.

This was the clearest demonstration of the ability of natural gas to change the lives of Indians in a real way. It also demonstrated that local governments could act, even if they needed to be pushed by the courts. The country took notice and began to pursue the use of natural gas more aggressively. India only imports about 25 percent of the gas it uses, and it is keen to increase domestic supply. Known reserves are concentrated in a few major provinces: Maharashtra and Gujarat in the west, and Andhra Pradesh and West Bengal in the east. In the south, Tamil Nadu has also developed natural gas fields, as have two smaller eastern provinces, Assam and Jharkhand.[48]

There are some potentially wonderful production-demand matchups in the natural gas story. But as India starts to take advantage of this bonanza, it starts to bump up against the mismatches that so often stall economic development. The biggest, in this case, is getting the gas to other critical states where it could be put to good use. While gas can be shipped, India can benefit more from the national pipeline system that is being planned. Currently, only two major gas lines exist, and they do not connect to major energy-starved cities such as Hyderabad or Bangalore.[49] Moreover, natural gas is a key feedstock for fertilizer. Yet the largely agricultural provinces in the north, such as Bihar and Uttar Pradesh, have yet to take full advantage of their natural gas resources.

King Coal Is Dead. Long Live the King

When it comes to coal, Indian policymakers have not applied the lesson that they have learned in the oil and gas sectors, that fuel sources respond to market signals. India uses a lot of coal, but it does not use it wisely or effectively.

By size India is the world's third-largest producer and consumer of coal, and most of it is located in the north and northeast. Coal use has grown by 75 percent from 2001 to 2011.[50] Coal is abundant across India's north and center, in the states that are most in need of energy—and energy reform. Uttar Pradesh and Bihar have relatively easy access to coal, yet they have some of the lowest rates of household electrification, at about 21 percent and less than 10 percent, respectively, and modest village electrification rates of 88 and 61 percent, respectively.[51]

Unlike the situation with oil and gas, the government still almost entirely controls coal use—and fritters away that control. First of all, it fails to charge end users. Furthermore, under the government's control, the production and transportation of coal are a case study in the ills often associated with state-owned companies. Sheltered from competition but burdened by regulations on opening mines, coal operators are inefficient and fail to invest in both mining and transportation.[52] A huge amount of coal either is stolen from the trains used to transport it or actually smolders away in transit. Moreover, fights with labor unions also have helped to drive up costs and hamper productivity. As a result, the coal rarely, if ever, leaves the region. When cities such as Chennai and Mumbai need a lot of coal, they tend to import it—despite the domestic abundance.[53]

Recent efforts by the central government to unlock India's coal reserves raised expectations, only to dash them. A new auction was planned for 2012 to allow coal prices to reflect the true costs of extracting and delivering the coal. That auction was to be tied to further liberalization of mining rules. Investors seemed lined up to initiate a new wave of energy investment. But that effort became embroiled in a bid-rigging scandal that helped to further tie up the government in controversy.

Of course, India's failure to take advantage of its coal wealth has had one ironic positive benefit: it has been good for the global climate. India already is a greenhouse gas giant: it is the world's third-largest national emitter (tied with Russia). But if it had fully exploited its coal resources, its emissions would be much greater. At 2 gigatons in 2011, its carbon emissions ranked far behind those of the United States (5.4 gigatons) and China (8.0 gigatons).[54] When adjusted for population, the average Indian emits four times less than the average Chinese and eleven times less than the average American. Of course, much of the low per capita figure also has to do with the fact that hundreds of millions of Indians are still not connected to the grid.

That disparity in per capita emissions has dominated India's position on global climate talks for two decades. Since the 1992 Rio Earth Summit, India has been the strongest voice for "common but differentiated" responsibilities. Those were enshrined in the famous 1997 Kyoto Protocol where developing countries avoided binding agreements to reduce their emissions until developed economies first dramatically slashed their own. For over a decade after Kyoto, India refused to discuss any binding limits.[55]

Still, India increasingly sees the local impacts of climate change and growing coal use. The biggest impact has been on changing weather patterns in South Asia. Over the last fifty years, rising temperatures have led to a nearly 10 percent reduction in the duration and rainfall levels of the annual monsoons that are vital to nearly all Indian agriculture. Moreover, the melting of Himalayan glaciers threatens the country's other vital water supply.[56] In addition, rising sea levels have put hundreds of millions of Indians at risk in low-lying population centers in the Kolkata and Chennai metropolitan regions—a reality brought home during the devastating 2004 tsunami.

So Indians now take climate change more seriously. Dr. Rajendra Pachauri, head of the Energy and Resources Institute in New Delhi, has become a global spokesman for the cause. For a decade, he has headed the Intergovernmental Panel on Climate Change—the UN-backed research body that collects and reviews the scientific evidence that human activity has been the main contributor to climate change. And little by little, his fellow Indians have begun to take notice.

Perhaps most surprising to Pachauri was the phone call he received from Narendra Modi, the chief minister of Gujarat. Like many in New Delhi, Dr. Pachauri had only heard of Modi because of his role in the infamous Gujarat riots of 2002. Modi called to request a briefing on climate change. Pachauri was suspicious, but he agreed to host Modi and several top advisors for a two-day seminar.

Modi returned home to Gujarat with the zeal of a convert. He launched the first state-level ministry to address the issue and promoted the use of renewables, especially solar.[57] Modi cites religion as inspiring his environmentalism—which comes as ironic to those who view him as a communal extremist.[58] As he told me, "For me, this is a moral issue. You don't have a right to exploit what belongs to future generations. We are only allowed to milk the earth, not to kill it." For the chief minister, it seems, all the world is a holy cow.

The Promise and Perils of Nuclear and Renewable Energy

With great fanfare, the biggest breakthrough in U.S.-Indian relations was inked in 2005. President George W. Bush and his Indian counterpart, Manmohan Singh, agreed to the famous Civilian Nuclear Agreement. The United States had decided that it would now sell advanced nuclear technology to India, even though India was not a member of the global pact against nuclear proliferation.[59]

In theory that would further advance the development of nuclear power in India. Westinghouse and General Electric were prepared to develop major facilities on the subcontinent. Nuclear power currently provides almost 5 percent of India's electricity, though the government plans to increase that proportion to 25 percent by 2050.[60] The central government has provided financing and technology. In practice, however, the "rush" to nuclear has been slow. Since the Bush-Singh agreement, not one commercial contract has been signed. India's fractious party politics explain much of the slowdown, as the opposition BJP has thrown up a number of road-blocks. But state and local politics also are a big part of that story.

Tamil Nadu has shown that turning on the nuclear switch is easier said than done. Nearly 400 miles south of the state's capital of Chennai, at the tip of the subcontinent, sits the completed Russian-built nuclear reactor at Kudankulam. The reactor was ready to go live in mid-2012, providing 2,000 megawatts of electricity. Yet as that year passed, it still sat dormant. The central government holds authority over nuclear energy and had built and paid for the reactor. Yet Indian states must approve any nuclear power installation, which means that Tamil Nadu's chief minister, J. Jayalalithaa, must sign off on opening the facility. It would appear to be a quick and easy decision. The reactor itself was over twenty-five years in development and was paid for by the central government.

Still, Jayalalithaa has proceeded with caution. She has instead backed the protests from local fishermen who fear "an Indian Fukushima," in the words of Gopal Gandhi, Mahatma Gandhi's grandson.[61] While several experts have vouched for the reactor's safety, South India was hit hard by the 2004 tsunami, and having a reactor sitting on that very coast stirs fears among the locals.

Many observers think that Jayalalithaa will ultimately concede to the math of economic development—and also use the controversy to extract additional concessions from Delhi. The biggest cost to her is to appear to value the energy-hungry industries in Chennai above the environmental safety of near-subsistence fishing communities in south Tamil Nadu.

That local fear of nuclear accidents has made its way to the national Indo-U.S. Civilian Nuclear Agreement and has affected the development of nuclear power across the entire country. To implement the agreement, parliament was very focused on the question of who would be liable if an accident were to occur. In a bow to local government concerns, it capped the liability of localities at $400 million. In contrast, the potential liability for the suppliers of parts and technology was limitless. As a result, foreign companies such as Westinghouse, General Electric, Siemens, and Areva are cautious about expanding business in India.

So when it comes to carbon-free energy, the biggest game in India is renewable power. India is already one of the world's largest producers of renewable energy, both in real terms and as a percentage of its energy production. All renewables combined constitute about one-third of all electricity generation in the country.

Hydropower is the biggest part of that total, providing about 23 percent of all Indian electricity. Hydropower installations are found across the country—in the Himalayan watersheds in the north and north east, the central mountains around Hyderabad, and the southern parts of the Ghats mountain ranges. These installations already supply eight times more electricity than what is provided by nuclear power, although the ability to expand hydropower is quite limited. Indeed, the biggest challenge to expanding hydropower is the battle between neighboring states when it comes to building and operating dams.

Tamil Nadu and Karnataka, for instance, have fought for several years over water rights surrounding the Cauvery River. In addition to using the water to meet drinking water and irrigation needs, Karnataka has two hydropower plants on the river, and Tamil Nadu has four. In January 2013, India's supreme court finally ordered Karnataka to release water to Tamil Nadu. Similar disputes have occurred between Gujarat and Rajasthan, and between West Bengal and neighboring Bangladesh.

Wind and solar power are the next renewable growth industries for India. In Tamil Nadu, wind power already accounts for 20 percent of electricity capacity. Other coastal regions are also trying to ramp up efforts to capture wind. And in a country where the average number of clear days numbers above 200, solar would appear to have a bright future. Already it is being adopted in remote locations to help bring simple electricity to small farms, for everything from pumping water from storage wells to helping charge battery-operated farming devices. And Narendra Modi has urged that India lead a global group of sun-drenched nations to make solar energy the next great leap forward.

FROM THE BOTTOM UP:
CONTINENTAL UNIONS AND MANAGING THE ENERGY CHALLENGE

There has been considerable commercial progress in the energy sector in both China and India, with different regional partners. Foreign firms like General Electric, Westinghouse, Hitachi, Siemens, and Areva sell gas and nuclear power plants, electric transmission equipment, and a range of other technologies to China and India, largely to the advanced coastal provinces and states. Chinese energy technology firms (most of which are located in the coastal province of Jiangsu) export solar panels and windmills to the west and even to India. Both emerging giants are investing in the development of fuel cells and electric batteries in the American heartland, and in oil sands and shale gas in more rural American areas.

Despite all this international exchange of goods and technology, it is important to be mindful that internal politics have external consequences. Just as international cooperation can lead to diverse local beneficiaries, distinct local voices and interests also can stop international cooperation. Central authorities in Beijing and New Delhi are subject to local pressure. The historic U.S.-India nuclear agreement in 2005 was a significant bilateral deal that broke with almost forty years of policy. But in the eight years since its signing, local opposition has won the day, particularly against new reactors and on the broader principle of who bears liability if there is an accident.

Trade battles have erupted on energy issues as well. From oil and gas to solar and wind, each country sees instances of unfair practices from counterparts. In each case, a domestic constituency in China or India comes with local political supporters who make their case to the national government The same is true when dealing with strategic energy issues, from the containment of nuclear aspirants such as Iran and North Korea to securing critical energy routes over land and sea.

The echo of local energy concerns can be heard on the biggest of global stages. In 2009 President Barack Obama and his European counterparts personally flew to global warming talks in Copenhagen, seeking to rescue the UN climate change treaty from the jaws of defeat. Chinese and Indian leaders participated as well, aware that their two countries will be the most important greenhouse gas emitters in the coming half century. With all of the "Big Four" players, states and localities shaped the negotiating positions taken by their leaders.

Europe is a leader in combating climate change, mostly because the three major European powers—Germany, England, and France—made costly decisions to shift from coal to nuclear power and natural gas in the late 1980s (just *before* the world became aware that carbon emissions caused climate change). American officials only took the issue seriously because states that hug the East and West Coast have been looking for action—regardless of political party affiliations. Republican governors often took the lead in those places, such as Schwarzenegger in California, Pataki in New York, and Romney in Massachusetts, each of whom actually signed state-level climate change laws. China and India each have states that are innovating in the fight against climate change and have been urging their leaders to take a more proactive stance.

But federal politics also limit what each of these continental unions can do. Poland, Slovakia, and Italy still have a long way to go to bring down their carbon emissions, making only a little progress in the last decade. As Europe contemplates deeper emission reductions, the question remains as to whether those three European Union members are committed to action.

In the United States, similar tensions exist. Senators from most of the American south and west have helped to kill national climate laws. And while Republican governors signed state-level climate laws into effect, Democrats in West Virginia, Louisiana, Nebraska, and Missouri helped lead the fight against national legislation.

China and India have similar internal political battles ahead. The poorer regions in China and India that are most desperate for growth are likely to view the effort to cut greenhouse gases as a luxury they cannot yet afford. That may be short sighted, but it certainly describes a reality that many Americans and Europeans know too well in their own systems, even if they are unaware of the economics of their Asian counterparts.

Behind each global policy challenge lies a Chinese province or Indian state that has its own agenda—just like Germany and Poland, or California, West Virginia, and Louisiana. Each sees energy or climate change policy through different lenses. Some important provinces and states are points of friction. Several others, however, could be the keys to success.

CHAPTER SIX

DIFFERENTLY THE SAME: INSIDE OUT DIPLOMACY

CHINA IS NOT only Beijing and Shanghai; India is not only New Delhi and Mumbai. The United States and Europe need to understand the range of important localities in the world's two largest nations, and they also must *actively engage* with those local communities and their leaders. On too many issues, American presidents or corporate CEOs have had productive talks with Indian and Chinese counterparts but are then disappointed because a regional leader opposes making a deal or refuses to implement a central government directive. And on a few key issues, important innovations are happening at the local state or provincial level that could usefully transfer around the world.

The opportunities are enormous—especially when one considers the range of local developments taking place. At least half a billion Chinese and Indians have moved into modernity in the last twenty years alone, and that number will increase in coming decades.[1] However, those successes have happened in certain regions and not in others. That will also be the case in the future. To influence these nations on major public policy issues or to cultivate their massive internal markets, one cannot simply make a single call to their political or financial capitals.

A CEO or cabinet secretary may think it easy to craft a "China strategy" or an "India strategy," given two political systems that, on paper, appear more centralized than those in Europe or the United States. In fact, China strategies and India strategies may be harder to design, let alone implement. Addressing a continental union requires understanding local economic, political, and cultural realities in cities such as Chengdu or Chennai, country-size jurisdictions such as Guangdong or Gujarat, or vast regions such as Inner Mongolia or Uttar Pradesh. Within China, Chengdu is as different from Guangdong as both are different from Inner Mongolia—just as Berlin is different from Barcelona and both are different from Brussels or Belgrade. In fact, in some ways, a Chinese province such as Guangdong may be more similar to the Indian state of Gujarat than it is to another Chinese region such as Inner Mongolia. Policy agreements, trade laws, or marketing strategies need to take that into account. Such deals can be hammered out in each nation's capital, but negotiators need to know how—and where and by whom—policies will be implemented and executed.

GETTING TO KNOW LOCAL SYSTEMS AND LOCAL LEADERS

By and large, the rise of local politics has been a positive force in both countries. It has helped many local regions grow their economies. But each system has its own strengths and weaknesses, and these will persist into the future as well.

China: Province-By-Province Reform

In China local experimentation has allowed some provinces to prosper, even if the central government is now trying to help less advanced provinces to catch up. Guangdong, Shanghai, Jiangsu, and Zhejiang took advantage of decentralization, liberalization, and local government entrepreneurialism. Now they all are struggling to produce globally competitive, higher-value-added goods and services. To do that, they will need to decrease the role of state-owned enterprises—or at least modernize them—and make financing more accessible and transparent. As they try to liberalize, these provinces are also on record as trying to implement a new wave of environmental and social regulations. And if that were not enough, the coast's political leaders have begun to experiment with granting a broader range of political rights for citizens to engage in public life, as well as civil liberties to protect citizens from arbitrary government action. That three-part economic, social, and political agenda will push these provinces to make changes that seemed like a luxury only two decades ago. And they will have to do all this while subsidizing the growth of inland provinces.

Those lagging inland provinces do appear to be making up lost ground, but they have a long way to go. Heartland success stories tend to be tales of state-led growth. Local governments have been major players, even more so than on the coast. The sustainability of inland growth—economically, environmentally, and politically—is not just a local concern, but a global one. Right now, the nature of progress in these areas is difficult to judge. Statistics are unreliable. Local governments, banks, and businesses lack transparency. For instance, it remains uncertain whether central authorities would be able to spot a banking collapse soon enough. They are clearly trying to get ahead of such a crisis right now, but it is unclear whether they are able to do anything about it. Local lending practices are worrisome enough that the central government has tried a series of steps to limit local excesses. But with the central government still calling for annual growth of over 7 percent a year, local governments are incentivized to spend money, whether or not they have it.

Officially, the central Chinese government recognizes the human and environmental limits to such aggressive growth targets. Local governments feel those limits in the form of protests. Working conditions, living conditions, migrant *hukou* status, lack of health and human safety standards, air pollution, and water degradation are all onerous enough that people are willing to take action against local authorities, whatever the consequences. In each case, everyday Chinese feel that they have nothing to lose by challenging the government. This has led to a "brittle authoritarian regime that fears its own citizens" and whose "leaders have a deep sense of domestic insecurity," in the words of the noted China scholar and former State Department official Susan Shirk.[2] Since the Arab Awakenings in 2011, spending in China on police and public security has grown to over $100 billion a year—exceeding that for China's military.[3] Much of this money is spent in cities such as Chengdu, Chongqing, Xi'an, and a dozen other heartland cities like them. It also is spent in the badlands of the Tibetan high country and the farthest reaches of Xinjiang.

In China's western plains and mountains, efforts to focus on economic or environmental sustainability, in and of themselves, may not be enough to offset the intrinsic ethnic issues. Furthermore, this is not purely an internal problem. Many of those restive western minorities have counterparts across the border, in places like Mongolia, Turkmenistan, Kazakhstan, Nepal, Bhutan, and (looking south) India, Bangladesh, and Burma. Leaders in Beijing and in the interior regions must find a way to embrace minority cultures and reconstruct China's national image as perceived across its borders. As it stands, many neighbors looking into China do not see a promised land or even a badland—they see a land of hardliners.

Across all these regions and issues, the Chinese political system faces two major challenges. First, it must consider expanding the list of public goods from simple economic growth to a wider range of social and political objectives. Second, it must consider coming to terms officially with the political pluralism that is popping up from place to place. China's central government allows for a diverse set of policies, adapted by local officials to local needs—as those officials see them. However, there is no established policy of recognizing the existence of distinct local interests as defined by local populations.

In explaining how political reform relates to economic reform, one noted Singapore diplomat, Kishore Mahbubani, draws a distinction between effective governance and democratic institutions.

The former leads to economic advancement; the latter is simply about representing public voices. Mahbubani presents a caricature of the Chinese view of the world, arguing that effective governance does not require democracy. In making governance a higher priority than representativeness, China's model over the last thirty years must be considered a success: "It is not perfect but it has lifted more people out of poverty, educated more people, increased their lifespans and generated the world's largest middle class. No other society in human history has improved human welfare as much as the Chinese government. It would be insane to deny that China has enjoyed 'good governance.'"[4] According to Mahbubani, the West should value outcomes as highly as political process, if not more so.

Yet traveling across mainland China should make anyone skeptical, at best, of Mahbubani's view of governance. Indeed, China has had great success in a few key places with populations and economic output that would dwarf most national economies, and in a few key sectors that have dramatically shaken and shaped global markets. In other regions or aspects of human welfare, however, China's focus on fast economic growth has often led to undeniably bad outcomes. In cities such as Chengdu, infrastructure and industry are still far behind those of the coast. Worse yet, the initial attempts to catch up have produced choking air pollution, questionable public finance, and displaced landholders. Moreover, if gains in jobs, skills, housing, health care, and other quality of life dimensions are to be sustained, it is critical for China's leaders to get the process right for incorporating civic input.

Chinese officials who are sympathetic to democratic reforms focus less on an either-or choice between growth and democracy and instead on the sequencing. Their approach has been to prioritize basic improvements in economic welfare first. Only after the country has generated considerable wealth would China address "externalities" such as impacts on public health, environmental damage, or social dislocation. And establishing more transparent and accountable governing processes—such as freedom of association, public debate, a free press, and elections—would likely follow these regulatory reforms.

The debate is now starting as to when political reform should happen—and where. A wave of reformers is experimenting with certain features of "liberal democracy" as necessary or even synonymous with good governance. Critically, those experiments are taking place in different provinces and localities, each addressing local needs. Guangdong's former party secretary Wang Yang emphasized the rule of law, protection of property and minority rights, and a freer press that can unearth and examine official corruption, environmental malfeasance, fiscal policy, and corporate reporting. Wang Yang is now vice premier, so many are watching closely to see if he will formally acknowledge private interests across the entire society as having intrinsic value. His policies are commonly contrasted with those of Bo Xilai, who not only championed state-led growth but also rolled back progress on rule of law and an independent judiciary.

Chinese experimentation is all based on local conditions, which has considerable implications for Western diplomacy. It places an even higher premium on American, European, and other foreign governments and businesses getting to know China's local developments and leaders. It is one thing to get a handshake in Beijing; it is quite another to have that agreement be implemented at the local level. That is as much the case in a trade, investment, or energy policy negotiation as it is in a private business deal. Foreign businesses already have entered the game of local bargaining. Absent a central government commitment to political and legal reform in all provinces, the West must prepare itself for a more well-informed, bottom-up approach that treats each province as an agent of change.

India: State-by-State Economic Reform

In India the local challenge is no less important, even if it is far different. As in China, there is considerable mixing of central and local authority. To this day, the central Indian bureaucracy reaches far deeper into the country than does the central Chinese Communist Party or government. Still, Indian state-level political leaders are now exerting local control and forcing their way into the national conversation.

Economic advancement in states such as Maharashtra, Gujarat, and Tamil Nadu has come from the efforts of both local entrepreneurs and political leaders. To be sure, states still face competitiveness hurdles. But that is partly because India's most successful states do not see economic growth as the only goal. Unlike in China, the institutions that protect and promote political pluralism also remain ends in and of themselves.

India's effort to balance growth, democracy, and multiculturalism is genuine. In the last twenty years, the central government has been less active in managing that balance, allowing each state to find its own equilibrium. The general trendline has been for states to embrace economic growth as a higher goal, although some states have succeeded more than others. Yet even in backward states such as Bihar and Uttar Pradesh, economic growth has moved up on the list of local priorities. The desire for growth now challenges the political dominance of caste and religious identity, especially among the lower castes. These states are now struggling to catch up in infrastructure, education, housing, roads, sanitation, and reliable energy. Of course, their development should not be judged just on GDP growth alone. In both Bihar and Uttar Pradesh, leaders should be applauded for focusing on more than GDP monotheism. They also have tried to expand access to water and power, to lower child mortality and female illiteracy, and to focus on law and order and property rights.

The forward states and cities already have tackled these basics and are now confronting a different set of challenges that come from being globally connected. Longtime residents of Mumbai and Chennai are still wary of all the foreign investment and internal migrants that have come to town. Globalization's brilliant rewards threaten traditional lifestyles. Again, success may not move forward in a straight line. The productive experiments that have connected these cities to global markets may ultimately lead to social and cultural detours and dead ends.

The intersection of local and global priorities can be seen in current efforts to develop a coherent national governing philosophy. The two major national political parties—the Congress Party and the BJP—are both aware of India's emergence as a global power but still cannot govern without regional coalition partners. India's federalism has held back central decisionmaking on critical policy issues such as investment rules, trade, energy, water resource management, and counterterrorism. It is even affecting traditional diplomatic and national security decisions. When Mamata Banerjee stops a cross-border water agreement, or Tamil Nadu's DMK party threatens to pull out of the government over policy toward Sri Lanka, the states and regional parties are becoming foreign policy players.

Across India—and much more so than in China—people speak freely about the distinct global issues that matter to them. Tamil Nadu looks to Singapore, Malaysia, Indonesia, and Thailand—and especially to Sri Lanka. Its people also care about the global tech revolution. Mumbai watches and weighs in on events in the Straits of Hormuz and piracy off the west coast of Africa. Gujarat cares about Middle East oil, and joins Jammu and Kashmir in a persistent focus on Pakistan.

This divergence of interests is healthy in any democracy. In the United States, the San Francisco Bay Area cares about worldwide intellectual property protection and H1-B visas, Florida cares about Latin America, New York cares about global finance and immigration, and California, Florida, and New York—as well as West Virginia and Texas—all have strong opinions about global climate change policy, based on their distinct local contexts.

India's former foreign minister Jaswant Singh summed this up for me. As I was trying to make sense of my time in India, he told me, "The rise of states is the most significant political development in the country today." Singh worries that the fracturing of parties will only lead to gridlock. "Indian foreign policy towards Sri Lanka should not simply be dictated by Madras, our approach to Pakistan determined in Jammu and Kashmir, our approach to Bangladesh in West Bengal."[5]

Harnessing and steering local dynamism remains a challenge. Federalism can become a problem when states fail to see the bigger picture. In today's globally integrated India, that means managing a parliamentary coalition and also working with chief ministers from opposition parties. Taken together, that is a difficult and dangerous juggling act. Top-down no longer seems to work; instead, leading requires listening and forging pragmatic partnerships.

That is the new reality. Regional parties provide more direct representation of India's states in New Delhi. And regional leaders increasingly act as intermediaries between their local populations and global interests and issues. The challenge for any national level Indian leader, as for his or her Western counterparts, is to craft a clear vision for the entire country and then work with state leaders and representatives to bring all of them along. This means that foreign governments must learn more about these states and work with the central government to engage them once a common objective has been determined—or perhaps even involve them in the shaping of that common objective.

China and India: Leadership Matters

With power increasingly diffuse in China and India, it is critical to get to know the leaders who make each system work—or not work. When presidents or CEOs visit these countries, they should insist on visiting the leader of at least one leading economic province or state outside the capital and also at least one aspiring inland region. Visiting foreign heads of state should always bring along provincial or state leaders from their own country—particularly from those jurisdictions that strategically match Chinese or Indian counterparts. Corporate leaders should bring manufacturing or marketing executives who are familiar with the strengths and weaknesses of "second cities" so that they can more accurately size up the opportunities and challenges.

Getting to know local leaders will require understanding political sensitivities. As of July 2013, the United States still had not issued a visa to Narendra Modi in India, even though he is among India's most effective economic leaders. Similarly, the new party secretary in the export superprovince of Guangdong, Hu Chunhua, had first learned how to rule by supervising crackdowns in Inner Mongolia and Tibet, but he appears to have demonstrated greater flexibility during each successive incident. It may not be wise for an American president to put either Gujarat or Guangdong as a first stop for a state visit. But this should not prevent governors, cabinet secretaries, or corporate executives from making such visits. Acquiring a better understanding of rising leaders is critical to understanding where these countries are going. Visits with these leaders should stress not only economic ties but also the importance of minority rights and religious liberties.

Local leaders and their economies are particularly critical for developing key global policy agreements. Not all places are made equal. Even in a globally wired economy, the world is not flat. In fact, it is still a rather lumpy world, with high hilltops and deep ravines in economic and social development.[6] The high hilltops are centers of innovation that cooperate and compete across continents. Their locations are not accidental. Each has brought together some combination of geography, historical and cultural characteristics, and also some element of effective local governance. So, if one is interested in state-of-the-art intellectual property protection in Shanghai or in recruiting more high-tech workers from Tamil Nadu, it is critical to understand the interests of and constraints on their political leaders.

Economic Diplomacy: Wingtips and Flats on the Ground

The United States still does not know the local economies and leaders in China and India as well as it should. While a few top officials know parts of China and India well, the U.S. government as a whole does not. As a result, it is not positioned to fully understand the challenges in all but a few of these countries' provinces and states.

The United States should immediately set a goal of doubling the number of consulates in each country within the next decade, even if that means shifting resources from Europe and Latin America.

The United States is significantly underrepresented across these two countries. As of 2013, there were only six U.S. consulates in China and five in India. That is one for every 200 million people in China and for every 240 million in India. By comparison, the United States has fifty-four consulates in the EU and fifty-five consulates in the Americas—roughly one consulate for every 10 million people.[7]

The thin official presence has economic consequences. The United States is overlooking economic and political opportunities in the provinces and states that are starting to climb the economic ladder most rapidly and where new markets are developing. The four U.S. diplomatic posts along China's coast—in Beijing, Shanghai, Guangdong, and Shenyang (near North Korea)—cover a region with over 500 million people and a $4 trillion economy. That is half the number of such posts in France—despite the fact that the French economy is only 60 percent as large as coastal China's and has only 13 percent as many people. The other two U.S diplomatic posts in China are in the megacities of Wuhan and Chengdu. Their regional responsibilities cover an area that has more than 800 million people and a $2 trillion-plus economy. Furthermore, this region has particularly important mineral and natural resources as well as foreign policy interests. In all these cases, the ability of the United States to know and understand these areas and develop economic opportunities is quite limited.

Similarly, the five U.S. diplomatic posts in India are situated in the megacities of New Delhi, Mumbai, Chennai, Hyderabad, and Kolkata. But this limited distribution misses important cities such as Ahmadabad, Bangalore, Jaipur, Lucknow, and Patna. Without more expansive diplomatic postings, American business pioneers are less likely to get the needed support and guidance of the U.S. government. Western government, business, and nongovernmental leaders need to act quickly. The opportunity to establish strong relationships with this new wave of rising stars will decrease over time.

In its relations with both China and India, the U.S. federal government—especially the State Department and Commerce Department—should make it a high priority to mobilize and coordinate the engagement of U.S. governors and mayors.

One positive trend is that U.S. governors and mayors have begun to lead trade missions to China and India, and vice versa.

State-level interest in China has received some central encouragement from Washington and Beijing. Secretary of State Hillary Clinton launched a U.S.-China Governors Forum in 2011 "to extend mutual understanding and interests beyond national governments to individuals, businesses, and state and provincial governments."[8] The first forum was first held in Salt Lake City, with the follow-up held in early 2013 in Beijing-Tianjin.

Since then, the National Governors Association has partnered with the Chinese People's Association for Friendship with Foreign Countries to forge a series of cooperative relationships, including sister-city pairings, university exchange programs, and partnerships on energy and environmental cooperation.[9] American governors have begun to hold one-on-one meetings with their provincial governor and party secretary counterparts, and a few meetings have led to concrete undertakings. Several states opened new offices dedicated to China. California's governor Jerry Brown led the way, launching a trade and investment outpost in Shanghai and also pursuing investment and trade agreements with leaders from Jiangsu and Guangzhou.[10] Similarly, Wisconsin, Virginia, and North Carolina all have aggressively pursued relationships in China.[11] The extent to which inland American states see benefit in forging similar bonds with counterparts in China's interior remains to be seen.

Getting to know regional concerns and interests also has a critical political and foreign policy dimension. When it comes to negotiating bilateral agreements with these countries, or even simply monitoring their internal economic developments, states and provinces may not themselves be frontline negotiators, but they are the places where policy is implemented. China's efforts to shift resources from a relatively prosperous coast to a growing but groaning interior are at the core of the top leadership's policy challenges and choices. Many of the last decade's battles over investor protection, intellectual property protection, and labor and environmental standards are now being replayed in the interior provinces. The coastal regions face a different set of policy implementation challenges, more akin to those faced by nations with upper-middle-income status. These include efforts to foster innovation, modernize banking rules, and create a high-tech workforce.

Direct policy engagement should be targeted. China's six-province emissions trading program, launched in the fall of 2012, is largely focused on the more advanced, coastal provinces. This has real potential synergies with emissions trading programs in American states such as California, New York, and Massachusetts that already are among our most advanced economic engines, combining manufacturing with high-end services. When California governor Jerry Brown met with his counterpart in Guangdong, they launched a state-to-province working group on climate change, renewable energy, and energy efficiency. He was matching the largest, most productive, and most energy efficient state in the United States with a peer state in China. Like California, Guangdong will have a cap-and-trade system that could be the model for much of the rest of China. Guangdong has about the same carbon footprint as California, even though it has about twice as many people and less than half the economic output. Likewise, the environmental and governance challenges associated with coal-fired electricity in China's interior are quite similar to those faced in America's industrial midwest. The opportunities and regulatory hurdles connected

173

with developing natural gas are also experiences that U.S. states should share with China's provinces.

India holds similar promise for greater state-to-state cooperation with the United States. Forward states such as Maharashtra, Gujarat, and Tamil Nadu are in the early stages of building bridges to "high hilltops" in the United States. The connections between Bangalore and the Bay Area are well known. But the world will increasingly hear about automotive powerhouses developing in Ahmadabad, Pune, and Chennai that will connect directly with Detroit. As M. Velmurugan, the head of Chennai's foreign investment office, explained to me, Ford Motor Company's decision to build its India manufacturing facility in Chennai was the single most important decision in turning Tamil Nadu into a manufacturing state in India. "That would not have happened had it not been for an active and engaged U.S. consulate."[12] That single investment led to the development of an automotive cluster that has benefited both India and the United States. Similarly, the biotech revolution that has been spearheaded in American cities such as Boston and Seattle also has natural partners in Chennai and Bangalore, an affinity that is only now starting to be exploited.

Thus it should not be surprising that American governors have begun to discover India. For almost a decade, Mark Warner—a cell phone service entrepreneur—has been promoting high-tech Virginia exports to India and direct investments from India, first as Virginia's governor and now as its senator.[13] More recently, Washington governor Christine Gregoire focused on India's growing aviation market—on the heels of the sale of Boeing 787 Dreamliners to Air India. Indians have reciprocated: officials from Andhra Pradesh traveled to Washington state in 2010 to connect with Seattle's leadership in information technology, biotechnology, skills development, and clean energy.[14] Governors from Delaware, Iowa, Kentucky, Maryland, and Wisconsin have led similar trips, and diverse American states—Arizona, Arkansas, Connecticut, Iowa, North Carolina, South Carolina, Utah, and Wyoming—are planning their own trade missions.[15] In theory those trips match economic strengths of American states with their counterparts in India.

This governor-led passage to India has lacked the same level of organization as the U.S.-China Governors Forum, which simultaneously brought together several governors from both sides as well as provincial party secretaries for extended discussions. The priority given to China over India makes some sense, given that the total trade volume in goods and services with China amounted to $539 billion in 2011, more than six times larger than India's total of $86 billion.[16] Still, American national leaders saw the potential of Indian states. Former secretary of state Hillary Clinton's trips included visits with Chief Minister Jayalalithaa in Tamil Nadu and with Mamata Banerjee in West Bengal.[17] Similarly, congressional Republicans visiting India met with Narendra Modi in Gujurat in March 2013.[18]

As India's regional leaders rise in influence, American governors and local leaders should coordinate their strategies toward India, both through groups such as the National Governors Association and the Conference of Mayors and League of Cities and with the support and guidance of the State Department and India's central government.

One area of emphasis could be helping India develop better interstate infrastructure. The United Kingdom was among the first to seize that opportunity, recently launching a $20–$25 billion "Bangalore to Mumbai Industrial Corridor"—an effort to guide private sector investment that will help provide better roads, trains, housing, Internet connectivity, and even technical and higher education. These are complex undertakings that could potentially help India more quickly adopt the kind of sophisticated systems that most industrial countries depend on. In India those systems often do not work well because they get mired in land acquisition and bureaucratic wrangling, particularly between national and state governments. In the case of the industrial corridor, the United Kingdom acting alone may actually complicate the problem. The

United Kingdom is notoriously skeptical of federal arrangements in Europe. Its representatives in India need to be sensitive to the complex relationship between local and central authorities that has developed there, which itself is an undoing of the top-down system India inherited from the British colonial regime.[19]

National Security Diplomacy:
Seeing Crises from the Bottom Up

Perhaps the greatest reasons for having a significantly greater diplomatic presence on the ground within China and India concern national and global security, which is very much tied up with the internal future of these two critical megacountries. If the United States and Europe do not know the many political entities inside China and India better, they risk missing the major political and security events of the day and being unable to evaluate or respond to them. When Bo Xilai's police chief, Wang Lijun, decided to turn state's evidence on Bo, he was forced to drive 200 miles in the middle of the night, crossing provincial lines from Chongqing into Sichuan, to find the nearest U.S. consulate in Chengdu. When the blind dissident Chen Guangcheng escaped house arrest, he also had to be secretly escorted nearly 350 miles from Shandong province to the U.S. embassy in Beijing. When the Gujarat riots happened in 2002, the lack of American presence made it harder for the United States to make an independent assessment of whether Chief Minister Modi or Gujarat officials were complicit in the killing of Muslims. It is impossible to know how many other critical situations the United States fails to track each year because of the lack of U.S. diplomatic postings.

Even a modest goal of doubling the number of consulates in both countries is likely to draw some criticism, both within the United States and abroad. In the former, it likely will be dismissed as yet another expensive government program at a time when budget battles are forcing cuts in all spending, domestic and foreign. In the past, key Republican national security officials such as Secretary of

State Condoleezza Rice and Defense Secretary Robert Gates called for a "rightsizing" of U.S. diplomatic presence, including greater civilian representation in India and China. Yet Congress still has not authorized the requisite funding in full, leaving American presence woefully thin on the ground. Getting the right allocation of diplomatic resources will require a push from a coalition of corporate and civil society organizations, including antipoverty, environmental, and human rights groups.

One can also expect some resistance within China and India to a deeper American and European presence. The prominent role that U.S. consulates played in recent internal Chinese dramas—such as the Bo Xilai and Chen Guangcheng cases—was embarrassing and difficult for Chinese authorities, even if applauded in the West for helping to advance the rule of law and to expose human rights violations. As a result, one can see why China's government might want fewer postings. Both national and local Chinese leaders might view more outposts as intrusive and hostile to their internal affairs.

Some Americans may make the case that local Chinese and Indian leaders should not be given a formal role in international diplomacy. For instance, even if provincial influence on China's internal politics is likely to grow, it is unclear whether that influence will be positive when it comes to foreign affairs. A decade ago, one noted scholar on China interviewed a number of regional leaders and found them to be uninterested in anything but narrow economic issues such as "economic growth to get tax revenue, create jobs, and keep stability." When local leaders do speak to broader foreign policy matters, they often are nationalistic in the extreme.[20] The same could be said about a range of Indian leaders, from Gujarat to Tamil Nadu.

I posed this last objection to various Chinese and Indian local leaders, journalists, and academics. Most had the exact opposite response. First, many were quick to point out that dozens of inland localities are actively seeking broader global exposure. They want the visibility and support that foreign postings provide to their businesses and the jobs that can bring. If the United States has an outpost in a foreign district, it is more likely that American investment will flow in that direction. And it is not just investment but also the technical support, academic exchanges, and tourist dollars that usually follow. As for the bellicosity of local leaders, Americans should get to know that reality rather than avoid it. Oftentimes, xenophobia in China or India is not well informed. Sometimes it may be a ruse, a convenient pose for an ambitious official seeking promotion in a system that favors outward displays of nationalism.[21] If nationalistic or xenophobic sentiments are genuine, they must be taken seriously. Though China's and India's formal national security and diplomatic policy machinery is streamlined, when it comes time to implement an international agreement provincial and state leaders often are far more influential than their diplomatic service counterparts. Perhaps more troubling, these local leaders may actually prevent their countries from developing national policies on issues that the rest of the world cares about.

LOCAL POLITICS AND GLOBAL GOVERNANCE

When it comes to negotiating global agreements with these two giants, we need to recognize that China and India are practically worlds unto themselves; thus we must be far more realistic about what can be accomplished.

Understanding the global implications of the rise of China's provinces and India's states means significantly revising how the West organizes and thinks about managing the big existential issues facing the planet. That starts with recognizing that all global politics are local.

Tackling climate change, preventing trade and currency wars, or fighting nuclear proliferation often requires getting big countries to agree to do big things. Together, the United States, European Union, China, and India are home to half the world's people, two-thirds of the world's economy, two-thirds of the world's greenhouse gases, and two-thirds of all nuclear power. On an annual basis, China and India are the largest and third-largest emitters of greenhouse gases, respectively. Both countries have large stockpiles of nuclear weapons. If the United States and EU cannot come to an agreement with China and India on major challenges, nothing will get done.

Still, the world will not come to order simply by creating a new "big four" grouping. Getting the leaders of those four continental unions to agree on any course of action may be necessary for global cooperation—but it is not sufficient. Power has become diffuse among nations.

In addition to these nations, a handful of critical countries—such as Japan, Brazil, Russia, Saudi Arabia, and South Africa—have tried to work together to manage global challenges. George W. Bush, in the final days of his presidency, pulled together leaders from the world's twenty most important national economies—the so-called G-20. This led to great speculation that this new grouping would become a board of directors for the planet, which could better steer the planet through rocky times.

China and India both wanted to make sure that within that group, they were able to protect their own national interests. They forged an awkward alliance with Brazil, Russia, and later South Africa to form the BRICS grouping to counterbalance advanced Western industrial democracies in the G-20 and various other global organizations.[22] This has led many global strategists to worry that power has become too diffuse in global politics, that if every country is a priority, no one is in charge. Perhaps we live in a "G-Zero" world, which is witnessing the end of power itself.[23]

Things actually may be even worse than they appear. Power is not only diffuse *between* these nations. The internal politics within China and India suggest that power is diffuse *within* the world's two biggest countries. Their own internal leadership crisis will make global leadership more difficult for them, just as federal politics in the United States and EU has made their global leadership more difficult. Big players have become bogged down and obsessed with complex internal power issues, and a rising number of smaller countries have stepped forward to lead in discrete realms and regions.

So if very, very big countries cannot get their own big internal pieces to agree, then the challenge becomes multiplied. But the answer is not simply to throw one's hands up in the air. It is time to pursue bottom-up solutions—especially in the four continent-wide unions. Of course, this process needs to start in the United States and Europe, where federal politics on financial and fiscal reform, trade agreements, and climate change often get in the way. Even while Western federal systems attempt those political gymnastics, China and India should be among the first places where Americans and Europeans mobilize their own local provinces and states for global purposes.

Directly engaging leaders of major provinces and states on global challenges is not a small undertaking. When it comes to China and India, perhaps the greatest concern for any global agreement is that the local jurisdictions in either country will either seek to block or fail to implement any binding global agreement that their leaders develop. The biggest Chinese provinces and Indian states already have larger populations than many members of the G-20, and some even have bigger economies. Getting international "binding commitments" is already difficult enough when rule of law and governance capacity are notoriously low in both countries. That is particularly true once one travels beyond the forward-leaning states or provinces. It may not be so much that China's or India's central leaders do not want to act. Rather, their greater concern may be that they do not have the power to act.

Again, that means the West should first show the way by getting its own federal houses in order. In the United States, this would be the equivalent of organizing a fiscal reform or financial reform summit among governors or actively including them in determining the scope of U.S. trade agreements or climate negotiations. In the case of climate change, for instance, the United States should work to pass domestic legislation to reduce greenhouse gas emissions that takes into account the concerns of governors and mayors. The United States then would be better positioned to negotiate a global agreement. But since the prospects for that are quite limited, the United States can and should build on successful experiments at the state and local levels. Without waiting for the federal government to act, U.S. state officials could become ambassadors to their counterparts in China and India and mentors for how to meet global targets.

What does that mean for negotiating with China and India about global order on one concrete issue or another? It means taking local institutions and leaders in these countries nearly as seriously as one would take similarly sized countries. The major provinces in China and major states in India do what all Western democracies do: balance economic growth with the challenge of representing their constituents' interests in a more sustainable, rules-based world.

State and provincial leaders should be part of global processes in a more visible way. That might include bringing governors, chief ministers, and provincial leaders to global climate change or trade negotiations, to educate them on the mechanics of these new agreements. This would be a major change in the way diplomatic business is done, but it would signal a desire to include localities more directly in global diplomacy and to design global agreements with end users in mind.

There could be real advantages to bringing representatives from major exporters, such as Guangdong or Chennai, to a World Trade Organization meeting, not to mention inland developing provinces such as Sichuan or Bihar. Global climate change talks would benefit demonstrably by having representatives from high energy consumers on China's or India's coast or from big coal-producing regions in China's or India's interior. If Governor Jerry Brown's efforts with Guangdong prove successful, one could imagine the United States and China encouraging cooperative efforts between other American states and Chinese provinces that have put in place mandatory laws curbing greenhouse gas emissions. Those

American states with emissions legislation account for one-fifth of U.S. emissions, even though they are home to about one-third of the American people and account for nearly two-fifths of the U.S. economy. In other words, our most carbon-efficient and productive states are taking the lead in reducing greenhouse gas emissions. Their counterparts in China are doing the same. The opportunities for cooperation are real.[24]

Similarly, one could imagine building out the effort to bring together forty global megacities to pursue greater action on climate change. This undertaking has largely been led by former and current European and American mayors, such as Ken Livingstone of London and Michael Bloomberg of New York, and has included fourteen EU cities and eleven U.S. counterparts. Right now, only four cities from China and India participate in that effort: Beijing, Hong Kong, New Delhi, and Mumbai. Expanding that list by four or five major cities from China or India would elevate the prominence of these places and help them to see their local problems as part of broader global challenges—and vice versa.[25]

There could even be benefits from bringing together, on a global stage, these major provinces and states to confer on big internal challenges, such as building infrastructure or addressing internal migration. For such issues and others, these large "internal nations" or even the smaller American states have useful experiences that they can bring to bear on finding solutions.

LOCAL GOVERNMENT AND THE FUTURE
OF LIBERAL DEMOCRATIC ORDER

Understanding the critical role of China's provinces and India's states also should lead us to think differently about the guiding theory of world order in Western policy circles: a world led by liberal democratic governments.

There is growing alarm in Western societies about the challenges facing a liberal democratic world order. Since the end of the cold war and the defeat of Soviet communism, foreign policy analysts have swung from optimism to pessimism and back again on whether modern democracies can build and maintain a peaceful international system. With an ever-growing number of countries aspiring to liberal democracy, many refer to this as a liberal democratic world order—not in the American sense of big-government liberalism but rather in the classical sense of liberalism that led to the establishment of constitutional democracies.

This new liberal democratic world order is premised on the idea that constitutional democracies do not fight one another and also that their respect for individual liberties and their embrace of the free flow of people, goods, ideas, and capital will lead to a more prosperous and harmonious world order. Those sets of values and institutions lay behind much of the contemporary global order. The primacy of liberal democratic domestic governance has been critical to a number of major security arrangements—such as NATO—as well as a web of high-standard regional trading regimes among industrialized nations, such as the North American Free Trade Agreement and the European Union.[26]

As attractive as that theory has been, most students of world affairs acknowledge that it has some profound flaws. The most glaring problem has been that liberal democracies have not been any less peaceful toward nonliberal democratic states.[27] Moreover, some of the great security dilemmas in the world exist with states that have adopted some liberal reforms (such as protection of private property or basic security for ethnic minority populations) or some democratic reforms (such as a free press, free expression, or multiparty elections) but not a fully elaborated combination of both *liberal* and *democratic* systems.[28]

China poses an obvious problem for proponents of a liberal democratic order. In many ways, parts of China resemble the eighteenth- and nineteenth-century industry-heavy trading nations of England and the Netherlands that were the homes of early economic liberal thinking. A strong central government has allowed a certain level of private property protection and also has provided basic physical security, enabling economic activity to flourish. But since China has not embraced political pluralism or democratic values, some more conservative thinkers see it as "a deeper and more serious challenge to the liberal order than was the Soviet Union."[29] Since property protection is tilted toward state-owned enterprises and, in particular, against individual or foreign ownership of property, the rules of China's economy are antithetical to the rules and norms that have produced global prosperity and integration for the last half century. More ominously, China's foreign policy is beyond the control of most civilian political authorities—a component critical to sustaining a liberal democratic peace.

On paper, India does have the opportunity to be a key player in a liberal democratic world order. As a result, many foreign policy thinkers imagine a natural alliance between the world's largest democracy and Western powers.[30] Given its residual fears of China, this alliance with the West would not just reflect India's values but also its self-interest. Yet India is still far behind China in shaking off socialist policies and embracing economic liberalism. That is, it has been difficult to know how committed a democratic India is to liberalism, especially the protection of property and individual security. As a result, it is unclear whether it shares the same priorities as Western powers—not just in foreign policy but on issues as wide ranging as trade and environmental agreements or the development of nuclear energy. Moreover, many Indians doubt that liberal democracy, as a value, really is paramount in the minds of Western policymakers. They remain rather suspicious about whether Western powers would come to their defense in a conflict with China given the deep trade and finance interdependence that has developed between the West and India's historic adversary to the northeast.

When one takes China's and India's local politics seriously, however, the liberal order thesis looks rather different in a few key regards. First, when China and India are viewed as complex continental unions, it becomes apparent what a major challenge it is simply to bring fully fledged liberal democratic order to the domestic politics *within* these massive places. It is far from clear that this is a priority for either country. Both countries are far more focused on managing what is, in effect, a world of their own than they are in getting those systems to correspond to Western theories of liberal democracy, let alone world order.

In some cases, "effective" governance in China or India is actually a higher priority for local leaders. That can actually be a threat to liberal or democratic values—or both. In China, while economic liberalism is advanced, political liberalism is still in a formative stage in a few key provinces—and it may not be progressing in a linear fashion. For instance, new information technologies now allow the Chinese state to monitor its own people or violate privacy or even property rights outside its borders. And, again, some Chinese provinces are further along in adopting those technologies than are others. In some Indian states, local democratic forces are not always necessarily liberal in the sense of protecting minority rights and individual freedoms or being receptive to global engagement. That is, communalism rather than tolerance is often the higher value.

Still, high hilltops of liberal democratic order exist in both places. In both countries, pluralism is real and emerging. While it is easy and in many cases appropriate to dismiss China as a nondemocracy, parts of China are more advanced in constituent services and community engagement than even certain Western, developed nations. Furthermore, the most competitive Chinese private firms are not seeking to remake the world system in China's image. These are the parts of China that want to join the liberal order as an equal partner because their firms have as much to gain from the enforcement of property rights—or as much to lose from the lack of enforcement—as businesses elsewhere do.

In India the challenge is not that the country falls outside the liberal democratic order. It is, most assuredly, the world's largest constitutional democracy forged by the greatest nonviolent revolution known to mankind. Democracy is deeply engrained in India as a practical matter; the political system both represents and contains India's enormous diversity. Rather, India's challenge is to live up to high *liberal* democratic expectations across a vast and diverse population—and to do so while representing the masses and also protecting minorities.

Ultimately, that brings the challenge back to the capitals, both in the East and the West. The capitals of China and India are well aware that they have to manage their diverse provinces and states. What they seem less aware of is that there are experiences that they can share with one another, and with their counterparts in the smaller but more economically advanced continental unions in America and Europe. Union systems learn slowly how to achieve compromise and consensus. By observing and cooperating with one another, there may be opportunities to learn how to forge domestic consensus more effectively. When that consensus is forced by the center on localities, it often requires political dark arts, obscured from the public eye. But when the localities themselves are brought into national decisionmaking, these continental unions can become even more effective global players.

For the West, the key is to think differently and act differently. Western capitals need to look past Beijing and New Delhi and understand the challenge within each country of governing over 1 billion people distributed into more than thirty jurisdictions, most of which could be major free-standing countries. As a result, Western capitals should adopt more realistic expectations about what can be done in bilateral, multilateral, and global negotiations. They must understand that the handshake on a bilateral agreement with China or India is only the beginning of the implementation process. In multilateral settings, it is often the fear of failed implementation that holds back national leaders. The execution of treaties, policies, or other agreements is hammered out through a myriad of local conversations. Those conversations in India and China are likely to be as complex as within our own federal systems, if not more so. As a result, the United States and the EU need to reallocate their human resources to these various localities and deploy a wider range of bottom-up "diplomats," including their many effective state and local leaders. And they should reserve judgment on exactly who or what is liberal and democratic in those countries, respecting the fact that Western political systems have been evolving on these issues for centuries.

The foundation for that approach is to give a new priority to inside-out and bottom-up diplomacy with China and India. Doing so means learning to respect and embrace the tension between the local, the national, and the global that is at the heart of federalism itself.

ACKNOWLEDGMENTS

THERE ARE MANY great research institutions in the world, but none more supportive, collegial, and interdisciplinary than Brookings. Three years of planning and execution went into this short book, along with considerable help from many Brookings colleagues.

The John L. Thornton Center on China houses a scholarly dream team. Many thanks to Jonathan Pollack, Jeff Bader, David Dollar, Erica Downs, Kevin Foley, Cheng Li, and Ken Lieberthal. At the Brookings-Tsinghua Center in Beijing, Wang Feng and Zhou Xuelian steered me through China's dynamic and complex intellectual scene, and Tao Ran, Arthur Kroeber, and Scott Moore all taught me a great deal.

Likewise, Brookings's deep bench of all-stars on India have taught me about the world's largest democracy, especially Barry Bosworth, Stephen Cohen, Tanvi Madan, Eswar Prasad, and Bruce Riedel. Vikram Mehta supported this book even before becoming chairman of Brookings India in New Delhi, and Subir Gokarn already has proven a great resource.

Governance Studies is Brookings's original research program, and its current roster lives up to that ninety-seven-year legacy. A number of scholars read and helped to improve this manuscript. Thanks especially to Darrell West, Bill Galston, Elaine Kamarck,

Tom Mann, Pietro Nivola, Jonathan Rauch, Walter Valdivia, Phil Wallach, and Ben Wittes. Bruce Katz, Amy Liu, and Joseph Parilla in Metropolitan Policy inspired the book's focus on cities and states. Tracy Gordon in Economic Studies taught me about fiscal federalism, and she was a diligent and fast reader. Kemal Dervis, Govinda Avasarala, Charles Ebinger, Nathan Hultman, Jon Huntsman, Michael O'Hanlon, and Anwar Shah all provided detailed and helpful comments.

My research assistants deserve more than simple thanks. Han Chen has been an insightful, resourceful, and tireless companion in research and writing, and a reality check on modern China. For ten weeks, Summer Jiakun Zhao served as our family's tour guide, travel agent, interpreter, research assistant, and adopted daughter. John-Michael Arnold, Kadeem Cooper, Alex Fife, Dana Gansman, and Amanda Mays all provided logistical support, as well as intellectual and research help along the way. Alexis Bataillon and Steve Bennett are dear and trusted colleagues, handling my day job as I traveled and wrote. Both are keen students of politics and policy, providing sharp comments and corrections.

The Brookings Press remains best in class. Bob Faherty has admirably led the press for twenty-nine years, and I'm honored that he supported this book from the outset. Moreover, he's been a friend for nearly a decade. Larry Converse, Chris Kelaher, Janet Walker, and Susan Woollen poured considerable energy into this book on matters large and small. Starr Belsky provided an excellent edit. The Brookings communications team, led by David Nassar, included Stephanie Dahle, Shawn Dhar, and Christine Jacobs who all have been terrific guides in taking these ideas into cyberspace and beyond.

Parts of this manuscript were delivered as lectures at Brookings, the Center for American Progress, Fordham University, the University of Virginia, the College of William and Mary, the University of Nevada Las Vegas (UNLV), the Indian Institute of Technology Madras, and the Tsinghua School of Public Policy and Management.

Special thanks go to Bill Brown, Rob Lang, Bernard Malamud, Alexandra Nikolich, Dennis Pirages, and Lindy Schumacher at Brookings Mountain West and the Lincy Institute, and to Tom Kaplan for hosting and participating in so many sessions where ideas were marinated and cooked. Thanks also to Adam Anthony, Nancy Busch, Jon Cannon, George Demacopoulos, Deborah Lawrence, Valerie Longwood, Aristotle Papanikolaou, and Michael Werz for giving me the opportunity to get feedback from their scholars and students. Fordham President Fr. McShane and UNLV President Neal Smatresk deserve extra credit for their friendship and encouragement.

Some world-class scholars who also happen to be dear friends provided valuable insights: Jeffrey Legro, Mark Leonard, Jim Ryan, and David Sandalow. Kate Ryan listened to sections of this during marathon training and also provided memorable lines for Kristen and me to recite as we traveled. Special thanks to Walter Isaacson and Krista Tippett for being inspirational writers and insightful readers. Thanks to Jon Landau for his friendship and encouragement.

Brookings is fortunate to have the Tsinghua School of Public Policy and Management (SPPM) as a partner—especially Xue Lan and Meng Bo, who are living proof of the vibrancy and openness of China's academic scene. I greatly benefited from conversations with Hu Angang, Chu Shulong, Qi Ye, Yu An, Yu Qiao, and Zhang Yanbin. SPPM and the Brookings-Tsinghua Center co-hosted a "think tank summit" where I met and learned from Fang Jin, Fu Xiao, He Fan, Jia Kang, Li Hua, Ma Xianfeng, Wang Yiming, Wen Xu, Yang Yudong, Yu Hui, Zhang Shuguang, Zhang Tuosheng, Zhu Xufeng, and Zuo Jun.

Others in Chinese universities and think tanks were also generous with their time. In Beijing that includes Patrick Chovanec, Di Dongsheng, Mark Dryer, Hu Shuli, Alvin Lee, Louise Qian Liu, and Tian Wei. Special thanks to Wang Wenfeng for a very careful reading of the text. Shanghai's Fudan University was most hospitable, thanks especially to Shen Dingli, and also to Chen Yun, Jing

Yijia, and Zhang Guizhong. I learned a great deal from a day at the Fung Institute in Hong Kong with Victor Fung, Andrew Sheng, Xiao Geng, and Louis Kuijs. Thanks also to Shirley Lin at the Chinese University of Hong Kong for detailed comments. Chengdu is a hothouse of committed scholarship. Chen Aimen of Sichuan University shared most of a day with us. Thanks also to Ma Xiao, Wang Yurong, and Yin Qingshuang at Southwest University of Finance and Economics.

Several institutes of the Chinese Academy of Social Sciences were generous with their time and resources. In Beijing, thanks to Zhang Yuyan and Huang Wei at the Institute of World Politics and Economics, and to Li Bin. In Shanghai, Huang Renwei provided a terrific overview of China's most dynamic city. In Chengdu, Du Shouhu taught me a great deal about Sichuan, as well as Chinese and Indian cooperation on climate change.

Similarly, India's academic and think tank community embraced this project. In New Delhi, special thanks to Pratap Bhanu Mehta, Partha Mukhopadhyay, and K. C. Sivaravakrishnan at the Centre for Policy Research; and to C. V. Madhukar and Priya Soman at the Parliamentary Research Service. Rajendra Pachauri at TERI is a resource to the world and was generous with his time. In Mumbai, thanks to Manjeet Kripalani, Hari Seshasayee, and Askshay Mathur at Gateway House. In Chennai, special thanks to Jessica Seddon Wallack at the Indian Institute of Human Settlements; Raj Cherubal at Chennai City Connect; and Sudhir Chella Rajan at IIT Madras. Many thanks also to Sophie Berkvist, Ram Madhav, Commodore Shekhar, and Lawrence Prabhakar Williams.

India has no shortage of world-class journalists, and I was fortunate enough to meet with the best of them— in particular, M. J. Akbar, Shekhar Gupta, Suhasini Haidar, Preetham Parigi, N. Ravi, Mala Singh, Amithab Srivastava, and Siddharth Varadarajan. Several Western journalists also were kind to share their wisdom and experiences: David Barboza, James Crabtree, Gardiner Harris, and Brian Rhodes.

ACKNOWLEDGMENTS

A number of Indian governmental and political leaders helped me understand the system's ins and outs. There is no greater Indian statesman than Jaswant Singh; he was also a generous teacher. Thanks also to Arun Jaitley, Saranyan Krishnan, Arun Meira, Rakesh Mohan, Nandan Nilekani, Urjit Patel, Suresh Prabhu, C. V. Shankar, Ashok Vardhan Shetty, and Mani Velemurugan. Thanks to two chief ministers and their staffs who sat for extended interviews: Nitish Kumar and Narendra Modi.

The United States is fortunate to be represented by diplomats who do their work with both professionalism and passion. In China, thanks to Jim Sciutto, Daniel Kritenbrink, Ryan Hass, Jeff Zaiser, Geoffrey Lyon, Robert Griffiths, Christopher Wurzel, Jim Mullinax, Camile Purvis Dawson, Steve Young, Matt Matthews, and Eitan Plasse. In India, Matthew and Asha Bey and their sons welcomed our entire family, including showing us Fisherman's Cove. Thanks also to Jennifer McIntyre, Peter Haas, Blair Hall, Peter Burleigh, Herro Mustapha, Angie Mizeur, and Max Hamilton. Senior U.S. government officials in Washington also made time in their busy schedules: Alyssa Ayers, Kurt Campbell, Derek Chollet, Michael Claussen, Bill Danvers, Karen Donfried, Michael Froman, Peter Ogden, Geoffrey Pyatt, and Pavneet Singh.

A number of business leaders lent considerable insight and advice in this project. McKinsey & Company welcomed me in practically every city we visited. I'm personally grateful to Dominic Barton and his assistant Katharine Bowerman, and also to Nicholas Leung, Ramesh Mangalaswaran, Adil Zainulbhai, and Jonathan Woetzel. Vassi Naidoo at Deloitte, a long-time friend and supporter of this effort, embraced this project immediately. Along with P. R. Ramesh in Mumbai, he provided wise counsel, contacts, and support. Lew Kaden at Citigroup was a constant source of insight and encouragement.

Special thanks also to Nicholas Logothetis for his friendship and support, and also to Emmanuel Androulakis for detailed comments. The entire firm of Greater Pacific Capital Partners embraced and supported the project, especially Ketan Patel who helped conceive, design, and review the project. Thanks also to his colleagues Madhabi Buch, Tulsi Manjeshwar, Akshaya Prasad, and Shelley Raja.

Members of China's business community shared their time and insights: in Beijing, Fengming Liu, Chris Deri, and Ted Dean; in Shanghai, Brenda Foster, Bob Theleen, and Pierre Cohade; in Hong Kong, Shengman Zhang, Richard Vuylsteke, and Vincent Chan; and in Chengdu, Yong Guo, Benjamin Wang, and Ao Zhiping; in Macao, Mike Mecca and Grant Bowie. Several friends, old and new, opened their homes to us: David, Lily, and L. J. Turchetti, as well as Han Feng, Mihalis Boutaris, Nikomachi Karakostanoglou, and Alkmene Boutaris. Peter Goff at Chengdu's Bookworm is an extraordinary wealth of insights, humor, and books. The Bookworm also serves Guinness.

India's business community was equally helpful. The project could not have happened without Rahul Bajaj and N. Kumar, in particular. Both provided guidance and assistance whenever I asked. Kumar and Bhavani adopted us for nearly a month. Gopal Srinivasan, Lalitha Gopal, Ramesh Rangalaswaran, Meenakshee, and Shivani also became our extended family in Chennai. The Confederation of Indian Industries deserves special thanks: Chandrajit Banerjee, Tarun Das, Kiran Pasricha, Sandhya Satwadi, Charu Mathur, Sujith Haridas, and Sreekumar Nair. Joshua Steiner and Antoinette Delruelle and their lovely kids hosted us in Mumbai, where they introduced us to *Modern Family*.

Special thanks to a number of other leaders who were particularly generous hosts and guides: in Chennai, T. T. Ashok, M. M. Murugappan, Subbu Murugappan, Vellayan, Lakshmi Narayanan, and V. Sumantran; in Mumbai, Ashwini Agarwal, Praveen Chakravarty, Ranjit Pandit, and Roopa Purushothaman; in New Delhi, Prema and Jyoti Sagar and Ravi Venkatesan; and in Ahmedabad, Sanjaybhai Jhaveri and Bhavit Jhaveri.

A number of Brookings trustees provided extraordinary insight, advice, encouragement, and connections on this project: Liaquat

Ahamed, Abby Cohen, Alan Dachs, Steve Denning, Ann Fudge, Bill Haseltine, Glenn Hutchins, Phil Knight, David Rubenstein, Antoine van Agtmael, and Tracy Wolstencroft.

The field research for this trip was a labor of love—particularly thanks to friends who traveled far to meet us along the way: Carter, Karen, Nadja, and Marcus Beauford; Jeannean Carver and Laurel Charles; Joe, Elvira, Ellie, Lucia, and Alice Hoskins; Janet Mitchell; and Caroline Clark. The world's greatest drummer accompanied us to Beijing's Drum Tower, but his favorite moment was seeing seven motorcycles in a spherical cage . . . "Hey!" Taking the world's most aggressively organic moms to McDonald's in the middle of China was almost as much fun. Lori Shineski's pre-trip video—and all those who starred in it—will outlive this book.

My Taunt Group brothers were always a mouse-click away. That was especially true of my actual brother Kary, whose regular Skype calls sustained me. The lowest point of this journey was in Shanghai when learning of our dear friend Stuart Wells's rapid decline. Stu had been a constant for exactly half of my life; it is still hard to imagine a world without him.

I was first pulled into government service by the greatest mind in American foreign policy, Jim Steinberg. On this project, he helped me construct an itinerary for China, design a framework for understanding the country, and refine the final manuscript. Jim has guided my career—including steering me to Brookings—and has been a great friend and treasured running partner.

Todd Stern taught me how to think strategically about the diplomacy and politics of climate change. He is also a terrific scholar and writer in his own right. His persistent focus on China and India, and their importance in future diplomatic efforts, was a constant motivation to complete the project. If the world solves the climate crisis, Todd will deserve considerable credit.

John Thornton has also been an intellectual, diplomatic, and managerial role model. He challenged my assumptions about China, but supported me in asking hard questions about its system.

His own writings are models of clarity, insight, and independent thinking. I hope this book has lived up to his core values of responsibility, courage, and empathy.

My nine years working for Strobe Talbott have been a dream come true. He encouraged the field research (and my leave of absence as managing director), and went out of his way to meet up with Swiss Family Antholis-Suokko during our long march. Having a preeminent statesman and world-famous author help shape this book is a gift. Getting his detailed comments and shameless promotion is a luxury. Having him as a true friend is a blessing.

That leaves my most important colleagues in this effort. My daughters, Annika and Kyri, suffered no shortage of hardships. They missed friends and home comforts, and endured endless meetings, airports, tour guides, drafty apartments, uncertain dining, and bad Internet service. The greatest joy of this trip was to learn from them. We thought we were introducing them to the world. Instead, they showed us that world through their eyes. We shared their wonder at riding elephants, holding baby pandas, being covered with butterflies, and riding Hong Kong's Space Mountain. They also demanded that we not look past the indignities of poverty and pollution. Their insistence on honesty and justice may have been our greatest lesson.

The other half of "we" is my wife, Kristen Suokko, who deserves my first and last thanks. She embraced the project from the start, and saw it through to the end. She postponed returning to her professional life one more year to play chief of staff, scheduler, diplomat, travel agent, chef, photographer, journal keeper, and school master. She listened to me describe the project so often that I feared she would start lip-syncing. She read and edited every blog and essay, and the entire manuscript, in great detail. But more than that, she was an intrepid cheerleader, intellectual side-kick, joyful muse, and steady metronome. This project was a return to our roots as work colleagues. It also was a great new adventure as partners and parents. This book is dedicated to her.

NOTES

CHAPTER 1

1. I first used this analogy to explain the scale of China and India—and the reason for our travels to these countries—to my two young daughters. But I also was delighted to see it made by Rob Giffords in his terrific *China Road: A Journey Into the Future of a Rising Power* (New York: Random House, 2007). The general concept of this book was also greatly influenced by Patrick Chovanec's "Nine Nations of China" essay in *The Atlantic,* November 2009.

2. In the United States and Europe, diverse political and social beliefs also cut across member states. That diversity of underlying public values also contributes to gridlock. Western democracies are defined, in part, by their embrace of diverse conceptions of the public good. In fact, that embrace of pluralism as a value helps allow Western democracies to *not* use force to maintain public order. But pluralism also makes it difficult for Western democracies to work toward common goals.

3. See "India's Poverty Will Fall from 51% to 22% by 2015: UN Report," July 8, 2011 (http://articles.timesofindia.indiatimes.com/2011-07-08/developmental-issues/29751472_1_extreme-poverty-india-and-china-report [September 2012]). According to the report, in "China and India combined, the number of people living in extreme poverty between 1990 and 2005 declined by about 455 million, and [an] additional 320 million people are expected to come out [of] poverty by 2015." Those living on less than $1.25 a day are considered poor.

4. After the end of the cold war, the prevailing theory—at least in the United States—was that liberal democracy should be the cornerstone of world order. As more nations adopt market economies and open political systems, nations will be less likely to go to war with one another—potentially ending the great plague of world history. Hence the controversial title of Francis Fukuyama's book, *The End of History.* However, while liberal democracies may have not gone to war with one another, they also have an uninspiring record in collaborating on major world challenges. See Francis Fukuyama, *The End of History and the Last Man* (New York: Free Press, 1992).

CHAPTER 2

1. Perhaps the most riveting personal account of the creation of the European Union is found in Jean Monnet, *Memoirs* (New York: Doubleday and Company, 1978).

2. Quentin Skinner, *Foundations of Modern Political Theory,* 1st ed. (Cambridge University Press, 1978); John Greville Agard Pocock, *The Machiavellian Moment,* rev. ed. (Princeton University Press, 2003).

3. Edmund Morgan, *Inventing the People: The Rise of Popular Sovereignty in England and America* (New York: W.W. Norton, 1988); Gordon Wood, *The Creation of the American Republic, 1776–1787* (University of North Carolina Press, 1969).

4. This view obviously held in the southern states. But some northerners also felt this to be the case. Stephen Douglas made the most explicit case for state sovereignty in his famous senate debates with Abraham Lincoln.

5. The President's Rule has become a misnomer, since the central government—under the prime minister—advises the president when to invoke the rule.

6. Tom Lasseter, "Dispute over Village Election Highlights China's Communist Party Challenge," *McClatchy,* October 29, 2012 (www.mcclatchydc. com/2012/10/29/172896/dispute-over-village-election.html).

7. "Election Bid a Tough Ask for China's Independent Candidates," CNN, July 25, 2011 (www.cnn.com/2011/WORLD/asiapcf/07/25/china.npc/index.html).

8. Legend has it that Henry Kissinger once asked his National Security Council staff, "Who do I call if I want to call Europe?" Kissinger now denies that he ever asked this, though he does not deny the core message: "It's a good statement so why not take credit for it?" Vanessa Gera, "Kissinger Says Calling Europe Quote Not Likely His," Associated Press, June 27, 2012.

9. Jonathan A. Rodden, *Hamilton's Paradox: The Promise and Peril of Fiscal Federalism* (Cambridge University Press, 2005), p. 10.

10. Chen Duxiu, the first general secretary of China's Communist Party, quoted in Yu Keping, *Democracy Is a Good Thing: Essays on Politics, Society, and Culture in Contemporary China* (Brookings, 2009). It is interesting to compare him with his American contemporary, U.S. Supreme Court justice Louis Brandeis, writing at almost exactly the same time: "A single courageous State may, if its citizens choose, serve as a laboratory; and try novel social and economic experiments without risk to the rest of the country." *New State Ice Co. v. Liebmann,* 285 U.S. 262 (1932).

11. China is one of the world's most fiscally decentralized countries. Along with Denmark, it stands alone as a centralized country that ranks similarly to federal countries in decentralization. See Claudia Dziobek, Carlos Guiterrez Mangas, and Phebby Kufa, "Measuring Fiscal Decentralization—Exploring the IMF's Databases," Working Paper WP-11-126 (Washington: International Monetary Fund, 2011). I am indebted to Scott Moore, doctoral research fellow at the Belfer Center, Kennedy School of Government at Harvard, for this observation.

12. See Government of Hong Kong, "Chapter 1 Drafting and Promulgation of the Basic Law and Hong Kong's Reunification with the Motherland," in *The Basic Law and Hong Kong—The 15th Anniversary of Reunification with the Motherland,* May

2012 (www.basiclaw.gov.hk/en/publications/book/15anniversary_reunification_ch1_1.pdf).

13. See Ken Lieberthal, *Governing China: From Revolution to Reform*, 2nd ed. (New York: W. W. Norton, 2003) pp. 179–97; Lieberthal, *Managing the China Challenge: How to Achieve Corporate Success in the People's Republic* (Brookings, 2011), chaps. 1–3. See also Tsui Kai Yuen and Wang Youqiang, "Between Separate Stoves and a Single Menu: Fiscal Decentralization in China," *China Quarterly* 177 (May 2004): 75. The excessive focus on GDP as an indication of national wealth has a long history of critiques. Perhaps there has been none more eloquent than Robert Kennedy. "Too much and too long, we seem to have surrendered community excellence and community values in the mere accumulation of material things. Our gross national product . . . if we should judge America by that—counts air pollution and cigarette advertising, and ambulances to clear our highways of carnage. It counts special locks for our doors and the jails for those who break them. It counts the destruction of our redwoods and the loss of our natural wonder in chaotic sprawl. It counts napalm and the cost of a nuclear warhead, and armored cars for police who fight riots in our streets. It counts Whitman's rifle and Speck's knife, and the television programs which glorify violence in order to sell toys to our children.

Yet the gross national product does not allow for the health of our children, the quality of their education, or the joy of their play. It does not include the beauty of our poetry or the strength of our marriages; the intelligence of our public debate or the integrity of our public officials. It measures neither our wit nor our courage; neither our wisdom nor our learning; neither our compassion nor our devotion to our country; it measures everything, in short, except that which makes life worthwhile. And it tells us everything about America except why we are proud that we are Americans." Robert F. Kennedy, address at University of Kansas, Lawrence, Kansas, March 18, 1968.

14. Deng Xiaoping, "The Central Leadership Must Have Authority," *People's Daily*, September 12, 1988 (http://english.peopledaily.com.cn/dengxp/vol3/text/c1910.html). See also Hong Yu, "The Rationale, Prospects, and Challenges of China's Western Economic Triangle in Light of Global Economic Crisis," *Asian Politics and Policy* 2, no. 3 (2010): 438.

15. Guangdong, along with coastal Fujian and Zhejiang provinces, is central to China's private sector, export-oriented manufacturing. Guangdong's strong private sector accounted for 43 percent of the province's GDP output in 2010. "Guangdong (GD) Province: Economic Situation, Research and Development (R&D), and General Remarks" (www.sinoptic.ch/guangzhou/pdf/2012/201203_Guangdong_Thesenpapier.Eco.and.RD_EU_en.pdf); "Zhejiang: Private Economy Accounts for over 60% of GDP," *Hexun News*, May 28, 2012 (http://news.hexun.com/2012-05-28/141850465.html); "Fujian's Private Enterprise Accounted for 66.5% of GDP and over 80% of Jobs," *FJNET*, January 30, 2012 (http://money.fjsen.com/2012-01/30/content_7736358.htm).

16. Zheng Yongnian, *De Facto Federalism in China: Reforms and Dynamics of Central-Local Relations* (Singapore: World Scientific Publishing, 2007), p. 36.

17. See, respectively, Lieberthal, *Governing China*, and *Managing the China Challenge*; Harry Harding, *China's Second Revolution. Reform after Mao*

(Brookings, 1987), p. 200; Zheng, *De Facto Federalism*. See also Susan Shirk, *China: Fragile Superpower* (Oxford University Press, 2007).

18. This practice dates back at least to the Sui Dynasty in the sixth century. My colleague Cheng Li calls it the "law of avoidance." See his excellent paper, "The Local Factor in China's Intra-Party Democracy," paper prepared for the conference "Democracy in China and Southeast Asia? Local and National Perspectives," March 15, 2012, Princeton University, p. 8.

19. The great exception is the People's Liberation Army: it is positioned across the country, but its appointments are made by the center.

20. See Cheng Li, "Local Factor in China's Intra-Party Democracy," p. 11.

21. Ibid., p. 5.

22. I am indebted to Anwar Shah, director of the Center for Public Economics in Chengdu, China, and Brookings nonresident senior fellow, for this metaphor. According to Ken Lieberthal, "The reforms [of 2001] have increasingly made cities the key level of organization for the economy. National-level regulations on many important urban issues such as health insurance and pensions, for example, are implemented in a different way in each major metropolis, with the city making the key decisions on how to take the national principles and turn them into actual programs within its jurisdiction." Lieberthal, *Governing China*, pp. 182–83.

23. Zheng, *De Facto Federalism*, p. 12.

24. Lieberthal, *Governing China*. See also Zheng, *De Facto Federalism*, p. 12.

25. Bo Xilai's case calls this harmony into question. For many it reinforces disillusionment with the Confucian ideal that leaders are, by definition, honorable and noble. When one leader is corrupt, it casts doubt on the whole lot. Bo's ultimate verdict and sentencing will be a Rorschach test for various Chinese audiences on the ability of the system to restore harmony.

26. See Cheng Li, "Introduction," in He Weifang, *In the Name of Justice: Striving for the Rule of Law in China* (Brookings, 2013), p. xvii–xlix. Cheng quotes Weifang: "The Chinese government's own info portal says this about checks and balances: 'Third, China's legislation structure is not one of checks and balances, where the legislation, administration and court stand independently to restrain one another. . . . The premier, however, does not have the right to approve or reject laws made by the NPC. Administrative laws and regulations shall not go against the laws passed by the NPC . . . and the NPC has the power to withdraw administrative laws and local regulations that go against the laws it has worked out.' This shows the internal relations of China's legislation structure—one of subordination, unification and supervision. It does not represent a relationship of restraint." See also "China's Current Legislation Structure," September 28, 2003 (www.china.org.cn/english/kuaixun/76212.htm).

27. Zheng, *De Facto Federalism*, pp. 50–56.

28. Min Jie, "Central and Local Governments: The Asset of Ambiguity," *News China Magazine*, June 2013 (www.newschinamag.com/magazine/the-asset-of-ambiguity).

29. The 2012 anti-Muslim riots in Assam have been quite disturbing and a real reminder of the ethnic tensions that always lie below the surface in modern India. See Prabin Kalita, "Assam Ethnic Violence Spreads to New Districts," *Times of India*, August 17, 2012 (http://articles.timesofindia.indiatimes.com/2012-08-17/

india/33248676_1_relief-camps-tarun-gogoi-ethnic-violence); Victor Mallet, "Ethnic Violence in India's Assam State," *Financial Times*, September 3, 2012 (www.ft.com/intl/cms/s/0/13dc81f8-f5d5-11e1-a6c2-00144feabdc0.html#axzz25oXVkpa7).

30. At the top, chief ministers in states live in the shadow of the constitution's "President's Rule," which allows the president of India to unseat any sitting chief minister and call for new state legislative elections. That rule was invoked over 100 times in India's first fifty years. See Robert L. Hardgrave and Stanley A. Kochanek, *India: Government and Politics in a Developing Nation*, 7th ed. (Boston, Mass.: Wadsworth, 2008). From the bottom up, India retained the "district collector" position from the British colonial administrative system; the district collector is appointed by New Delhi as effective chief executive in each of India's 1,000 administrative units, each of which has a population of about 1 million people.

31. I am indebted to Anwar Shah for reinforcing this point to me.

32. Mahatma Gandhi was killed by a Hindu nationalist, Nathuram Godse, who feared Gandhi had conceded too much to Muslims and other minorities in creating the nation. Indira Gandhi (no relation to Mahatma Gandhi) was killed by her Sikh bodyguards after she had ordered a military operation against a Sikh temple in Amritsar where a local Sikh leader was allegedly planning an armed uprising. Rajiv Gandhi was assassinated by Tamil extremists in South India, who felt that he had not been sufficiently vigilant in protecting their kin in Sri Lanka.

33. Future chapters will explore which Indian states and Chinese provinces have benefited more than others since liberalization.

34. In coalitions led by the Congress Party, Congress held 97 percent of seats in the coalition in 1984 but only 79 percent in 2009.

35. "Criteria for Backward States to Be Revised," *Indian Express*, March 26, 2013 (www.indianexpress.com/news/criteria-for-backward-states-to-be-revised/1093487/).

36. *Wall Street Journal* reporter Tom Orlik has laid this out in two recent pieces with the same title: "Lies, Damned Lies, and Chinese Statistics," *Wall Street Journal*, July 25, 2012 (http://online.wsj.com/article/SB10000872396390444840104577548932454533806.html), and "Lies, Damned Lies, and Chinese Statistics: Who's Cooking Beijing's Books?" *Foreign Policy*, March 20, 2013 (www.foreignpolicy.com/articles/2013/03/20/lies_damned_lies_and_chinese_statistics).

37. Iacob N. Koch-Weser, "The Reliability of China's Economic Data: An Analysis of National Output," paper prepared for the U.S.-China Economic and Security Review Commission, January 28, 2013 (http://origin.www.uscc.gov/sites/default/files/Research/TheReliabilityofChina%27sEconomicData.pdf).

38. Orlik, "Who's Cooking Beijing's Books?"

39. Neil Munshi, "Chart of the Week: The Great Indian GDP Growth Revision Conundrum," *Financial Times*, September 3, 2012 (http://blogs.ft.com/beyond-brics/2012/09/03/chart-of-the-week-the-great-indian-gdp-revision-conundrum/#axzz2OCyCvTUt).

40. Amy Kazmin, "Oops! India Revises Its GDP Data," *Financial Times*, September 2, 2010 (http://blogs.ft.com/beyond-brics/2010/09/02/oops-india-revises-its-gdp-data/#axzz2OCyCvTUt); C. R. L. Narasimhan, "Official Statistics Need to Be Reliable," *Hindu*, July 10, 2011 (www.thehindu.com/business/Economy/official-statistics-need-to-be-reliable/article2216561.ece).

41. Ankush Agrawal and Vikas Kumar, "How Reliable Are India's Official Statistics?" *East Asia Forum,* April 6, 2012 (www.eastasiaforum.org/2012/04/06/nagaland-s-demographic-somersault-how-reliable-are-india-s-official-statistics/).

CHAPTER 3

1. Michael Forsythe, "China Eclipses U.S. as Biggest Trading Nation," Bloomberg, February 10, 2013 (www.bloomberg.com/news/print/2013-02-09/china-passes-u-s-to-become-the-world-s-biggest-trading-nation.html).

2. Compare with Nicholas Lardy, *Sustaining China's Economic Growth after the Global Financial Crisis* (Washington: Peterson Institute for International Economics, 2012), chapter 1. Lardy is quite thorough in putting into context the extensive public spending in the stimulus campaign. While he believes there may be considerable overinvestment and nonperforming loans at the provincial level, he also thinks that ultimately these can be paid off over time, that demand will eventually catch up to supply as more people move from farms to the cities, and that many public investments do not necessarily have revenue attached to them but eventually pay for themselves in growth over time. See also Jonathan Laing, "Falling Star," *Barron's,* July 2, 2012 (http://online.barrons.com/article/SB5000142405311 1903857104577467200405790354.html); Fubing Su and Ran Tao, "Visible Hand or Crippled Hand: Stimulation and Stabilization in China's Real Estate Markets, 2008-2010," in *The Global Recession and China's Political Economy,* edited by Dali L.Yang (New York: Palgrave, 2012), pp. 71–100.

3. Zhang Qian and Yao Chun, "Full Text: Report on China's Central, Local Budgets," *People's Daily Online,* March 19, 2013 (http://english.people.com.cn/102774/8174523.html).

4. The saying is thought to have originated in Zhejiang during the thirteenth-century Yuan dynasty but is used as a common idiom now. See "The Phrase 'The Mountains Are High, and the Emperor Is Far Away' Comes from Which Emperor? [in Chinese]," Xinhua, November 3, 2012 (http://news.xinhuanet.com/xhfk/2012-11/03/c_123909316.htm).

5. Michael Forsythe, "Xi Travels to China's Guangdong Echoing Deng Visit in 1992," Bloomberg, December 10, 2012 (http://www.bloomberg.com/news/2012-12-10/xi-travels-to-china-s-guangdong-echoing-deng-xiaoping-1992-visit.html).

6. Deng Xiaoping, "The Central Leadership Must Have Authority," *People's Daily,* September 12, 1988 (http://english.peopledaily.com.cn/dengxp/vol3/text/c1910.html). Cited in Hong Yu, "The Rationale, Prospects, and Challenges of China's Western Economic Triangle in Light of Global Economic Crisis," *Asian Politics and Policy* 2, no. 3 (2010): 437–61.

7. In 2011 Guangdong's exports were $532 billion, and those of the United Kingdom were $479 billion. See HKTDC Research, "Guangdong: Market Profile," November 26, 2012 (http://china-trade-research.hktdc.com/business-news/article/Fast-Facts/Guangdong-Market-Profile/ff/en/1/1X000000/1X06BUOU.htm); Central Intelligence Agency, "United Kingdom," CIA World Factbook, May 7, 2013 (www.cia.gov/library/publications/the-world-factbook/geos/uk.html).

8. Zhang Zhiming, *Inside the Growth Engine: A Guide to China's Regions, Provinces and Cities* (Hong Kong: HSBC Global Research, December 2010), p. 71.

9. Many of those manufactured goods involve the assembly of parts that were made and designed elsewhere, and that does not count the machinery and equipment made elsewhere that are used to build roads, factories, and homes in the province. Still, Guangdong's trade surplus is an impressive $100 billion. During the Eleventh Five-Year Plan, the value of Guangdong's private sector as a portion of GDP rose to 50.4 percent in 2011, up from 48 percent in 2007.

According to the policy requirements, Guangdong provides 250 million yuan of special funds to support the financing of small and microenterprises and tax cuts for small and medium-size enterprises. See Sheng Zheng, "Guangdong Private Enterprises Average Survival of 3.2 Years, Experts Have Called for Reducing the Burden [in Chinese]," *21st Century Network,* May 24, 2012 (http://money.msn. com.cn/internal/20120524/04551412590.shtml).

State-owned enterprises and entities directly controlled by state-owned enterprises accounted for more than 40 percent of China's nonagricultural GDP. If the contributions of indirectly controlled entities, urban collectives, and public town and village enterprises are considered, the share of GDP owned and controlled by the state is approximately 50 percent. See Andrew Szamosszegi and Cole Kyle, *An Analysis of State-Owned Enterprises and State Capitalism in China,* report for the U.S.-China Economic and Security Review Commission (www.uscc.gov/Research/ analysis-state-owned-enterprises-and-state-capitalism-china).

10. As recently as 2010, foreign-owned companies accounted for over 60 percent of all "Chinese" exports. See "China's Trade Surplus: Made in China by Foreign-Owned Factories," *People's Daily Online,* December 10, 2010. (http:// english.people.com.cn/90001/90778/90861/7227376.html).

11. While Wang Yang was careful to distance government from the responsibility to provide happiness, provincial officials are fascinated by the Western social science effort to better understand happiness. Willy Lam, "Wang Yang: The Future Torchbearer of Reform?" *China Brief* 12, no. 11 (2012): 2–5 (www.jamestown.org/ uploads/media/cb_05_05.pdf).

12. Guangdong has the third-highest Internet penetration in China at 60.4 percent, behind Beijing and Shanghai but far higher than the national average of 38.3 percent. China Internet Network Information Center, "29th Statistical Report on Internet Development in China," January 2012 (www.apira.org/18B97D12-F515-46D4-81DE-E7A3AF2B8AA0/FinalDownload/DownloadId-479F680710C7B8AE 951A003003399EE6/18B97D12-F515-46D4-81DE-E7A3AF2B8AA0/data/upload/ The29thStatisticalReportonInternetDevelopmentinChina_hbwnp5.pdf).

"Five provinces—Beijing, Guangdong, Jiangsu, Shandong and Zhejiang— yielded 40.1% of mobile web traffic in the first quarter of 2012. More specifically, the analysis showed that the amount of people logging on through a handset was higher than for personal computers in Beijing, Fujian, Guangdong, Shaanxi, Sichuan and Tianjin." See WARC, "Mobile Web Use Rises in China," May 28, 2012 (www. warc.com/LatestNews/News/Mobile_web_use_rises_in_China.news?ID=29894).

"Guangdong takes number one spot in mobile data traffic. . . . Guangdong and Jiangsu provinces have two of the highest volumes of mobile data traffic, which stands at 15.2 percent and 7.4 percent of total China traffic respectively." Betty

Tian, "Baidu Releases 2012 Q1 Mobile Internet Development Trends Report," *Baidu Beat,* May 24, 2012 (http://beat.baidu.com/?p=5398).

13. Lam, "Wang Yang: The Future Torchbearer."

14. Shanghai Municipal Statistics Bureau, *Shanghai Statistical Yearbook 2012* (Beijing: China Statistics Press, 2012), "Table 3.2: Shanghai Annual GDP Growth 1978–2011[in Chinese]" (www.stats-sh.gov.cn/tjnj/nj12.htm?d1=2012tjnj/C0302.htm).

15. Indeed, Hu's and Wen's own rise was seen by many as a response to the "Shanghai clique," as it is known. Jiang Zemin, China's president in the 1990s and himself a head of the Shanghai clique, had filled many top leadership posts with his supporters. That angered leaders from other regions and appears to have been one reason why the inland-oriented group gained power in the 2000s. See Cheng Li, "Power Shift in China—Part I," *YaleGlobal Online,* April 16, 2012 (http://yale global.yale.edu/content/power-shift-china-part-i).

16. In Shanghai, most of the economic activity is from services (also known as the tertiary industry, 57.3 percent), some from manufacturing (secondary industry, 42.1 percent), and almost none from agriculture (primary industry, 0.7 percent). National Bureau of Statistics, *China Statistical Yearbook 2011* (Beijing: China Statistics Press, 2011).

17. See HKTDC Research, "Zhejiang: Market Profile," December 17, 2012 (http://china-trade-research.hktdc.com/business-news/article/Fast-Facts/Zhejiang-Market-Profile/ff/en/1/1X000000/1X06BVYH.htm); "Shanghai: Market Profile," December 5, 2012 (http://china-trade-research.hktdc.com/business-news/article/Fast-Facts/Shanghai-Market-Profile/ff/en/1/1X000000/1X06BVOR.htm); "Jiangsu: Market Profile," December 7, 2012 (http://china-trade-research.hktdc.com/business-news/article/Fast-Facts/Jiangsu-Market-Profile/ff/en/1/1X000000/1X06BV87.htm).

18. Douglas J. Elliott, "Building a Global Financial Center in Shanghai: Observations from Other Centers," June 10, 2011 (www.brookings.edu/research/papers/2011/06/10-shanghai-financial-center-elliott).

19. Cheng Li, "The Local Factor in China's Intra-Party Democracy," paper presented at the 2012 Association for Asian Studies Annual Conference "Democracy in China and Southeast Asia? Local and National Perspectives," Toronto, March 15–18, 2012, p. 12.

20. Shanghai's state-owned enterprises and state-held enterprises contribute 765 billion yuan in value-added tax and other business taxes, a rather high share at 69 percent. See Szamosszegi and Kyle, *Analysis of State-Owned Enterprises.*

21. Foo Choy Peng and Barry Porter, "Suzhou: Sino-Singapore Bid Fails Test," *South China Morning Post,* June 30, 1999 (www.singapore-window.org/sw99/90630sc.htm).

22. In 2010 private enterprises made up 53 percent of the province's output. See Daxue Consulting, "Overview of Jiangsu Economy" (http://daxueconsulting.com/overview-of-jiangsu-economy [April 2013]).

23. "Critics Worry Jiangsu's Growth Has Too Much Government," *Want China Times,* May 21, 2012 (www.wantchinatimes.com/news-subclass-cnt.aspx?cid=1102&MainCatID=&id=20120521000013).

24. The zones are demonstrations of "open economy, concentrated locations of FDI, international trade and technological innovation." See China Jiangsu

Provincial Economic and Trade Office in Europe, "General Survey (2012)" (www.china-jiangsu.org/1doc.htm).

25. Jasper Becker, "China Must Change, Warns Lee Kuan Yew," *South China Morning Post*, September 30, 1999.

26. See profiles of Alibaba in *The Economist*, December 29, 2010, and March 23, 2013. Jack Ma and Alibaba have not been without controversy. Both were embroiled in a dispute with Yahoo!, one of Alibaba's major shareholders, in 2011, over Jack Ma's ownership and control of Alipay, a subsidiary arm that helps clear payments for products. See Nadia Mamouni and Jennifer Saba, "Yahoo, Alibaba Reach Deal Over Alipay," Reuters, May, 31, 2011. Alibaba also dismissed a few senior managers after a scandal over the fraudulent rating of some of its larger vendors. See "Alibaba and the 2,236 Thieves," *The Economist*, February 22, 2011.

In addition, Alibaba and Yahoo!China earned notoriety in Western human rights circles when they provided private email exchanges and the identity of the journalist and poet Shi Tao, who was reporting on the tenth anniversary of the Tiananmen Square crackdown. As a result of those correspondences, Shi Tao currently is serving a ten-year sentence. See Marc Gunther, "Yahoo's China Problem," *Fortune*, February 22, 2006; Lysette Kent, "China, Multinational Corporations, and Internet Privacy Issues: An Incoherent Landscape," *Public Purpose*, Spring 2011 (www.american.edu/spa/publicpurpose/archives.cfm).

27. Xinhua, "Zhejiang: Private Economy Contributes over 60 Percent of GDP [in Chinese]," May 26, 2012 (http://news.xinhuanet.com/fortune/2012-05/26/c_112041450.htm).

28. Sheng, "Guangdong Private Enterprises."

29. Zhang, *Inside the Growth Engine*, p. 71.

30. Malcolm Moore, "Credit Crisis in China's Richest Province Zhejiang," *The Telegraph*, August 28, 2012 (www.telegraph.co.uk/finance/financialcrime/9504692/Credit-crisis-in-Chinas-richest-province-Zhejiang.html).

31. Gabriel Wildau, "Bad Loans at Wenzhou Banks Surge as China's Economy Slows," Reuters, October 8, 2012 (www.reuters.com/article/2012/10/09/china-economy-wenzhou-idUSL3E8L905F20121009).

32. Jiangsu has a unique political culture. Local bureaucrats take an entrepreneurial outlook and lobby the central government for resources and policies to boost investment, including from abroad. Competition has been intense between local governments in Jiangsu, although some cooperation on regional development plans has occurred as well. See Wong C., Qian H., and Zhou K., "In Search of Regional Planning in China: The Case of Jiangsu and the Yangtze Delta," *Town Planning Review* 79, no. 2 (2008): 295–329.

33. This is the main theme of *China 2030: Building a Modern, Harmonious, and Creative Society*, a joint research project of the World Bank and the Development Research Center of China's State Council (www.worldbank.org/content/dam/Worldbank/document/China-2030-complete.pdf).

34. Zheng Yangpeng, "High-End Manufacturing Holds the Key," *China Daily*, March 1, 2013 (http://africa.chinadaily.com.cn/weekly/2013-03/01/content_16266779_2.htm).

35. Alan Beattie and Joshua Chaffin, "China Takes Solar Power Dispute to WTO," *Financial Times,* November 5, 2012 (www.ft.com/intl/cms/s/0/b5b8a1cc-2768-11e2-8c4f-00144feabdc0.html).

36. Loretta Chao, "U.S., China Tout Progress over IP," *Wall Street Journal,* April 12, 2012 (http://online.wsj.com/article/SB10001424052702303624004577339351934437474.html).

37. Jonathan Landreth, "What Chinese Companies Want: Intellectual Property Protection," *Christian Science Monitor,* April 13, 2012 (www.csmonitor.com/World/Asia-Pacific/2012/0413/What-Chinese-companies-want-intellectual-property-protection).

38. Lardy, *Sustaining China's Economic Growth;* Douglas J. Elliott and Kai Yan, "The Chinese Financial System: An Introduction and Overview," paper (Brookings, forthcoming).

39. Deng, "Central Leadership Must Have Authority."

40. "Three Trillion in Government Transfers, Eastern China Is Providing a Transfusion for the West [in Chinese]," *21st Century Business Herald,* March 24 2011 (www.21cbh.com/HTML/2011-3-25/1NMDAwMDIyODg1Nw_2.html).

41. Ibid.

42. Ibid.

43. International Finance News, "Tax Reform: New Western Development Dynamics [in Chinese]," *QQ Finance,* July 08, 2010 (http://finance.qq.com/a/20100708/002347.htm).

44. See Kent Kedl and others, *China Business Report: 2011–2012* (American Chamber of Commerce in Shanghai, February 2012), pp. 59, 63–65. More than half of those surveyed (58 percent) considered manufacturing in China for Chinese consumers as their top strategic goal, and an equal number (58 percent) reported that maximizing market reach was the top reason that they had for investing outside of Shanghai. Yet current investment beyond the coast was limited to only about a quarter of all firms. Still, looking forward, the number one inland investment location was consistently Chengdu, with Xi'an and Chongqing regularly ranking in the top four.

45. For these purposes, I am counting all seven provinces that have territory west of China's midpoint: Gansu, Inner Mongolia, Sichuan, Tibet, Qinghai, Xinjiang, and Yunnan. China marks its midpoint at 103.23 degrees east longitude. Chengdu sits just to the east of that at 104.03 degrees east, Chongqing is further east at 106.34 degrees east, and Xi'an is even further east at 108.54 degrees east. See "China's Geographical Center Marked," *People's Daily,* September 14, 2000 (http://english.people.com.cn/english/200009/13/eng20000913_50419.html).

46. Chen Aimin and Gao J., "Urbanization in China and the Coordinated Development Model—The Case of Chengdu," *Social Science Journal.* 48, no. 3 (2011): 500–13.

47. Hong, "Rationale, Prospects, and Challenges," p. 448.

48. Data can be found using the form on the Shanxi Economic Information Portal (http://data.sei.gov.cn/yearnew/a_search200809.asp).

49. Ge Honglin, "2009 Chengdu Municipal Government Work Report [in Chinese]," March 11, 2010 (www.chengdu.gov.cn/GovInfoOpens2/detail_allpurpose.jsp?id=rWdw5TgF7cMl6CmZ14K7).

50. National Bureau of Statistics, "Table 11-3. Main Social and Economic Indicators of Provincial Capitals and Cities Specially Designated in the State Plan (2009),"in *China Statistical Yearbook 2011* (Beijing: China Statistics Press, 2011).

51. See in particular Wei Zhang, "Can the Strategy of Western Development Narrow Down China's Regional Disparity?" *Asian Economic Papers* 3, no. 3 (2005): 1–23.

52. Kelvin Soh and Aileen Wang, "China's Local Debt Pileup Raising Risk of Hard Landing," Reuters, October 10, 2011 (http://in.reuters.com/article/2011/10/10/idINIndia-59796920111010).

53. Lynette H. Ong, "Fiscal Federalism and Soft Budget Constraints: The Case of China," *International Political Science Review* 33 no. 4 (2012): 455–74.

54. Economist Intelligence Unit, *Building Rome in a Day: The Sustainability of China's Housing Boom,* report (London, March 2011), p. 2.

55. Zhang, *Inside the Growth Engine,* p. 76. HSBC Holdings is a renamed entity, formerly known as the Hong Kong and Shanghai Banking Corporation.

56. Ibid., p. 77.

57. Zhang Monan, "China's Hidden Debt Risk," *Caijin,* March 21, 2013 (http://english.caijing.com.cn/2013-03-21/112612002.html).

58. "Xi'an 'Twelve Five': International Features, Brand Development Services Outsourcing [in Chinese]," *China Outsourcing,* June 18, 2011 (http://mag.chnsourcing.com.cn/catelog/article/12406.html).

59. Li Fusheng, "IT Companies Flock to Xi'an," *China Daily,* September 25, 2012 (www.chinadaily.com.cn/cndy/2012-09/25/content_15780390.htm).

60. See James Fallows, *China Airborne* (New York: Pantheon, May 15, 2012), for a terrific telling of this story through the lens of Xi'an's early attempts to develop itself as a center of aerospace research, development, and manufacturing.

61. Ibid.

62. Chongqing was split out from Sichuan province in the early 1990s and established as a free-standing province-level municipality.

63. Bo was not solely responsible for this. In fact, Wang Yang had been his predecessor before being transferred to Guangdong. Still, in the five years when Mr. Bo held the reigns, Chongqing's GDP growth sizzled at an average 15.8 percent, compared to 10.5 percent for China as a whole. Even accounting for a bit of local exaggeration in the data, that is impressive. Industry plays an outsize role, accounting for 55 percent of output, compared to 47 percent nationally. Services have been squeezed out, accounting for 36 percent of the total compared to 43 percent nationally. See Tom Orlik, "China Real Time Report. The Chongqing Economy: An Illustrated Primer," *Wall Street Journal,* May 17, 2012 (http://blogs.wsj.com/chinarealtime/2012/05/17/the-chongqing-economy-an-illustrated-primer/); "Chongqing's GDP Growth Rate Ranks No.1 in China," *China Times,* January 20, 2012 (www.thechinatimes.com/online/2012/01/2007.html).

64. Dexter Roberts, "China Gambles on Affordable Housing," *Businessweek,* April 26, 2012 (www.businessweek.com/articles/2012-04-26/china-gambles-on-affordable-housing).

65. About 3.6 million have signed up for an urban *hukou* (household registration) as of December 2012. Not all farmers want to make the switch, despite Chongqing's best efforts. Rural hukou holders benefit from agricultural subsidies and cash

rewards not available to urban hukou holders. They can also have two children. Urban living costs are much higher, and urban life is more stressful, given the need to find jobs and affordable housing and to pay school tuition and medical expenses. Having land means that farmers have their own safety net to fall back on. See Jing Ulrich, Amir Hoosain, and Ling Zou, "Urbanization, Hukou Reform and Investment Implications," J.P. Morgan Hands-On China Report, March 13, 2012 (www.jpmorgan.com); Dai Liu, "Chongqing's Framework of Urban-Rural Supplementary Reforms Takes Shape," *Chongqing News*, December 31, 2012 (http://english.cqnews.net/html/2012-12/31/content_23067055.htm); "Farmers in Chongqing Say 'No Thanks' to Hukou," *People's Daily*, September 29, 2010 (http://english.peopledaily.com.cn/90001/90776/90882/7153618.html); Miguel Elosua and Ai Chi-Han, "Urban or Rural Household Registration?" *Urbachina*, November 20, 2012 (http://urbachina.hypotheses.org/1521); "Chongqing Urban Household Registration Reform Policy FAQs [in Chinese]," *Fabang.com*, November 1, 2010 (www.fabang.com/a/20101116/209590.html); Xhang Yanling and Zhang Tao, "Chongqing's Call to Urban Conversion," *Caixin*, August 25, 2010 (http://english.caixin.com/2010-08-25/100173950.html).

66. For a gripping account of this before the public disgrace of Bo Xilai and Wang Lijiun, read He Weifang, "An Open Letter to Legal Professionals in Chongqing," in *In the Name of the Justice: Striving for the Rule of Law in China* (Brookings, 2013), p. 1–6. According to many in China, Bo and Wang Lijun seemed to attack—and seize the assets of—major private sector figures associated with Wang Yang. The most prominent was Wen Qiang, the former deputy police chief who was convicted and executed on counts of bribery.

67. Cheng Li, "Remarks at the National Committee for U.S.-China Relations," April 13, 2012, p. 1, as shared by the author.

68. Chen Yao, "The New Situation of East-West Interaction: The Transference and Acceptance of Industrial Cluster [in Chinese]," in *Annual Report on Economic Development in Western Region of China 2008*, edited by Yao Huiqin and Ren Zongzhe (Beijing: Social Sciences Academic Press, 2008), pp. 298–308.

69. According to the American Chamber of Commerce in Shanghai, Chengdu beat out Chongqing, Xi'an, and Wuhan as the next most likely place where their members will expand investment. See Kedl and others, *China Business Report: 2011–2012*.

70. Huang Zhiling, "Fortune Global Forum Chooses Chengdu Thanks to Western China Market," *China Daily*, April 12, 2012 (www.chinadaily.com.cn/regional/2012-04/12/content_15026905.htm).

71. "A Video of the World's Largest Building: The Chengdu New Century Global Center," *GoChengdoo*, October 10, 2012 (www.gochengdoo.com/en/blog/item/2805/a_video_of_the_worlds_largest_building_the_chengdu_new_century_global_center).

72. Financing schemes for local real estate development have become a hot topic. See Ong, "Fiscal Federalism." See also Fubing Su and Ran Tao, "State Fragmentation and Rights Contestation: Rural Land Development Rights in China," *China and World Economy* (2013, forthcoming); Fubing Su and Ran Tao, "Asian Tiger or Fragile Dragon? Understanding China's Development Model," unpublished work; Su and Tao, "Visible Hand or Crippled Hand."

73. "China Foxconn Workers Riot at Chengdu Restaurant," BBC, June 8,2012 (www.bbc.co.uk/news/world-asia-china-18363929).

74. See Xie Liangbing, "Central Government Investigates Chengdu's Hukou Reform," *Economic Observer*, December 9, 2010 (www.eeo.com.cn/ens/Politics/2010/12/09/188529.shtml); Zou Si, "Lessons from Chengdu's 'Hukou Unification Model' of Reform and Its Main Problems [in Chinese]," *Chengdu.cn*, November 22, 2012 (http://news.chengdu.cn/content/2012-11/22/content_1095011.htm).

75. Su and Tao, "State Fragmentation."

76. Tom Orlik, "Tensions Mount as China Snatches Farms for Homes," *Wall Street Journal*, February 14, 2013 (http://online.wsj.com/article/SB1000142412788 7324906004578287182123200020.html).

77. Jonathan Watts, "Chinese 'Rocket Man' Wins Record Payout over Farmland Dispute in Beijing," *The Guardian*, July 9 2010 (www.guardian.co.uk/world/2010/jul/09/chinese-rocketman-wins-payout); Su and Tao, "State Fragmentation."

78. See Hong, "Rationale, Prospects, and Challenges," pp. 437–61. See also Min Jie, "Central and Local Governments: The Asset of Ambiguity," *News China Magazine*, June 2013 (www.newschinamag.com/magazine/the-asset-of-ambiguity). "In recent years, local governments have become dependent on profits from the real estate industry, one of China's only truly lucrative private business sectors. Much of this money has come in the form of "land grant fees," paid by developers to local government officials, as no private citizen in China has the right to own land. In some localities, these fees account for more than half of total local government revenue. There is no indication as to what might replace them."

79. Huang Bihong and Chen Kang, "Are Intergovernmental Transfers in China Equalizing?" *China Economic Review* 23, no. 3 (2012): 534–51 (www.sciencedirect. com/science/article/pii/S1043951X12000028).

80. Chinese Academy of Social Sciences, Institute of Finance and Trade Economics, "12th Five Year Plan and Financial System Reform [in Chinese]," Research Institute for Fiscal Science, Ministry of Finance, January 5, 2012 (http://cks.mof. gov.cn/crifs/html/default/caizhengtizhi/_content/12_01/04/1325642622508.html).

81. Zhang, *Inside the Growth Engine*, p. 119.

82. "About Xinjiang," CCTV English, June 14, 2011 (http://cctv.cntv.cn/lm/rediscoveringchina/20110614/105069.shtml).

83. Xinjiang also receives a great deal of development assistance from other parts of the country. The central government launched a "pairing assistance" program in 2010. The nineteen provinces and municipalities involved have invested more than $466 million (3 billion yuan) and helped implement 150 pilot projects in the region. See Yao Bin, "Xinjiang Takes Off," *Beijing Review*, August 8, 2011 (www.bjreview. com.cn/Cover_Stories_Series_2011/2011-08/08/content_382089.htm).

84. Zhang, *Inside the Growth Engine*, p. 120.

85. Xinjiang has twenty-nine ports of entry bordering eight countries with whom extensive economic and trade ties are being established. Yao, "Xinjiang Takes Off"; Wang Huimin, "Xinjiang Progressing toward Prosperous Future," *People's Daily Online*, July 5, 2011 (http://english.peopledaily.com.cn/90001/90780/7430135.html).

86. Ben Blanchard, "China to Spend \$4.6 bln on Airports in Restless Xinjiang," Reuters, Jan 31, 2011 (www.reuters.com/article/2011/01/31/uk-china-airports-idUKLNE70U01P20110131).

87. Yao, "Xinjiang Takes Off."

88. Gabe Collins and Andrew Erickson, "Xinjiang Poised to Become China's Largest Coal Producer: Will Move Global Coal, Natural Gas, and Crude Oil Markets," *China SignPost,* September 20, 2012 (www.chinasignpost.com/wp-content/uploads/2012/09/China-SignPost_65_Xinjiang-Poised-to-Become-Chinas-Largest-Coal-Producer_20120920.pdf).

89. Xinjiang accounted for 35 percent of PetroChina's total natural gas production in 2010. PetroChina plans to produce 30 billion cubic meters a year by 2015 and is increasing the capacity of its gas pipeline from Xinjiang to Guangdong. Sinopec wants to increase its natural gas production to 5 billion cubic meters a year by 2015. See "Big Sky, New Horizons for Xinjiang: Part 3," CNTV, June 11, 2011 (http://english.cntv.cn/program/rediscoveringchina/20110611/101308.shtml); Shai Oster, "China Launches Energy Tax in Xinjiang," *Wall Street Journal,* June 2, 2010 (http://online.wsj.com/article/SB1000142405274870356160457528218179 2884798.html).

90. Selig S. Harrison, "China's Discreet Hold on Pakistan's Northern Borderlands," *New York Times,* August 26, 2010 (www.nytimes.com/2010/08/27/opinion/27iht-edharrison.html?_r=0).

91. Erica S. Downs, "China Buys into Afghanistan," *SAIS Review* 32, no. 2 (2012): 65–84.

92. Xinhua, "Maintaining Social Stability in Xinjiang a Long-Term Task: Official," March 3, 2012 (http://news.xinhuanet.com/english/china/2012-03/03/c_131444268.htm). See also Joshua Kucera, "Central Asia: What Is China's Policy Driver?" *Eurasia Net,* December 18, 2012 (www.eurasianet.org/node/66314).

93. Edward Wang, "China Announces New Top Official for Tibet," *New York Times,* August 26, 2011 (www.nytimes.com/2011/08/27/world/asia/27tibet.html?_r=0).

94. For two different and interesting accounts of the origins, goals, and reporting on the 2008 Tibetan riots, see Chen Li and Lucy Montgomery, "The 2008 Tibet Riots: Competing Perspectives, Divided Group Protests and Divergent Media Narratives," in *Transnational Protests and the Media,* edited by Simon Cottle and Libby Lester (New York: Peter Lang, 2011), pp. 225–41; Human Rights Watch, *"I Saw It with My Own Eyes": Abuses by Chinese Security Forces in Tibet: 2008–2010* (New York, July 2010).

95. Institute for Ethnic Studies of Sichuan Province, "A Summary of Tibetan History and Culture in Sichuan [in Chinese]" (www.iessp.com/newsdetail11867.htm [February 2013]).

96. United Nations Development Program, *Access for All: Basic Public Services for 1.3 Billion People,* China Human Development Report 2007/08 (http://hdr.undp.org/en/reports/national/asiathepacific/china/China_2008_en.pdf).

97. Stephen Kurczy, "Beijing Boasts of 'Leapfrog Development' in Tibet," *Christian Science Monitor,* January 25, 2010 (www.csmonitor.com/World/Global-News/2010/0125/Beijing-boasts-of-leapfrog-development-in-Tibet).

98. Xinhua, "China to Spend $46.89 Billion for Development of Tibet," *Economic Times,* September 14, 2011 (http://articles.economictimes.indiatimes.com/2011-09-14/news/30154403_1_lhasa-zangmu-hydropower-station-hao-peng).

99. Shanghai, Jilin, and Yunnan received the most tax rebates in eastern, central, and western China, respectively; Hainan, Jiangxi, and Guizhou received the lowest amount in each region. Tibet had the highest per capita general-purpose transfers in the nation at 3,846 yuan. The six coastal provinces (or municipalities) received no general transfers. Tibet also received the most specific-purpose transfers in the west and nationally. Shanghai and Jilin received the most specific-purpose transfers in the eastern and central areas, while Guangdong received the least. See Huang and Chen, "Are Intergovernmental Transfers in China Equalizing?"

100. Xinhua, "China to Spend $46.89 Billion."

101. "Three Trillion in Government Transfers."

102. Kurczy, "Beijing Boasts of 'Leapfrog Development.'"

103. Jamil Anderlini, "Hit-and-Run Sparks Mongolian Protest against China," *Financial Times,* May 25, 2011 (www.ft.com/intl/cms/s/0/51769a96-86f8-11e0-92df-00144feabdc0.html); Minxin Pei, "China Has Another Way to Defuse Ethnic Strife," *Financial Times,* June 5, 2011 (www.ft.com/intl/cms/s/0/e6db53f6-8fa9-11e0-954d-00144feab49a.html#axzz2FQanrTdh).

104. Hohhot and Xilin Gol, "Little Hu and the Mining of the Grasslands," *The Economist,* July 14, 2012 (www.economist.com/node/21558605).

105. "No Pastoral Idyll: Turbulence in Inner Mongolia Makes Managing China No Easier," *The Economist,* June 2, 2011 (www.economist.com/node/18775303).

106. Andrew Jacobs, "China Extends Hand and Fist to Protesters," *New York Times,* June 1, 2011 (www.nytimes.com/2011/06/02/world/asia/02mongolia.html).

107. Human Rights Watch, *Crackdown in Inner Mongolia,* Asia Watch Report (New York, July 1991), p. 17 (www.hrw.org/reports/pdfs/c/china/china917.pdf).

108. Hohhot and Gol, "Little Hu and the Mining of the Grasslands."

109. Wu Zhong, "Green Motives in Inner Mongolian Unrest," *Asia Times,* June 8, 2011 (www.atimes.com/atimes/China/MF08Ad01.html).

110. Zhang, *Inside the Growth Engine,* p. 97.

111. This study was done by the China Economy Research Institute in Beijing, cited in Wu, "Green Motives."

112. Xinhua, "Key Policies to Boost Inner Mongolia's Development," *China Daily,* June 16, 2011 (www.chinadaily.com.cn/bizchina/2011-06/16/content_12712673.htm).

113. Tom Orlik, "China Real Time Report. Ominous Ordos: Dispatch from a Chinese Ghost Town," *Wall Street Journal,* December 5, 2011 (http://blogs.wsj.com/chinarealtime/2011/12/05/ominous-ordos-dispatch-from-a-chinese-ghost-town/).

114. Hohhot and Gol, "Little Hu and the Mining of the Grasslands."

115. See Cheng Li, "Hu Chunhua: One of China's Future Leaders to Watch" (www.brookings.edu/about/centers/china/top-future-leaders/hu_chunhua).

116. See Su and Tao, "Asian Tiger or Fragile Dragon?"; Fubing Su, Ran Tao, and Dali L. Yang, "Rethinking the Institutional Foundations of China's Hyper Growth," in *The Oxford Handbook on the Politics of Development,* edited by Carol Lancaster and Nicholas van de Walle (New York: Oxford University Press, forthcoming).

117. See Min, "Central and Local Governments."

CHAPTER 4

1. Directorate General of Commercial Intelligence and Statistics, "Annual Report 2009–2010: Foreign Trade Performance of India" (Kolkata: Ministry of Commerce, Government of India, 2010), p. 5 (www.dgciskol.nic.in/annualreport/book_3e.pdf).

2. Steven Rattner, "India Is Losing the Race," *New York Times,* January 19, 2013 (http://opinionator.blogs.nytimes.com/2013/01/19/india-is-losing-the-race/).

3. Brookings colleague Tanvi Madan has aptly captured this as India running a triathlon, compared to China's marathon. See Tanvi Madan, "China's Marathon Is India's Triathlon," February 4, 2013 (www.brookings.edu/blogs/up-front/posts/2013/02/04-india-china-madan).

4. Gujarat is India's tenth-largest state by population and ranks fifth in GDP. Large states that did not make my G-7 include Madhya Pradesh (73 million, sixth in population, and twelfth in GDP); Karnataka (61 million, ninth in population, and seventh in GDP); and Rajasthan (68 million, eighth in population, and eighth in GDP).

5. Directorate of Economics and Statistics, Planning Department, *Economic Survey of Maharashtra 2011–2012* (Mumbai: Government of Maharashtra, 2012).

6. Ibid.

7. In 2010 Guangdong had about $20 billion in foreign direct investment. Billy Wong, "Guangdong: Market Profile" (http://china-trade-research.hktdc.com/business-news/article/Fast-Facts/GUANGDONG-PROVINCE/ff/en/1/1X000000/1X06BUOU.htm).

8. Katherine Boo, *Behind the Beautiful Forevers: Life, Death, and Hope in a Mumbai Undercity* (New York: Random House, February 2012).

9. Thackeray famously opposed Western rituals such as Valentine's Day as a sign of foreign encroachment on Hindu traditions.

10. Getting an exact figure on these populations is a challenge. Estimates vary from 6.5 to 9 to 12.4 million—depending, in part, on whether the slums in question belong to Mumbai proper or the immediate outlying areas. See Akshaya Mishra, "Slum Population Shifts Preference as Big City Cramps Space," *Firstpost,* October 21, 2011 (www.firstpost.com/mumbai/slum-population-shifts-preference-as-big-city-cramps-space-113013.html); Bhavika Jain, "62% of Mumbai Lives in Slums: Census," *Hindustan Times,* October 17, 2010 (www.hindustantimes.com/India-news/Mumbai/62-of-Mumbai-lives-in-slums-Census/Article1-614027.aspx).

11. "Halfway to Paradise: A Half-Built Bridge Symbolizes the Urgency and the Frustrations of Improving India's Infrastructure," *The Economist,* December 22, 2012 (www.economist.com/news/christmas-specials/21568582-half-built-bridge-symbolises-urgency-and-frustrations-improving-indias).

12. In a January 2012 survey by *India Today,* Modi ranked as India's top performing chief minister and as the top pick for national prime minister. The percentage who favored him had doubled over the previous year, vaulting him past the Congress Party's Rahul Gandhi. Modi was picked by 24 percent of those surveyed, far ahead of Gandhi, who received 17 percent. That was a major shift from the

previous year, when Gandhi received 21 percent to Modi's 12 percent. See "Who Should be the Next PM?" *India Today,* January 28, 2012.
Much of the rest of this section appeared previously on the Brookings website. See William J. Antholis, "India's Most Admired and Most Feared Politician," March 16, 2012 (www.brookings.edu/blogs/up-front/posts/2012/03/16-modi-antholis).

13. All quotes of Modi are from my interview with him on March 2, 2012, at the chief minister's residence in Gandhinagar, Gujarat.

14. Narendra Modi, "Blueprint for Infrastructure in Gujarat 2020 (Big 2020)" (www.gidb.org/cms.aspx?content_id=316).

15. Official Gujarat State Portal, "MOUs—An Economy of Abundance: Vibrant Gujarat" (www.gujaratindia.com/business/mous-signed.htm).

16. This famous text message was widely reported later in the Indian and international press. See Shilpa Kannan, "Gujarat State in the Fast Lane of Indian Economy," BBC, February 26, 2012 (www.bbc.co.uk/news/business-17156917).

17. See Gujarat Infrastructure Development Board, "Gujarat Economic Profile" (Gandhinagar, July 2011) and "Infrastructure Initiatives in the State of Gujarat," paper prepared for the Steering Committee Meeting of the Development Account Project for South Asia, UN Economic and Social Commission for Asia and the Pacific, Bangkok, February 2009.

18. Central Statistics Office, National Statistical Organization, "Women and Men in India," 14th issue (New Delhi: Government of India, 2012).

19. Modi had been formally elected and sworn in on February 26, 2002, having been acting chief minister for six months, mostly overseeing response to Gujarat's 2001 earthquake. The Godhra train burning happened the following day, and the riots occurred two days later.

20. See U.S. Commission on International Religious Freedom, "International Religious Freedom Act of 1998" (www.uscirf.gov/index.php?option=com_content &id=349&Itemid=45), Section 604(a).

21. Amol Sharma, "Q&A: Gujarat Chief Minister Narendra Modi," *Wall Street Journal,* August 28, 2012 (http://blogs.wsj.com/indiarealtime/2012/08/29/qa-gujarat-chief-minister-narendra-modi/).

22. "Peace, Harmony and Unity: Narendra Modi to Fast for Three Days," *Times of India,* September 13, 2011 (http://articles.timesofindia.indiatimes.com/2011-09-13/india/30148879_1_gulbarga-society-narendra-modi-gujarat-chief-minister).

23. "Newly-Formed Gujarat Assembly's First Session on Jan 23," *Zee News,* January 18, 2013 (http://zeenews.india.com/state-election-2012/gujarat/newly-formed-gujarat-assembly-s-first-session-on-jan-23_823771.html).

24. Nehru family members who have led the Congress Party include Indira Gandhi, his daughter; Rajiv Gandhi, Indira's son; Sonia Gandhi, Rajiv's wife and Indira's daughter-in-law; and Rahul Gandhi, Indira's grandson.

25. Over thirty U.S. states have overseas offices, in addition to offices within their own states for trade promotion. See the State International Development Organizations, "2010 Annual Survey of State International Economic Development Agencies" (http://apps.csg.org/sidoprofiles/).

26. See Ministry of Statistics and Program Implementation of India, "State Domestic Product," February 27, 2013 (http://mospi.nic.in/Mospi_New/upload/SDPmain_04-05.htm).

27. Department of Economics and Statistics, *Statistical Handbook of Tamil Nadu 2012* (Chennai: Government of Tamil Nadu, 2012) (www.tn.gov.in/deptst/ ForeignTrade.pdf).

28. The U.S. consulate in Chennai serves a territory of about 168 million people, covering the states of Tamil Nadu (population 72 million), Karnataka (61 million), Kerala (33 million), and the Union Territories of Andaman and Nicobar Islands (79,944), Pondicherry (1.2 million), and Lakshadweep Islands (64,429).

29. For now, many Chinese and Indians still want to obtain visas, attend U.S. universities, and join the American workforce. Those H-1B applicants aspire to work not only in Palo Alto and Cambridge but also in towns like Columbus, Indiana, and Bloomington, Illinois—places that may not be epicenters of high tech but are often where important industrial innovations are developed. See Neil G. Ruiz and Shyamali Choudhury, "Opinion: Demand for H-1B Visas High among Program's Biggest Critics," *National Journal,* July 18, 2012 (http://nationaljour-nal.com/thenextamerica/workforce/opinion-demand-for-h-1b-visas-high-among-program-s-biggest-critics-20120718); Neil G. Ruiz , Jill H. Wilson, and Shyamali Choudhury, "The Search for Skills: Demand for H-1B Immigrant Workers in U.S. Metropolitan Areas," Metropolitan Policy Program Report, July 18, 2012 (www. brookings.edu/research/reports/2012/07/18-h1b-visas-labor-immigration).

30. Conversation with Matt Beh from the U.S. consulate in Chennai, January 2012.

31. Government of Tamil Nadu, *Vision Tamil Nadu 2023: Strategic Plan for Infrastructure Development in Tamil Nadu* (Chennai, March 17, 2012) (www. scribd.com/doc/86455032/TN-Vision-2023).

32. Interview with Raj Cherubal, January 2012, in Chennai. See also Raj Cherubal, "The Coming Mutinies: India Will Evolve into a Confederation of City-States," *Pragati: The Indian National Interest Review,* no. 8 (November 2007): 19–20.

33. Registrar General and Census Commissioner, "Census of India 2011: Pro-visional Population Totals" (http://censusindia.gov.in/2011census/censusinfodash-board/index.html); Census Bureau, "State & County QuickFacts: Arkansas" (http:// quickfacts.census.gov/qfd/states/05000.html).

34. "Bihar Grew by 11.03%, Next Only to Gujarat," *Times of India,* January 3, 2010 (http://timesofindia.indiatimes.com/business/india-business/Bihar-grew-by-11-03-next-only-to-Gujarat/articleshow/5405973.cms).

35. Indo-Asian News Service, "Bihar Registers 16.71 Per Cent Growth Rate," *NDTV,* July 17, 2012 (www.ndtv.com/article/india/bihar-registers-16-71-per-cent-growth-rate-244446).

36. When Lalu Prasad was chief minister, he signed an agreement to split off the southern part of Bihar into a new state, Jharkand. Under Prasad it was the poorest part of Bihar and now is one of the poorest states in India. *Outlook India* quotes Nitish Kumar as initially opposed to Jharkand separating from Bihar in 2000. But splitting off poverty-stricken Southern Bihar into Jharkhand may have contributed to the improvements in Bihar's statistics after 2000. The Jharkhand region also has a substantial number of Naxalites, also referred to as communists or Mao-ists, regarded as India's most serious internal security threat. See "I Had Initially Opposed Bifurcation of Bihar: Nitish," *Outlook India,* May 7, 2012 (http://news.

outlookindia.com/items.aspx?artid=761886); "Senior Maoist 'Arrested' in India," BBC, December 19, 2007 (http://news.bbc.co.uk/2/hi/south_asia/7151552.stm).

37. Faizan Ahmad, "Bihar Ranks Poorest despite Giant Strides," *Times of India,* February 23, 2011 (http://articles.timesofindia.indiatimes.com/2011-02-23/patna/ 28626349_1_lakh-tonnes-economic-survey-capita-income); Press Information Bureau, Government of India, "Statement: Per Capita Net GDP at Current Prices," March 2012 (http://pib.nic.in/archieve/others/2012/mar/d2012032902.pdf).

38. Government of Bihar, Finance Department, *Economic Survey 2011–12,* February 2012 (http://indiagovernance.gov.in/files/Economic-Survey-2012-En.pdf).

39. See "Statement-4" in Government of Bihar, "Census Statistics," 2001 (http:// gov.bih.nic.in/Profile/CensusStats-03.htm); Ministry of Home Affairs, Office of the Registrar General and Census Commissioner, *Census of India 2011, Provisional Results* (New Delhi: Government of India, 2011).

40. See in particular Ed Luce, *In Spite of the Gods: The Rise of Modern India* (New York: Doubleday, 2007). Luce gives a brilliant account of Nitish's predecessor—and one-time mentor—Lalu Prasad Yadav, who manipulated various lower castes "by focusing on what divides them. It is much closer to ethnic politics than to class politics." Lalu and other Bihari officials also colluded with local protection and kidnapping rackets.

41. Unless otherwise noted, all quotes from Nitish Kumar are from an interview with him at the chief minister's residence, Patna, Bihar, March 6, 2012.

42. See especially Bibek Debroy and Laveesh Bhandari, *Corruption in India: The DNA and the RNA* (New Delhi: Konark Publishers, 2012), chap. 6, section 4: "The States Lead the Way." Bihar edged out Gujarat as the state that most effectively files corruption charges, brings criminals to trial, and successfully convicts those accused.

43. Government of Bihar, *Economic Survey 2011 –12.*

44. Recall that the poorer southern part of Bihar was split off to create the new province of Jharkhand in 2000. See note 36.

45. Government of Bihar, *Economic Survey 2011–12.*

46. Ibid.

47. Taken from the website of Mayawati's Bahujan Samaj (Majority People's) Party. See "About the Bahujan Samaj Party (BSP)" (www.bspindia.org/about-bsp.php).

48. Ashutosh Varshney, "India in Transition: The Challenge in Uttar Pradesh," University of Pennsylvania, Center for the Advanced Study of India, August 30, 2009 (http://casi.ssc.upenn.edu/iit/varshney).

49. Avinash Celestine, "Can Akhilesh Singh Yadav Make UP Find Economic Dynamism Like Bihar?" *Economic Times,* March 11, 2012 (http://articles.economic-times.indiatimes.com/2012-03-11/news/31143353_1_sp-government-samajwadi-party-land-acquisition).

50. Registrar General and Census Commissioner, "Census of India 2011."

51. See Government of Andhra Pradesh, Planning Department, *Socio- Economic Survey Report 2011–2012* (Hyderabad, 2012), table 2.5.

52. "Andhra Pradesh: The State That Would Reform India," *The Economist,* August 31, 2000 (www.economist.com/node/354212). See also Keith Bradsher, "A High-Tech Fix for One Corner of India," *New York Times,* December 27, 2002 (www. nytimes.com/2002/12/27/business/a-high-tech-fix-for-one-corner-of-india.html).

53. See Government of Andhra Pradesh, *Socio-Economic Survey Report 2011–12,* table 2.5.

54. Ministry of Statistics and Program Implementation of India, "Gross State Domestic Product at Current Prices," March 1, 2012 (http://mospi.nic.in/Mospi_New/upload/State_wise_SDP_2004-05_14mar12.pdf); M. H. Suryanarayana, Ankush Agrawal, and K. Seeta Prabhu, "Inequality-Adjusted Human Development Index for India's States," paper (New Delhi: United Nations Development Program India, 2011) (www.undp.org/content/dam/india/docs/inequality_adjusted_human_development_index_for_indias_state1.pdf).

55. Government of India, Planning Commission, "Growth Rate of Gross State Domestic Product in Industry Sector State-wise (2000–01 to 2011–12)" (http://planningcommission.nic.in/data/datatable/0512/databook_40.pdf).

56. See reference to central bank figures in "The City That Got Left Behind," *The Economist,* January 7, 2012 (www.economist.com/node/21542446?zid=306&ah=1b164dbd43b0cb27ba0d4c3b12a5e227).

57. Government of India, "Growth Rate of Gross State Domestic Product."

58. Urmi A. Goswami, "Land Acquisition Bill: Kamal Nath Calls for All-Party Meet," *Economic Times,* March 2, 2013 (http://articles.economictimes.indiatimes.com/2013-03-02/news/37390047_1_rehabilitation-and-resettlement-bill-land-acquisition-public-purpose).

59. "Nano Wars: Tata Threatens to Make the World's Cheapest Car Somewhere Else," *The Economist,* August 28, 2008 (www.economist.com/node/12010079).

60. Amol Sharma, "Mamata Banerjee's No-Confidence Bid Flops," *Wall Street Journal,* November 22, 2012 (http://blogs.wsj.com/indiarealtime/2012/11/22/mamata-banerjees-no-confidence-bid-flops/).

61. Janaki Fernandes, "Mulayam Singh Yadav's Support for UPA Could Impede Reforms' Initiative," *NDTV,* September 21, 2012 (www.ndtv.com/article/india/mulayam-singh-yadav-s-support-for-upa-could-impede-reforms-initiative-270284).

CHAPTER 5

1. Federation of American Scientists, "Status of World Nuclear Forces" (www.fas.org/programs/ssp/nukes/nuclearweapons/nukestatus.html).

2. Joanna Lewis, "Energy and Climate Goals of China's 12th Five-Year Plan," Pew Center on Global Climate Change, March 2011 (www.c2es.org/docUploads/energy-climate-goals-china-twelfth-five-year-plan.pdf).

3. Edward Wong, "On Scale of 0 to 500, Beijing's Air Quality Tops 'Crazy Bad' at 755," *New York Times,* January 12, 2013 (www.nytimes.com/2013/01/13/science/earth/beijing-air-pollution-off-the-charts.html?_r=0); Evan Osnos, "One Nation Under Smog: The Rules for Beijing Living," *New Yorker,* January 14, 2013 (www.newyorker.com/online/blogs/evanosnos/2013/01/one-nation-under-smog-the-rules-for-beijing-living.html).

4. Li Wenfang, "Academic Claims Air Pollution Is More Frightening Than SARS Virus," *China Daily,* February 1, 2013 (www.chinadaily.com.cn/china/2013-02/01/content_16192311.htm).

5. Laurie Burkitt, "Beijing 'Airpocalypse' Reflected in Online Shopping Stats," *Wall Street Journal,* January 16, 2013 (http://blogs.wsj.com/chinarealtime/2013/01/16/beijing-airpocalypse-reflected-in-online-shopping-stats/).

6. Laurie Burkitt and Brian Spegele, "Why Leave Job in Beijing? To Breathe," *Wall Street Journal,* April 14, 2013 (http://online.wsj.com/article/SB100014241278 87324010704578418343148947824.html).

7. U.S. Energy Information Administration, "China," September 4, 2012 (www.eia.gov/countries/cab.cfm?fips=CH).

8. Only 5 percent of China's coal comes from abroad, mostly from Australia and Indonesia. International Energy Agency, "FAQs: Coal" (www.iea.org/aboutus/faqs/coal/). However, those imports are rising quickly.

9. In 2011 Inner Mongolia produced almost 990 million tons; Shanxi, 870 million tons; and Shaanxi, 405 million tons. Combined, these provinces accounted for 64 percent of China's 3.52 billion tons of coal produced in 2011. Yu Xiangming, "NDRC Production Guide: Coal Production for This Year Will Be Limited to 3.65 Billion Tons," Xinhua, August 15, 2012 (http://news.xinhuanet.com/energy/2012-08/15/c_123584088.htm). Xinjiang and Ningxia are also undergoing rapid growth in coal production. Xinjiang produced 120 million tons of coal in 2011, sending 20 million tons eastward. See "Xinjiang's 2011 Coal Production Exceeds 120 Million Tons. Transports East Total 20 Million Tons," *Yaxin.com,* January 6, 2012 (http://news.iyaxin.com/content/2012-01/06/content_3254636.htm).

10. These figures are for primary energy consumption. See, respectively, Statistical Bureau of Guangdong Province and Survey Office of the National Bureau of Statistics in Guangdong, *Guangdong Statistical Yearbook 2012* (Beijing: China Statistics Press), "Table 7-2 Total Consumption of Energy and Its Composition" (www.gdstats.gov.cn/tjnj/2012/table/7/07-02.htm); Shanghai Municipal Statistics Bureau, *Shanghai Statistical Yearbook 2011* (Beijing: China Statistics Press, 2011), "Table 5.10 Coal, Petroleum, Electricity Balance Sheet (2010)" (www.stats-sh.gov.cn/tjnj/nje11.htm?d1=2011tjnje/E0510.htm); Hu Wei-xi and others, "Jiangsu Province Coal Consumption Forecast under the Restraint of Carbon Emission [in Chinese]," *Energy and Energy Conservation,* November 12, 2012 (www.nyyjn.org/jienengjianpai/1894.html), table 1.

11. Sichuan derived 65 percent of its energy from coal in 2008; in Shaanxi that proportion was 60 percent in 2007, and in Chongqing the figure was 66 percent in 2008. See, respectively, Statistical Bureau of Sichuan Province and Survey Office of the National Bureau of Statistics in Sichuan, *Sichuan Statistical Yearbook* (Beijing: China Statistics Press, 2009), "Table 6-3 Total Consumption of Energy and Its Composition" (www.sc.stats.gov.cn/); People's Government of Shaanxi Province, "2007 Shaanxi Energy Savings Results," May 2008 (http://english.shaanxi.gov.cn/english/templates/articleChinese.jsp?sSeq=2864& sFlag=Y&chinesehtml=/articleAboutgov/chinadoc/chinaone/governmentdoc/200805/2864_1.html); National Bureau of Statistics of China, "Chongqing Energy Supply and Demand Gradually Rising, Energy Savings Being Achieved," August 31, 2009 (www.stats.gov.cn/tjfx/dfxx/ts20090828_402583239.htm).

12. Beijing Municipal Statistics Bureau and Survey Office of the National Bureau of Statistics in Beijing, *Beijing Statistical Yearbook 2012* (Beijing:

China Statistics Press, 2012), table 4-12 (www.bjstats.gov.cn/nj/main/2012-tjnj/content/mV84_0412.htm); Li Jing, "Beijing's Coal Use to Be Capped," *China Daily,* August 30, 2011 (www.chinadaily.com.cn/cndy/2011-08/30/content_13215820. htm); Tianjin Government, "Notice about the Pilot Implementation of the Program for Low-Carbon Tianjin [in Chinese]," 2012 (www.tj.gov.cn/zwgk/wjgz/szfbgtwj/201203/t20120330_174424.htm).

13. Li Xiaohui, "China Asked to Set Ceiling on Coal Output, Official," *iStockAnalyst,* August 11, 2010 (www.istockanalyst.com/article/viewiStockNews/articleid/4400044).

14. Frik Els, "2,900 Mines Closed Down in China's Coal and Rare Earth Region," *Mining.com,* September 22, 2012 (www.mining.com/2900-mines-closed-down-in-chinas-coal-and-rare-earth-region-73692/).

15. "Energy Brings Wealth to West China," *China Daily,* May 21, 2012 (www.chinadaily.com.cn/bizchina/2012-05/21/content_15346624.htm).

16. Joel Martinsen, "The Rich Lives of Coal Bosses," *Danwei,* October 11, 2007 (www.danwei.org/business/its_a_good_time_to_be_a_coal_b.php).

17. This very general estimate is the subject of considerable debate and controversy, even among those who fully accept the role that manmade emissions have in warming the atmosphere. This is partly due to debates about how long greenhouse gases linger and partly due to incomplete understanding of the role of clouds and of other aerosols in heating the atmosphere. But the estimate is robust enough that it provides a useful benchmark. See William Antholis and Strobe Talbott, *Fast Forward* (Brookings, 2010), chapters 1–3; see also Malte Meinshausen and others, "Greenhouse-Gas Emission Targets for Limiting Global Warming to 2 °C," letter, *Nature,* April 30, 2009, pp. 1158–62 (www.nature.com/nature/journal/v458/n7242/full/nature08017.html).

18. Kenneth G. Lieberthal and David B. Sandalow, "Overcoming Obstacles to U.S.-China Cooperation on Climate Change," January 2009 (www.brookings.edu/research/reports/2009/01/climate-change-lieberthal-sandalow).

19. See comments by Kenneth Lieberthal in "The Road Ahead for China's Economy" (Brookings, April 16, 2013), pp. 136–37 (www.brookings.edu/~/media/events/2013/4/16%20china%20economy/20130416_china_economy.pdf). See also Matthew Brown, "Fracking Is Flopping Overseas," *Businessweek,* May 3, 2013 (www.businessweek.com/articles/2012-05-03/fracking-is-flopping-overseas).

20. Jen Alic, "U.S. Companies Poised to Launch Chinese Shale Boom," December 30, 2012 (http://oilprice.com/Energy/Natural-Gas/US-Companies-Poised-to-Launch-Chinese-Shale-Boom.html).

21. "China Pays Top Dollar for Gas Imports," *South China Morning Post,* February 08, 2013 (www.scmp.com/business/commodities/article/1145564/china-pays-top-dollar-gas-imports).

22. Robert M. Cutler, "China's Gas Imports Jump," *Asia Times,* June 24, 2011 (http://atimes.com/atimes/China_Business/MF24Cb01.html); Jing Yang, "China Piped Gas Imperils $100 Billion LNG Plans: Energy Markets," Bloomberg, October 10, 2012 (www.bloomberg.com/news/2012-10-10/china-piped-gas-imperils-100-billion-lng-plans-energy-markets.html); Song Yenling, "China Imports Uzbekistan Gas via Pipeline for First Time in August," September 24, 2012 (www.platts.com/RSSFeedDetailedNews/RSSFeed/NaturalGas/7091999); International Energy

Agency, "Oil and Gas Emergency Policy—China 2012 Update" (www.iea.org/publications/freepublications/publication/name,28189,en.html).

23. U.S. Energy Information Administration, "China."

24. Ibid.

25. China is the third-largest importer from Venezuela, behind the United States and the Caribbean, and the fourth-largest importer from Russia. See, respectively, U.S. Energy Information Administration, "Venezuela" (www.eia.gov/countries/cab.cfm?fips=VE), and "Russia" (www.eia.gov/countries/cab.cfm?fips=RS).

26. See the following reports from the U.S. Energy Information Administration: "Sudan" (www.eia.gov/cabs/sudan/Full.html);"Iran," (www.eia.gov/emeu/cabs/iran/full.html); "Angola" (www.eia.gov/emeu/cabs/angola/full.html).

27. Charles K. Ebinger and Kevin Massy, "Energy and Climate: Black to Gold to Green," January 17, 2013 (www.brookings.edu/research/papers/2013/01/energy-and-climate-black-to-gold-to-green).

28. Mark Fulton and others, "Hydropower in China: Opportunities and Risks," Deutsche Bank Group, October 31, 2011 (www.dbcca.com/dbcca/EN/investment-research/investment_research_2399.jsp). Sichuan province had 32.82 gigawatts of installed hydropower capacity at the end of 2011. See Interfax-China, "Sichuan Ranks First in Hydropower Production," May 29, 2012 (www.interfax.cn/node/20312).

29. Sharon LaFraniere, "Possible Link between Dam and China Quake," New York Times, February 6, 2009 (www.nytimes.com/2009/02/06/world/asia/06quake.html?pagewanted=all&_r=0).

30. Qi Ye, presentation at the Third Annual Review of Low-Carbon Development in China, Brookings, December 14, 2012, transcript, p.12 (www.brookings.edu/events/2012/12/14-low-carbon-us-china).

31. Hao Xin, "China's Booming Solar and Wind Sector May Be Put on Hold," Science Insider, March 9, 2012 (http://news.sciencemag.org/scienceinsider/2012/03/chinas-booming-solar-and-wind-se.html).

32. Scott Clavenna, "China's Wind Market: Growing, but Challenged by Grid Realities," GreenTech Media, November 1, 2012 (www.greentechmedia.com/articles/read/Chinas-Wind-Market-Growing-but-Challenged-by-Grid-Realities).

33. Hao, "China's Booming Solar and Wind Sector."

34. "Henan Province of China Announces Energy Consumption Target for 2015," Climate Connect News, April 17, 2012 (www.climate-connect.co.uk/Home/?q=node/2166)

35. International Atomic Energy Agency, Power Reactor Information System, "China: Country Statistics," February 28, 2013 (www.iaea.org/pris/Country Statistics/CountryDetails.aspx?current=CN).

36. U.S. Energy Information Administration, "China."

37. International Atomic Energy Agency, "China: Country Statistics."

38. Tian Shuangyue, "Guangdong Commission Appeals: Reduce the Energy-Saving Target for Guangdong's Twelfth Five-Year Plan [in Chinese]," China News, December 9, 2010 (www.chinanews.com/ny/2010/12-09/2710285.shtml).

39. Haibing Ma, "Can China Do a Better Job Delegating Its 2015 Energy and Emissions Targets?" WorldWatch Blogs, January 14, 2011(http://blogs.worldwatch.org/can-china-do-a-better-job-delegating-its-2015-energy-and-emissions-targets/).

40. Bruce Springsteen, "Badlands," *Darkness on the Edge of Town* (New York: Columbia Records, 1978).

41. Chennai's national English-language newspaper, *Hindu*, regularly prints the load-sharing schedule for the state. It confirmed what we discovered: R. A. Puram loses power at 2 p.m. (www.thehindu.com/todays-paper/tp-national/tp-tamil nadu/revised-load-shedding-schedule/article4464496.ece).

42. Directorate of Economics and Statistics, Planning Department, *Economic Survey of Maharashtra 2009–2010* (Mumbai: Government of Maharashtra, 2010).

43. See Charles K. Ebinger, *Energy and Security in South Asia* (Brookings, 2011), p. 49.

44. Ibid., p. 54.

45. Interview with Narendra Modi, Gandhinagar, Gujarat, March 2, 2012.

46. "Sustained Diesel Price Hike Key to Reform: India Ratings," *Moneycontrol. com,* January 19, 2013 (www.moneycontrol.com/news/fitch-research/sustained-diesel-price-hike-key-to-reform-india-ratings_810237.html).

47. Urvashi Narain and Ruth Greenspan Bell, "Who Changed Delhi's Air?" discussion paper (Washington: Resources for the Future, 2005) (http://ageconsearch. umn.edu/bitstream/10466/1/dp050048.pdf).

48. U.S. Energy Information Administration, "India," March 18, 2013 (http:// www.eia.gov/countries/cab.cfm?fips=IN).

49. In early 2013, the Petroleum and Natural Gas Regulatory Board received a proposal from the Indian Oil Corporation to expand its natural gas pipelines from a port in Tamil Nadu to Bangalore and other cities. See Petroleum and Natural Gas Regulatory Board, "EOI NG Pipeline Public Notice" (www.pngrb.gov.in/newsite/ NG-Pipeline-eoi-ng10-2012.html).

50. Ministry of Statistics and Program Implementation, Central Statistics Office, *Energy Statistics 2012* (New Delhi, March 2012), p. 45.

51. Andreas Kemmler, "Regional Disparities in Electrification of India—Do Geographic Factors Matter?" Working Paper 51 (Zurich: Swiss Federal Institutes of Technology, Center for Energy Policy and Economics, November 2006) (www. cepe.ethz.ch/publications/workingPapers/CEPE_WP51.pdf); Directorate of Economics and Statistics, *Economic Survey.*

52. Ebinger, *Energy and Security,* p. 35.

53. Ibid., p. 36.

54. See Jos G. J. Olivier, Greet Janssens-Maenhout, and Jeroen A. H. W. Peters, *Trends in Global CO$_2$ Emissions,* report (The Hague: PBL Netherlands Environmental Assessment Agency, 2012), "Table A1.2 Trends in CO$_2$ Emissions per Region/ Country, 1990–2011" (http://edgar.jrc.ec.europa.eu/CO2REPORT2012.pdf).

55. At the 2009 Copenhagen summit, India briefly flirted with assuming some obligations, but that possibility evaporated after Jairam Ramesh, then chief negotiator for India, was subsequently reassigned to the Ministry for Rural Development.

56. "IPCC's Dr. Rajendra Pachauri: Himalayan Glaciers Are Undoubtedly Melting," *Telegraph,* December 7, 2011 (www.telegraph.co.uk/earth/environment/ climatechange/8939801/IPCCs-Dr-Rajendra-Pachauri-Himalayan-glaciers-are-undoubtedly-melting.html).

57. Some have questioned his environmental commitments. See, for instance, Kinjal Desai, "'Convenient Action' Conveniently Ignores?" *Daily News and Analysis,* June 23, 2011.

58. Gandhi promoted rurally oriented development and was an early and committed environmentalist. Many in the Western environmental movement were influenced by Gandhi, who looked to Thoreau and others. Modi packages a copy of Gandhi's autobiography along with his own, recently released book *Convenient Action.* His detractors, of course, see this as painfully ironic, if not downright cynical. See Narendra Modi, *Convenient Action: Gujarat's Response to Challenges of Climate Change* (Macmillan Publishers India, 2011) (www.narendramodi.in/convenient-action-2/).

59. India had long objected to the nonproliferation treaty because it locked into place a small handful of nations as the sole members of the nuclear club, which at the time of the signing did not include India.

60. Ministry of Statistics and Program Implementation, *Energy Statistics 2012;* World Nuclear Association, "Nuclear Power in India," September 2012 (www.world-nuclear.org/info/inf53.html).

61. See "Indian Fukushima Possible: Gopal Gandhi," *Hindustan Times,* November 7, 2011 (www.hindustantimes.com/India-news/NorthIndia/Indian-Fukushima-possible-Gopal-Gandhi/Article1-766082.aspx). Gopal is a former governor of West Bengal.

CHAPTER 6

1. Citing the 2011 UN Millennium Development Goals Report, a *Times of India* article stated that, in "China and India combined, the number of people living in extreme poverty between 1990 and 2005 declined by about 455 million, and [an] additional 320 million people are expected to come out [of] poverty by 2015." "India's Poverty Will Fall from 51% to 22% by 2015: UN Report," *Times of India,* July 8, 2011 (http://articles.timesofindia.indiatimes.com/2011-07-08/developmental-issues/29751472_1_extreme-poverty-india-and-china-report).

2. Susan Shirk, "Introduction," in *China: Fragile Superpower* (Oxford University Press, 2007).

3. Cheng Li, "Introduction," in He Weifang, *In the Name of Justice* (Brookings, 2012), p. xlii.

4. See "Mahbubani on 'What Is Governance?'" Governance Blog, March 26, 2013 (http://governancejournal.net/2013/03/26/mahbubani/). See also Kishore Mahbubani, *The Great Convergence: Asia, the West, and the Logic of One World* (New York: Public Affairs Press, 2013).

5. Phone conversation between Jaswant Singh and the author, March 23, 2012.

6. I am deeply indebted to Bruce Katz and the Brookings Metropolitan Policy Program, which has developed this paradigm over the course of the last decade.

7. That does not include U.S. missions to various international organizations such as the UN in New York and Geneva, the Organization for Economic Cooperation and Development in Paris, the Organization of American States in Washington.

It also excludes missions to non-EU countries or candidates such as Switzerland, Norway, Iceland, Turkey, Serbia, and Ukraine.

8. Hillary Rodham Clinton, "Memorandum of Understanding Concerning the Establishment of the U.S.-China Governors Forum to Promote Sub-National Cooperation," Department of State, January 19, 2011 (www.state.gov/secretary/rm/2011/01/155075.htm).

9. Reta Jo Lewis, "Outcome of U.S.-China Governors Forum," Department of State, July 19, 2011 (http://fpc.state.gov/168721.htm).

10. William Bradley, "Jerry Brown Leaves the Party behind in China," April 17, 2013 (www.huffingtonpost.com/william-bradley/jerry-brown-china_b_3104447.html).

11. During the 2013 forum, the Wisconsin Center China was officially opened. Wisconsin Economic Development Corporation, "Governor Scott Walker Announces Opening of Wisconsin Center China to Help Wisconsin Companies Reach New Markets," April 18, 2013 (http://walker.wi.gov/Default.aspx?Page=5242d319-2220-4540-9148-8242d769c828). North Carolina also signed a memorandum of understanding with Zhejiang. See also Lewis, "Outcome of U.S.-China Governors Forum."

12. Interview with the author, January 27, 2012, in Chennai, Tamil Nadu. For a profile of M. Velmurugan, see M. Ramesh, "Tamil Nadu: Where Wooing Investors is a Way of Life," *Hindu Business Line,* March 25, 2011.

13. Stuart S. Malawer, "Governor Warner's Trade Mission to India," *Virginia Lawyer,* June-July 2005 (www.vsb.org/docs/valawyermagazine/jul05india_malawer.pdf). Similarly, in 2006 Governor Tom Vilsack of Iowa led a trade mission to India, focusing heavily on soybean exports, given the need for vegetable protein for many vegetarian Indians. "Governor Vilsack to Lead Trade Mission to India," press release, February 23, 2006 (https://votesmart.org/public-statement/155770/governor-vilsack-to-lead-trade-mission-to-india).

14. K. Rajani Kanth, "Andhra, Washington Sign Pact for Trade Cooperation," *Business Standard,* October 3, 2012 (www.business-standard.com/article/economy-policy/andhra-washington-sign-pact-for-trade-cooperation-112100303025_1.html).

15. Beth Musgrave, "Gov. Steve Beshear Visits India on Third Foreign Economic Development Trip This Year," September 12, 2012 (www.kentucky.com/2012/09/12/2333622/gov-steve-beshear-visits-india.html). Likewise, Wisconsin's former governor Jim Doyle led a similar trade mission; see "Gov. Doyle Leading Trade Mission to India," *Business Journal,* May 13, 2008 (www.bizjournals.com/milwaukee/stories/2008/05/12/daily22.html).

Maryland governor Martin O'Malley led a major trade mission in 2011, establishing agreements for collaborations in mobile applications, engineering and architecture, health technology and management, and medical research. India was Maryland's twelfth-largest export market in 2010 ($233 million in goods and services) and the state's thirteenth-largest import market, at more than $465 million. Office of Governor Martin O'Malley, "Governor O'Malley Kicks Off Historic India Trade Mission," November 28, 2011 (www.governor.maryland.gov/blog/?p=3026).

16. In 2011 total exports to India came to $33 billion; total imports, $53 billion. Goods exports totaled $21.6 billion; goods imports, $36.2 billion. Services exports were $11.6 billion; services imports, $16.9 billion. In 2011 total exports to China came to $129 billion; total imports, $411 billion. Goods exports totaled $104 billion; goods imports, $399 billion. Services exports were $25 billion; services

imports, $11 billion. See, respectively, Office of the United States Trade Representative, "India" (www.ustr.gov/countries-regions/south-central-asia/india); "China" (www.ustr.gov/countries-regions/china-mongolia-taiwan/peoples-republic-china).

17. Tridivesh Singh Maini, "Clinton's Southern India Sojourn," *Diplomat,* July 22, 2011 (http://thediplomat.com/indian-decade/2011/07/22/clintons-southern-india-sojourn/); "Hillary Clinton Arrives in Kolkata for 3-day India Visit," *Hindustan Times,* May 06, 2012 (www.hindustantimes.com/India-news/WestBengal/Hillary-Clinton-arrives-in-Kolkata-for-3-day-India-visit/Article1-851474.aspx).

18. "U.S. Delegation Meets Gujarat CM Narendra Modi, *New Delhi Post,* March 28, 2013 (www.tndpost.com/news/top-news-story/us-delegation-meets-gujarat-cm-narendra-modi.html#.UZwPoLWsiSo).

19. James Crabtree, "UK to Help India Build 'Mega-Project,'" *Financial Times,* February 18, 2013.

20. See Shirk, *China,* p. 43.

21. Ibid.

22. The acronym BRIC (before South Africa joined) first appeared in Jim O'Neill, "Building Better Global Economic BRICs," Global Economics Paper 66 (New York: Goldman Sachs, November 30, 2001) (www.goldmansachs.com/our-thinking/archive/archive-pdfs/build-better-brics.pdf).

23. Ian Bremmer, *Every Nation for Itself: Winners and Losers in a G-Zero World* (New York: Portfolio, 2012); Moises Naim, *The End of Power* (New York: Basic Books, 2013).

24. See William Antholis, presentation at the Third Annual Review of Low-Carbon Development in China, Brookings, December 14, 2012 (www.brookings.edu/events/2012/12/14-low-carbon-us-china).

25. See C40Cities Climate Leadership Group (www.c40cities.org).

26. The most compelling case for the foundations of the liberal democratic peace was made by Michael Doyle, "Kant, Liberal Legacies and Foreign Affairs," parts 1 and 2, *Philosophy and Public Affairs* 12, nos. 3 and 4 (1983): 205–35 and 323–53, respectively; see in particular page 222. These pieces provided the intellectual underpinnings for Francis Fukuyama, "The End of History?" *National Interest,* Summer 1989, and *The End of History and the Last Man* (New York: Free Press, 1992), and launched an extensive literature on if, how, and whether liberal democracies are more inclined toward peace.

27. See, in particular, Doyle, "Kant, Liberal Legacies," part 2.

28. See Amy Chua, *World on Fire: How Exporting Free Market Democracy Breeds Ethnic Hatred and Global Instability* (New York: Doubleday, 2003).

29. See Stephen Szabo, "China's Challenge to the Liberal Order, India's Attraction to It, and the Possibilities for Western Revitalization in Light of the Global Embrace of Democratic Norms," May 29, 2012, in the National Intelligence Council's online forum *Global Trends 2030* (http://gt2030.com/2012/05/29/chinas-challenge-to-the-liberal-order-indias-attraction-to-it-and-the-possibilities-for-western-revitalization-in-light-of-the-global-embrace-of-democratic-norms/). See also G. John Ikenberry, "The Future of the Liberal World Order: Internationalism after America," *Foreign Affairs,* May-June 2011, pp. 56–68.

30. The most compelling case for this was made by Robert Kaplan, *Monsoon: The Indian Ocean and the Future of American Power* (New York: Random House, 2010).

INDEX